CHANGING THE RULES

Best wishes

Jenny Kelsey

Also by Jennifer C. Kelsey

A Voice of Discontent

CHANGING THE RULES
WOMEN AND VICTORIAN MARRIAGE

JENNIFER C. KELSEY

Matador
9 Priory Business Park,
Wistow Road, Kibworth Beauchamp,
Leicestershire. LE8 0RX
Tel: 0116 279 2299
Email: books@troubador.co.uk
Web: www.troubador.co.uk/matador
Twitter: @matadorbooks

ISBN 978 1785890 291

British Library Cataloguing in Publication Data.
A catalogue record for this book is available from the British Library.

Printed and bound in the UK by TJ International, Padstow, Cornwall
Typeset in 11pt Bembo by Troubador Publishing Ltd, Leicester, UK

Matador is an imprint of Troubador Publishing Ltd

*For all my dear family and friends for their continued love and support,
and the delightful members of the University of the Third Age
who have encouraged me to move away from the library,
and the laptop, to the podium and the stage.*

Contents

Acknowledgements

Every effort has been made to gain the correct copyright permissions for works quoted.

The quotation from Vera Brittain's *Honourable Estate* is included by kind permission of Mark Bostridge and T.J. Brittain-Catlin, Literary Executors for the Estate of Vera Brittain 1970.

Extracts from *A London Child of the Seventies* by Molly Vivien Hughes (1934): 144w (pp.6-7 & 38), *The Making of a Schoolgirl* by Evelyn Sharp (1989): 176w (pp.25-6, 28, 33, 41 & 92), and *Lark Rise to Candleford* by Flora Thompson (2011 edition): 33w (pp.148-9), by kind permission of Oxford University Press.

The quotation from *Alas Poor Lady* by Rachel Ferguson, reprinted by Persephone Books in 2006, has also been included with their kind permission.

Special thanks go to Dr Catherine Pope of 'Victorian Secrets' for her friendly and helpful advice regarding Florence Marryat and her permission to use the quotation (about the butter) on page 146 in Chapter Six.

The wonderful collections and resources of the British Library give me infinite pleasure; I have learned so much there over the years. I continue to be very grateful for its existence and for all the helpful staff who work there.

Front Cover Illustration
The Divorce Court © The British Library Board
(The Graphic 8/1/1870, p128)

Foreword

After taking a short course at Birkbeck College some years ago, I decided to write a trilogy about women that aimed to make our journey to the present day a much more personal one than is commonly found in history books. Rather than focusing purely on facts and figures, endless statistics and only the occasional name, I wanted to discover the real emotion – the passion – that drove women forward in their quest for change. To do this I have relied on the works of the women themselves, their fiction and their non-fiction, in order to pick up the details that often get left behind. My first book, *A Voice of Discontent,* concerned the women writers of the long eighteenth century who had dared to voice their opinions through the medium of print. That was a fascinating voyage of discovery for me. This second book in the trilogy, *Changing the Rules*, continues that journey.

PART ONE

INTRODUCING THE SUBJECT

Chapter One
The Question Of Marriage

George Eliot actually agreed with me or, at least, I like to think she would have done if we had ever met. She once wrote:

> *See the difference between the impression a man makes on you when you walk by his side… or look at him in his home, and the figure he makes when seen from a lofty historical level, or even in the eyes of a critical neighbour who thinks of him as an embodied system or opinion rather than as a man.*[1]

In all of her novels there is a very strong sense of realism: the characters; the settings; the events – but most of all through the intense thought and emotion contained within the work. These emotions, I believe, cannot be conveyed by just factual recording or post-event analysis. Like George Eliot, I leave that to the historians.

When I first became engaged in the study of women's history I had wanted to avoid yet another rewrite of what most people already knew. I wanted to use more experiential writings to gain a greater understanding of the emotions of the time, to learn how women felt about their lives and experiences, and to see how they had used their literature to convey them. If you have looked at my first book, *A Voice of Discontent*, you will know how important the women writers of the long eighteenth century were – for they had used their individual written responses to their own experiences in order to raise the level of awareness of many women's issues that otherwise were to have been ignored.

So now I move forwards into the Victorian era – an amazing period of mega changes in so many walks of life. Inventions. Discoveries. Empires and Exhibitions. The Famous and the Fabulous. The Great

---

[1] George Eliot, *Adam Bede*, 1859

Age of Reform. When Victoria came to the throne, in 1837, the problems for women were much the same as they always had been; the time was not yet ripe for radical reform for them. Progress on such a fundamental scale would take many years to achieve and during the process there were to be many different forms of discontent. In 1886 a (male) Victorian novelist called George Moore was to make a very astute observation:

> The history of a nation as often lies hidden in social wrongs and domestic griefs as in the story of a revolution, and if it be for the historian to relate the one, it is for the novelist to dissect and explain the other.[2]

I do not think George Eliot would have disagreed with that, but I wonder how she would have felt about a rather amusing quote concerning women writers that I found the other day. It is by George Henry Lewes, who was to be George Eliot's partner, written a year before he actually met her.

> Women's proper sphere of activity is elsewhere. Are there no husbands, lovers, brothers, friends to coddle and console? Are there no stockings to darn, no purses to make, no braces to embroider? My idea of a perfect woman is one who can write but won't.[3]

I wonder if he ever changed his mind or did he indeed realise in time that perfect partners are hard to find? Either way, when we look at the history of this country, the work of the women writers has a crucial role to play. Regardless as to whether we focus on contemporary fiction or non-fiction we cannot escape the fundamental truth as pointed out by Mrs Humphrey Ward:

> The picture is seen through a woman's eyes. A man would have reported it differently. But… the woman's impression and the woman's reports are no less vital, no less necessary to the utterance of a generation than a man's.[4]

---

[2] George Moore, *A Drama in Muslin*, 1886
[3] George Henry Lewes, *A Gentle Hint to Writing Women*, 1850
[4] Mrs Humphrey Ward, *Marcella*, 1894

This same point was particularly well reinforced by George Paston (Emily Morse Symonds) in 1898. In her novel *A Writer of Books* a male historian was in conversation with a young female novelist:

> '*We have plenty of opportunities at getting a masculine point of view, but it is only in comparatively recent times, that we have had female writers who possessed ideas of their own and dared to express them. We laugh sometimes at their grammar and their logic, but it must not be forgotten that the work of those who thought for themselves will be invaluable documents for the social historian of the future... We can follow the development of the thought of man from the first dawn of history, but the thoughts of woman are buried in her grave.*'
>
> '*And whose fault is that?*' asked Cosima.
>
> '*The fault of our fathers of course, who held that the pen was no less unfeminine a weapon than the sword. But prejudices never go unpunished and the penalty of that prejudice is that we have lost half the history of the human race... Just think of the light that would have been thrown on history... if Jane Austen had gone out to America with the Pilgrim Fathers, or Charlotte Bronte had been a school-fellow of Lucrezia Borgia's!... Therefore tell us what you and your sisters think and feel, what you have seen and suffered; deliver your soul in short, and never mind the grammar!*'

Even though many men did not seem to like women operating outside of the domestic sphere, by choosing to dismiss their efforts, such men were blatantly ignoring the important contribution that women could actually make to the world. Florence Nightingale once said that if 'there were none who were discontented with what they have, the world would never reach for anything better'. I think that this was certainly true as far as women were concerned.

It has now generally been accepted that the lot of most women in the past has not been a particularly favoured one. From my own research for my first book I found there were many common themes amongst the expressed concerns of women from at least the eighteenth century. Many had been aware of the limitations of receiving a poor education, had suffered problems trying to obtain suitable employment, had often faced unreasonably limited expectations of their own abilities, and had had to endure being placed in subservient positions both legally and socially from birth. Only the privileged few could avoid all of these social handicaps; most just had to accept them as a way of life.

Eighteenth-century women writers like Mary Wollstonecraft had been keen to point out that it was not just that women were prevented from being given a chance to succeed; key decisions were regularly being made about a woman's life without even considering that she might have a valid opinion of her own, let alone asking her for it. In other words, assumptions had been repeatedly made about a woman's abilities, wants and needs without any reference to her. For many years few had thought to question those assumptions or dared to question the rights of others to make them. Over time, though, that situation was changing and, as we shall see, during the Victorian period there were to be frequent challenges to it. This, for example, was written in 1874:

> *Without denying the self-evident proposition that whatever a woman can do she has a right to do, the question at once arises, what can she do?... I will add the further question, 'Who will decide what can she do?'... Let us pause and consider... Why not in all matters that pertain to her – especially in that question of what can she do – ask her directly and pay some heed to her answer? If she does not know, who does?* [5]

Identifying a problem, though, even being able to see clearly where some of the faults could lie, was never going to be enough. First of all, the contribution that women's opinions could make to the process of change had to be recognised as being valid in itself, before it could take on any important role. Women had to gain a voice and to use it effectively. It had to be heard by the right people and by enough people. In the words of my scientific son, 'You have to reach a critical mass before something happens.' This seems to have been a problem for women right across the world, but over time women have made their mark – and using literature is one of the more effective means they have found for doing so.

One direct example of this concerns the issue of slavery in the

---

[5] Mrs E.B.Duffy, *No Sex in Education; Or, An Equal Chance for Both Boys and Girls*, 1874

United States. It has long been acknowledged that the novelist Mrs Harriet Beecher Stowe made a highly significant contribution in the fight for abolition by exposing the life of the slaves in her work. In the preface of one novel, the nineteenth-century American feminist Mrs Elizabeth Cady Stanton was to comment, 'I have long waited for some woman to arise and do for her sex what Mrs Stowe did for the black race in *Uncle Tom's Cabin*.'[6] It was unfortunate that Mary Wollstonecraft's *A Vindication of the Rights of Woman*[7] had not played as significant a part in reform as Mary had wished it might have done at the time, even though it was to do so in later years. As the eighteenth century passed and the Victorian period unfolded, women were to increasingly recognise the role of the printed word in the path of their progress, and the importance of their own contributions to that path from both fictional and non-fictional work. In one of her novels Caroline Norton was to state, 'I was thinking of a power apart from political discussion, the simple power of publication. How many wrongs have been redressed that never would have been known, without the aid of the press?'[8] In the preface to one of her other novels she also stated that 'individual protests are the small hinges on which the great doors of change forever turn.'[9]

Caroline was to play a leading role, albeit a somewhat notorious one, fighting for changes that would initially affect her own life and then subsequently the lives of many other women. We will encounter her frequently in later chapters. Others were to write in similar vein, even though neither they nor their works are so well known today. Thus, for example, Marion Read referred to her own work as 'a drop of water in the ocean' and hoped that drop by drop 'at last they may wear a passage through the hard rock of the customs and prejudices of ages.'[10]

When their fictional works were criticised by contemporaries, women writers would continue to justify their literary efforts because of the (sometimes) covert meanings within them. Caroline herself believed 'a novel is as likely a mode as any other – more likely with some minds – of waking attention to certain facts.'[11]

6 Helen H. Gardener, *Pray You, Sir, Whose Daughter?* 1892
7 Mary Wollstonecraft, *A Vindication of the Rights of Woman*, 1792
8 Caroline Norton, *Stuart of Dunleath*, 1851
9 Caroline Norton, *Lost and Saved*, 1863
10 Marion Reid, *A Plea for Woman*, 1843
11 *Lost and Saved*

Intrinsic to their writing was a genuine belief that even though change may be slow to materialise it would eventually come, through the spreading of the knowledge of life's injustices and then encouraging the growing desire to correct them. A common theme scattered throughout both fiction and non-fiction works by female authors during the nineteenth century was the belief that women had the ability to change the status quo. During a public address in 1894 Mary Haweis announced 'in women's hands – women writers' hands – lies the regeneration of the world'. Their contribution to society, to the world of work, even to government itself could ultimately save the planet.

One of the reasons why I find the Victorian period so fascinating is because so many different types and classes of people, males and females alike, all joined in the debate about women. There is an abundance of evidence to prove it. It was openly discussed in private, as well as in public meetings; it was written about in books, journals, and newspapers; it was also increasingly considered within that most important setting – Parliament itself. In order to give a balanced view of the time, it has therefore been necessary to include more works by men, both in their support of women's issues and in their criticism of them. Fierce debate would rage on the nature and capabilities of women, new scientific evidence would be used to prove arguments on either side, and right at the heart of it all was the critical subject of marriage.

When I was studying the eighteenth century I noted that marriage played a fundamental part throughout each stage of a woman's life; her early education and experiences prepared her for it. As she grew up she learned accomplishments to help her attract and acquire a husband; she spent her subsequent life as a wife, most likely later as a mother and then perhaps as a woman separated from her husband, probably through his death. At all stages she was identified by the role she would play in life relative to a man and within each period the notion of marriage carried a large hidden agenda for her. It is undeniable that for most women marriage was to be the key event of their lives; few women would determinedly choose never to marry.

Life for a woman was thus not such a simple issue, although for years it seemed to have followed a particular set pattern that never really seemed to change. It 'was not the smooth road it looked, but a rough path enough cut into dangerous ruts, through which generations of men and women followed each other without ever being able to mend the way.'[12]

As my research led me into the Victorian period, I wanted to focus on the institution of marriage, to see how women experienced it and whether they actually found it a satisfactory institution as far as they were concerned. Of course there were many ways to look at marriage – from the religious perspective; the social; the legal; the economic; and yes, even the purely romantic. According to established Church doctrine, marriage was an honourable estate and it fulfilled three fundamental purposes:

> *It was ordained for the procreation of children to be brought up in the fear and nurture of the Lord… it was ordained for a remedy against sin and to avoid fornication, and thirdly it was ordained for the mutual society, help and comfort that the one ought to have of the other.*[13]

Young girls were sold the idea of marriage by being told how much they would benefit from it and, in no uncertain terms, what they would risk if they did not accept those terms. The justification of marriage 'for your own happiness', even when there was no love in a relationship, occurs so frequently in the novels of the eighteenth and nineteenth centuries that it is unnecessary to cite them. Marriage was supposed to bring the girls all the benefits of a promising future – a husband; a home; a family; security and stability – and yet there was heavy criticism at the time of foreign novels, particularly from France, that foretold of romance and roses rather than showing the harsher realities of life.

There were, however, other motives for accepting a proposal of marriage, motives that give a rather different perspective of the lives of many women, whether married or single. The following quotations are all from Victorian novels, describing marriage, but the authors themselves had a very broad experience of life on which to base their work.

> *A woman made herself worthwhile by marriage and devotion to her husband and her children, if she had any. In herself she was nothing.*[14]

---

[12] Margaret Oliphant, *The Perpetual Curate*, 1864
[13] *The Book of Common Prayer*, 1662
[14] Dinah Mulock Craik, *Agatha's Husband*, 1853

It was the chance of rescue from the dreariest life of drudgery that a poor dependent creature ever lived, and I took it. [15]

Why do we marry? In nine cases out of ten, to be kept. What infamy to be forced to sell ourselves for an existence… Marriage was her sole profession; a husband her sole source of income, and in securing these where she could, though he might outrage her womanhood, she only yielded to necessity. [16]

It is not hateful to all girls, for a few – one or two – have told me they were glad. The others were indifferent or frightened or pious or resigned. I think that very few would be married if it were not for the flattery and the triumph and the full of the wedding, and if there were anything else to do. [17]

A woman's life was assessed through her marriage; it was important to know how much her future husband earned, whether he had property, if his family was important, what was his profession or means of employment, where they would live when married, how many servants would be in the household, and so on. In addition to these factors even the very number of children a wife bore during the marriage could be seen as a criteria of success that was based on her husband's achievements – not her own. A woman was a success *if* she married – and particularly *if* she made a *good* marriage. Many novels worked towards a predictable conclusion with the successful pairing off and marriage of key characters. What followed afterwards regarding the women was of no particular importance or interest to the reader – or at least according to some of the publishers of the day. In the eighteenth century when novels for women, by women, had first really became popular, marriage still seemed to close the door on a woman's life – there was no afterword. Nobody seemed to expect anything more of a married woman beyond rearing the family.

Frances Trollope, successful writer and mother of the more famous Anthony Trollope, was one amongst many women who challenged this view of their lives: 'Unless my life be permanently cut short my

[15] Mary Elizabeth Braddon, *Milly Darrell*, 1873
[16] Eliza Lynn Linton, *Rebel of the Family*, 1880
[17] Emma Frances Brooke, *A Superfluous Woman*, 1894

history does not end here, although the event which usually concludes the history of a woman may be said to be reached.'[18] In her other works Frances was to look not only at life *during* marriage, but she was also to show what real pleasures could be in store for a woman *post-marriage*, as a widow. Widow Barnaby – a very merry widow indeed – was given her own trilogy: *The Widow Barnaby* (1839), *The Widow Married* (1840), and *The Widow Wedded* (1843).

Although the idea of marrying primarily for love, rather than actual convenience or financial benefit, was becoming increasingly popular over time, how any marriage would develop was dependent upon other factors too. For a woman, while the role she would play within marriage depended to a huge extent on what she and her partner considered the marriage was for, marriage was also dependent upon what the two parties considered the woman herself was actually capable of achieving. John Stuart Mill, who later published his well-known *The Subjection of Women* (1869), was very clear on this point. In 1832 he had written, 'The question of marriage cannot be considered by itself alone. The question is not what marriage ought to be, but a far wider question of what woman ought to be.'[19] Both he and co-writer Harriet Taylor knew only too well that men's views of women were not always complimentary and could have a profound effect on a woman's experience of marriage.

There are innumerable examples of this across the centuries. During my recent research I came across one that I felt was particularly thought-provoking, written by George Paston:

> *The man never lived who in his heart regarded women as human beings, as anything but inferior animals created expressly for the use or pleasure of his sex. 'Wine, women and song', in that line our position is summed up, we come midway between a bottle of champagne and a music hall ditty. What duties or responsibilities can a man owe towards creatures who stand lower than a bottle in the scheme of creation?*[20]

It was an original question and deserved some serious attention. There was likely to be the world of difference between a marriage where two

---

18 Frances Trollope, *The Life and Adventures of a Clever Woman*, 1854

19 John Stuart Mill and Harriet Taylor, *Early Essays on Marriage and Divorce*, 1832 in *Essays on Sex Equality* (ed.) Alice S. Rossi, University of Chicago Press, 1970

20 George Paston, *A Writer of Books*, 1898

individuals mutually respected each other and a marriage where only one individual counted; one with a woman respected and the other a woman scorned. Would she be the angel of the house or would she be the slave? Many of the criticisms of marriage as an institution were to do with power and control, with the man holding the key advantages – all reinforced by law. As many women writers had shown, if abused, the life of a married woman could be one of abject misery. In 1861 an Edinburgh physician, Dr George Drysdale, described marriage as:

> *One of the chief instruments of degradation for women... It delivers woman bound into the hands of man and tempts him to use his gift of superior strength; it is in short the instrument in numberless cases of making the man the tyrant and the woman the slave.*[21]

Others held similar views. Fifty years after the publication of *A Vindication of the Rights of Woman*, an event had taken place in the United States that marked a watershed in the history of women. In 1848 the first ever Woman's Rights Convention was held in Seneca Falls, USA. At their tenth convention, held in New York in 1860, marriage had been one of the key topics under debate. Even allowing for cultural and legal differences between Britain and the United States, the situations in the two countries were really very similar. An early speaker, Elizabeth Cady Stanton, had already noted that when a man married it was not necessary for him to change his life at all – he could still remain 'in the full tide of business or pleasure'. For a woman, though, at the time, it was a very different matter. Susan B. Anthony continued the attack:

> *Woman has never been consulted; her wish has never been taken into consideration as regards the marriage contract. By law, public sentiment and religion, from the time of Moses to the present day, woman has never been thought of as other than a piece of property to be disposed of at the will and pleasure of man. She has no voice whatever in saying what shall be the basis of the relation. She must accept marriage as man proffers it and nothing more.*

---

[21] Dr George Drysdale, *The Elements of Social Science, or Physical, Sexual and Natural Religion*, 1861

At the time these ideas were considered to be radical, but they were not unknown either in America or in England. Where women had no political voice and no political power they were governed by laws entirely created by males. So the laws that applied to married persons were created by men who thought they were best qualified to make decisions on behalf of women; until women were in a position to show that they as a sex seriously challenged those decisions, and had sufficient support from the power holders themselves, nothing would change. In spite of generations of young women being told they should marry and ask no questions, for 'who are you that should question an institution that has lasted for centuries?' [22] marriage had undoubtedly been the subject of much detailed discussion and debate, and would continue to be so for generations to come.

George Meredith, a Victorian novelist who was very much a supporter of women, once said, 'The subject of marriage is kept too much in the dark. Air it! Air it!' I wonder if he was satisfied with the amazing response from the readers of *The Daily Telegraph* to an article by Mona Caird, entitled '*Marriage*', printed in 1888, which asked the question, is marriage a failure? One of her basic points had been that she believed modern wifehood was not based on her self-respect as a woman, 'but from the fact of her subjection to a man'. Harry Quilter was asked to collate all the replies and subsequently published his work; his own introductory words give a full flavour of what had taken place:

> *Wives and mothers, maids and bachelors, spinsters and husbands, clerks and curates, priests and publicans, saints and sinners gathered themselves into one compact mass of respondents, and hurled their woes, their joys, their experiences, their doctrines and themselves at the head of The Daily Telegraph. To the honour of Englishmen be it said, the Editor stood firm beneath the shock of 27,000 letters! He had sown the wind and he was to reap the whirlwind! Day by day the inevitable three columns appeared in the journal, day by day we read of the havoc wrought by club or cup, by temper or neglect, or learned the secrets of domestic joy or single wretchedness. Seasons changed, summer passed away. Baldwin fell from the clouds, and Edison's*

---

[22] Mona Caird, *The Morality of Marriage*, 1897

voice was brought us in a box. Imperial diaries came out and were suppressed, grouse were cleared from the moors and partridges shot in the stubble, but still with the inevitableness of fate, the regularity of time and the persistency of a Scotch lawyer, the three columns of perplexed curates, city barmaids, observant bachelors and glorified spinsters maintained their hold upon the journal, and their claim upon the public attention. [23]

In only six weeks there were 27,000 letters to the editor. It is mind-boggling. From the famous, like the author Jerome K. Jerome and Archdeacon Blunt, through the ranks of the populace and even down to 'THE DOG', everyone, it would seem, had something to say to the editor on the matter. Overall the responses chosen by Quilter were in favour, showing that marriage was *not* a failure per se, but they still clearly illustrated the fact that there was plenty of room for improvement. As it stood marriage could be a risky business – and this view reinforced what women had been saying elsewhere. There was, for example, the somewhat pessimistic view that:

All marriages are a great risk. My wonder is not that they are sometimes unhappy, but that they are ever happy at all. I should counsel no young girl to change her state unless she thoroughly knows and deeply loves the man she marries. [24]

There was a similar notion that 'marriage is, at best, a lottery with more blanks than prizes' [25] and from the novel *The Root of All Evil* came the slightly humorous slant that 'marriage was a lottery, that it was, and the greatest mercy in this life was being able to think that there was none of it in heaven.' [26]

This idea of marriage as a lottery caught my attention. Queen Victoria herself is known to have described it as such, and years earlier Jane Austen had done the same thing; I seriously doubt if she was the first to do so. Although I had decided to focus on marriage in this second book, I had initially been uncertain on how to approach

23 Harry Quilter, *Is Marriage A Failure?* 1888
24 Dinah Mulock Craik, *A Brave Lady*, 1870
25 Eliza Lynn Linton, Our Civilisation, *Cornhill Magazine* 27, June 1873
26 Florence Marryat, *The Root of All Evil*, 1879

it – but the responses to *The Daily Telegraph* feature had unwittingly pointed me in the right direction. Marriage was still being considered as a game – was it indeed a game of chance? It could provide an interesting and original framework to my study of women and their writings during the Victorian period.

Firstly, there were the players – the men and the women – and how they had learned the rules of the game, as children, before they even started to play. Then there were the rules themselves – well established, with years of tradition, but now under threat for a variety of reasons. Suddenly, I had so many new questions to answer. Was the game of marriage really random or did it have a real bias? Was the dice really loaded, in favour of men, and if so how had that been achieved? And more importantly how did the umpires, the referees and the rule-makers of the establishment respond to the changes that the women desired?

Whether or not the women were to obtain the changes they wanted within marriage was very much dependent on how well the proposed changes fitted in with the desires, and needs, of those who already controlled the game. Church, society and the law controlled the rules of marriage, so how could any changes actually come about? And were the Victorian women, particularly the women writers, actually able to play any significant part in achieving those changes? It was at last time to turn to the literature again, to discover what women had to say on the subject, and to see whether they were indeed able to have any effect on the outcome of the game.

PART TWO

CONDITIONING THE PLAYERS

Chapter Two
Duty and Submission

In order to play a game there are two basic prerequisites. You need the players and you need the rules. The potential players in the marriage game were the adults, the men and the women, but, rather than learning the rules on the spot, the process of learning had begun many years earlier when the players of the future were mere children.

Marriage and the family were keystones in the very foundations of English society and together had upheld a very stable construction. European countries had suffered from violent disruption and upheaval; revolutionary ideas had both shocked and influenced the world, but in the main, English society had continued along the same social pathways that it had trodden for years. Ways and means had been found to maintain that stability through systems, beliefs and values that seemed to work. So generations of men and women were groomed to accept, adopt and then, in turn, pass these on to their own children. Society, law and religion added further constant reinforcement; there will be more on this throughout the book.

During the Victorian period, then, the stable family unit, headed by the paterfamilias, was still the mainstay of society and the fundamental rules of play were learned within its parameters. From a very young and tender age boys and girls would be prepared for their adult roles, but in what forms did this education take place? The journey from being a carefree girl, for example, running perhaps a little wild as a small child, to a more sombre, certainly serious, Victorian wife and mother who performed her daily duties with humble diligence was certainly no small step. It required years of training, practice and self-control. What would it have been like to experience it? What was she told that calmed her down, what made her put aside her own wants, needs and desires as she grew older and devote herself to catering for the needs of others – more specifically for her father, her brothers, and then her husband? Was she being altruistic, a doting and dutiful daughter, and afterwards a loving wife and mother or was it a total self-sacrifice? Other writers have focused on how girls became women, their intellectual education and accomplishments, and including perhaps the process of learning to run a household. My concern in this chapter lies more with the development of a girl's understanding, and accepting, of her future role, how the requirements of duty and submission in a wife were taught to her, and how she frequently learned not only to accept them but also to justify their very existence.

I have read a great deal about 'separate spheres' in recent years: the principle of two worlds – one the female domain contained within the home boundary, the other the outside world, the territory of the male. Some believe the boundaries between them were hard and fast, others that there were overlaps between the two and, to a certain extent, men and women having a role to play within both. One thing, however, is certain: marriage for many women meant that a wife was largely confined to and around her home. While some women undoubtedly did have to work for a living, for those in the middle classes at least, it was generally accepted that a husband should be providing for his wife and that included keeping her at home.

In 1792 Mary Wollstonecraft had referred to the virtually limitless power that could be exercised by a husband within marriage, and expressed her hope that 'the divine right of husbands, like the divine right of kings, may... in this enlightened age, be contested without danger.'[1] She believed that marriages should be based on common affection and mutual respect, a partnership between equals. She did not agree with marriages of convenience nor with those where a wife was merely a toy for, or servant of, the husband. Although Mary did much to raise the consciousness of many other women through her work, little real change in the accepted form of married life had actually taken place by the mid-nineteenth century.

In 1854 a female journalist wrote an article about her, which deplored the lack of progress for women during this period:

We have the same fight to fight that she had, and the same things remain undone that she would fain have forwarded with a helping hand. Who will take this stigma of cowardice and the slave's degradation

---

[1] *A Vindication of the Rights of Woman*

from the women of England? Who will show that we have minds as
subtle and wills as strong as Mary Wollstonecraft of the past? Who
will prove that, if they will, our women shall be free and noble? [2]

There is a key phrase in this last sentence:'if they will'. In spite of many
calls for women to take on the responsibility for the development of
their own future, according to publications dating from as early as
1700 to at least the mid-nineteenth century, the majority of women
seem to have given the impression that they *were* satisfied with the
limited opportunities and the social restrictions imposed upon their
sex in the material world. To cite just two examples:'How astonishing
is it that the oppressions of these men, who are the authors of such
mischief, should so long have passed unnoticed?'[3] and 'Not that they
revolted but that they have borne it so long is the cause of wonder'.[4]

At the very least women seem to have accepted that the status
quo was not likely to change during their own lifetime. It is possible
that part of this acceptance was due to the realisation that life could
become very difficult if they opposed family and/or friends. Olive
Schreiner was to describe this situation very clearly:

But what does it help? A little bitterness, a little longing when we are
young, a little futile searching for work, a little passionate striving for
room for the exercise of our powers – and then we go with the drove.
A woman must march with her regiment. In the end she must be
downtrodden or go with it; and if she is wise she goes.[5]

It is difficult to understand the complex reasons for this compliance
without paying full attention to the upbringing and personal education
of children, long before they grew into adulthood. During my earlier
research I had learned that one of the fundamental reasons that so few
women had actually tried to challenge the system (rather than just
decry it) was because of their earlier conditioning, but I had failed
to appreciate just how extensive and effective this system was for
conditioning both sexes. In order to illustrate this it will be necessary

2   Eliza Lynn Linton,'Mary Wollstonecraft', *The English Republic*, 1854
3   Mary Ann Randall, *The Female Advocate*, 1799
4   Eliza Lynn Linton,'The Modern Revolt', *Macmillan's Magazine*, 1870
5   Olive Schreiner, *The Story of An African Farm*, 1883

to open the front door of a Victorian household and examine the common experiences of both boys and girls who would grow up accepting that men and women, husbands and wives, would not be equal. To a large extent this chapter will be about the girls – the boys will be considered more in Chapter Three.

One of the fundamental principles that underpinned much of Victorian society and permeated every level within it was the acceptance of personal duty. Masters and servants, workers and tenants, men and women all had ideas of what their own roles involved and what their own personal responsibilities might or might not be. From a very early age children too would be taught their duty, to their parents, to their siblings and to the people around them. However, what was perceived as the duty of men versus women, boys versus girls, was often vastly different.

We should remember the critical role that religion played at the time in the acceptance and fulfilment of personal duty. Children and adults alike were constantly taught and reminded of this through the lessons read in church, the weekly sermons, and in home readings of the Bible and other such religious works. Duty may involve personal sacrifice at times, but for Christian followers there was no disgrace or shame in that. Far from it; after all, according to the scriptures wasn't the ultimate example of self-sacrifice undertaken on our behalf by Jesus himself? Women were taught that accepting a lowly and humble position (for example, that of a wife) and acknowledging the superior authority of the men (in this case a husband) offered a constant opportunity to imitate the humility and sufferings of the Lord. There are many references to women's love of self-sacrifice in literature and its links to religious belief; some could be a little extreme:

> *The fact was that this woman delighted in self-sacrifice, however exercised. She believed that on the wings of self-sacrifice a soul may mount into high and pure air; in short that by self-sacrifice that soul might follow the footsteps of the great self-sacrificer – Christ himself.*[6]

As a wife, a woman would be expected to meet the domestic needs of her husband and family; as a daughter she would have been expected to contribute towards the fulfilment of those needs, generally by helping

---

[6]   L.T.Meade, *Bel Marjory*, 1878

her mother. Children would witness the dominance of their father's will and the acceptance of it by their mother. They were taught to accept the authority of their father within the family and the authority of such patriarchal institutions as the Church without. In her famous work *The Cause,* Ray Strachey stated, 'The grip of convention was so strong and so much entangled with parental feelings that to outrage it in any aspect seemed like a sin.'[7]

Outside the family home the main thinkers and doers, the decision makers, the chief wage owners would be male, supported in their thoughts and actions by women who may have rarely, if ever, challenged them. Young children would observe and experience a system that would in turn influence their own behaviour. Just as a small boy reached a certain age and was taken out of dresses and started to assume his masculine role by wearing trousers, so too a young girl would learn that, when she reached a certain age or stage, she may have to start wearing longer dresses and learn to modify her own behaviour accordingly, but her preparation for her future role as a woman, as a wife, would have begun long before that.

Sarah Stickney Ellis was one of the most popular writers of conduct literature in the nineteenth century. She wrote a whole series of books concerning the moral education and duties of women, starting with *The Women of England* (1839), closely followed by *The Daughters of England* (1842), *The Wives of England* (1843) and *The Mothers of England* (1844). These books were to be in print for many years, giving detailed guidance on what she perceived the roles and responsibilities for each of these groups to be, and how to achieve them. Contained within them was a fundamental lesson for girls growing up; Sarah's aim, mentioned very early on in the first chapter, was:

> *For girls leaving school or completing their education, it is to answer the inquiry what is my position in society, what do I aim at? ... As Christian women then I address you. As women the first thing of importance is to be content to be inferior to men – inferior in mental power, in the same proportion that you are inferior in bodily strength... look at your duties first, examine them well, submit yourself without reserve to their chains.*[8]

[7]   Ray Strachey, *The Cause,* 1928
[8]   Sarah Stickney Ellis, *The Women of England,* 1839

Such types of comment are not rare in Victorian literature and you come across them in all sorts of places. From serious tomes, doctrinal works, and other conduct literature right through to fiction for both mature women and young girls, printed in books and in periodicals, women were told to obey men. Even the *Girl's Own Paper*, an immensely popular publication in the 1880s, would still recommend submission to a man's will to a future generation of women. However, following this advice was not to be without personal cost for, in order to fulfil her wifely duties, a woman would frequently be required to sacrifice something in herself.

> *As for me, I daily wished more to please him, but to do so, I felt daily more and more that I must disown my own nature, stifle half my faculties, wrest my tastes from their original bent, force myself to the adoption of pursuits for which I had no inclination.*[9]

A similar awareness could be found later in a lesser-known article by Lady Wilde (mother of Oscar Wilde):

> *Hitherto the chief dogma of a woman's education has been simply husband worship. She was taught that if she studied it was simply to qualify herself as a companion to her husband; if she talked it was just enough to show that she appreciated his profounder wisdom. She was to resign all individual taste, to dress only as he pleased, obey meekly as he ordered and, whatever might be his faults, to give him unqualified homage as to a visible god.*[10]

In 1809 the writer and blue stocking Elizabeth Montague had written a perceptive if somewhat cynical comment in one of her letters, 'As for the intrinsic value of woman few know it and nobody cares'.[11] Throughout the nineteenth century many women (including Sarah Ellis), whether they were conservatives or radicals, novelists or journalists, did much to try to change that negative attitude by stressing the important role that women, as mothers, had to play as primary carers for their children. In addition to providing their initial

---

[9]   Charlotte Brontë, *Jane Eyre*, 1847
[10]   Lady Wilde, *The Bondage of Women*, in *Social Studies*, 1893
[11]   quoted in Walter Lyon Blease, *The Emancipation of English Women*, 1910

general education a mother was responsible for transmitting early notions of duty – for both sexes – and her own ideas and beliefs would inevitably have some bearing on the subsequent development of theirs. She therefore should be considered a key element in any process of conditioning.

The nature/nurture argument (over whether behaviour characteristics are due more to genetic/family inheritance or whether they were acquired through life) had already been underway during the eighteenth century, and indeed has continued right up until the present day, but during the Victorian period few would argue about the importance of having a good mother. This, for example, came from the preface of *Home Influence*:

> *The moral of the following story the author acknowledges is addressed to mothers only, for on them so much of the responsibility of Home Influence devolves. On them, much more than any other, depends the well doing and happiness, or the error and grief, not of childhood alone, but of the far more dangerous period of youth… The author's only wish is to aid by the thoughts, which in some young mothers anxious and eager to perform their office, her story may excite. To daughters also she hopes it may not be found entirely useless, for on them rests so much of the happiness of home, in the simple thought of and attention to those little things which so bless and invigorate domestic life.* [12]

One of the clear messages that the author, Grace Aguilar, wanted to convey was that *any* action the mother took could have a long-term effect on her children, not just in terms of their education but also the actual quality of life they experienced and the future people they might become. It was an important point, although one that could be taken to extremes – in his lecture *Of Queens' Gardens* (1865) the writer and critic John Ruskin was to assert that women had such immense domestic influence that they could ultimately be held responsible for all the evil, disharmony and war in the world. Certainly the rearing of children was a huge responsibility and should not be taken lightly.

Another highly successful writer of the period, Edward Bulwer Lytton, also had very strong views on the subject. He stated:

---

[12] Grace Aguilar, *Home Influence*, 1847

There is so divine a holiness in the love of a mother, that, no matter how the tie that binds her to her child was formed, she becomes as it were consecrated and sacred; and the past is forgotten, and the world and its harsh verdicts swept away, and when that love alone is visible; and the God, who watches over the little one, sheds his smile over the human deputy, in whose tenderness there breathes his own. [13]

It is unfortunate that in real life he did not consider his own wife to be such a mother, and his performance in the role of a good father is also somewhat questionable, but as a rule both parents had an important role to play in the development of their children. We may have a mental image of a strict or stern paterfamilias ruling over his extensive Victorian family; perhaps he is bewhiskered with a benevolent smile upon his face as he distributes presents near a decorated Christmas tree. His own attitude towards women in general, and his wife in particular, could set a very strong pattern of behaviour for his family to follow. Even if he treated women with respect and love he could still see them very much as an inferior species. He could also be someone who was personally feared rather than loved, tyrannical rather than kindly or wise.

There are some sombre warnings in literature of what happened when a father failed to take on his full family responsibilities. Dissipated husbands, as in *Home Influence* (Grace Aguilar, 1847), *The Tenant of Wildfell Hall* (Anne Bronte, 1848), and *A Brave Lady* (Dinah Mulock Craik, 1870), show only too clearly the damage that could result when the moral welfare of the young was not taken seriously and they were actively encouraged to take up bad habits:

Though her husband would spend weeks and even months at a time away, the impressions she so earnestly and prayerfully sought to instil in her son's own heart were or appeared to be completely destroyed by her husband's interference the whole time of his sojourn at home. It was his pleasure to thwart her every plan, laugh at her fine notions, make a mockery of all that was good, and holy, and self-denying, and all in the presence of his children. [14]

---

[13]   Edward Bulwer Lytton, *Night and Morning*, 1841
[14]   Grace Aguilar, *Home Influence*

When a father was heavily involved in business affairs, virtually the whole process of moral education could often be left to the mother, with the father taking on the occasional but visibly leading authoritative role of conducting family prayers or being the final arbiter of domestic affairs. It is possible to find occasional humour highlighting the difference between mothers taking on their serious task and the fathers' lack of relevant knowledge, or perhaps experience, in this area. In her book *For Lilias* Rosa Nouchette Carey used the illustration of a widower with four young daughters:

> *Mr Brooks … was a man who did not understand children. It embarrassed him to keep up a long conversation with them. They had a tiresome habit, Ada especially, of asking questions he could not answer, especially on Biblical subjects, and them regarding his puzzled face with round critical eyes. 'I don't believe papa knows,' Ada said once, when she found herself outside the library door. 'He only said, "Humph, Humph," like a big bee, when I asked him once if he were not sorry for the poor devil – I am because he is so wicked. I do hate to be humphed at like that.' Her sister tried to defend him… 'Of course papa knows all the kings of Israel and Judea, only he could not remember the name of David's grandson all of a sudden, and you learned it last Sunday. Papas always know everything,' finished Dora, with the beautiful faith of childhood.[15]*

In the majority of families the upbringing of the young was considered to be a woman's task and this was generally a duty performed by the mother herself or a suitable mother substitute (for example, a female relative, an elder daughter, or a paid employee like a governess or nurse). Even if a governess was employed to teach and look after the children, time spent with a mother was often considered to be of far greater importance because of her own moral guidance and influence over them. Any mother who failed to perform this duty of care was at serious fault. She would be at least partly to blame for the future failings of her children, and her failings would be considered sinful in the eyes of God. In the popular novel *Dora Thorne* a young mother had been unable to take care of her children, but the grandmother

---

[15] Rosa Nouchette Carey, *For Lilias*, 1885

was now handing over control and gave the simple instruction, 'To you, Dora, I must leave the highest and best training. Teach them to be good and to do their duty. They have learned all when they have learned that.'[16]

Lessons of duty were likely to begin in simple form when children were very young and generally under their parents' care, the primary commands being that they should obey their parents and love God. Whether receiving instruction at home or in church, from the Bible or other carefully selected personal reading matter, the message was generally the same for all children: 'What does it matter – what does anything matter – if we only do our duty and love each other, and submit to the Divine Will?'[17]

Fulfilling one's duties may not always be pleasant, but they were deemed necessary. In a letter to Robert Southey in 1837 Charlotte Bronte once wrote:

> *Following my father's advice... I have endeavoured not only attentively to observe all the duties a woman ought to fulfil, but to feel deeply interested in them. I don't always succeed, for sometimes when I am teaching or sewing, I would rather be reading or writing; but I try to deny myself; and my father's approbation amply rewarded me for the privation.*[18]

Being dutiful and good also meant being obedient. Wives were taught to obey their husbands; they solemnly took the vow during the marriage service and many took their promise very seriously. There is much to say on this topic in a later chapter, so for the time being I will leave it as a simple statement of fact. Children were similarly taught to obey their parents. It too was a fundamental rule. It was sinful to disobey. Mirroring the need to accept the laws of society and the rules of government, members of the family had to accept the rules of the family, as dictated by the head of the household, generally the father.

One of the duties an elder daughter frequently had to take on was becoming a mother substitute, whether on an occasional or permanent

---

[16] C.M.Braeme, *Dora Thorne*, 1877
[17] Rosa Nouchette Carey, *Not Like Other Girls*, 1884
[18] quoted in Elizabeth Gaskell, *The Life and Works of Charlotte Bronte and Her Sisters*, ca.1895

basis, and she could earn the respect and even admiration of others if she was successful in the role. Grace, for example, in *Not Like Other Girls* had to take on this role and the subject was under discussion:

> *I cannot think your sister an object of pity. Think what a good and useful life she is leading. She must be a perfect treasure to her mother, and I dare say they all love her dearly ... oh how happy she must be ... To be the centre and support of a large family circle – the friend and trusted confidante of each. What a wonderful creature this Grace must be! And how could [her brother] speak of her in that pitying tone? No life of her own! Well what life could she want better than this? To be the guide and teacher of her younger sisters, and be loved by them so dearly! Oh I think she is to be envied! Her life must be so full of interest.* [19]

A tragic carriage accident had occurred at the beginning of the classic story *The Daisy Chain*[20]. The virtuous mother had been killed and the elder daughter had become bedridden. The role of mother substitute had not yet been firmly established, so the next older girl, Ethel, had been able to pursue some of her own activities freely. Unfortunately, that meant that when a younger child wandered unattended, and unseen, into the room she was in, literally played with fire and got burned, Ethel was blamed. She was blamed primarily for her inattention – although the father, the other older boys and the servants who were all in the house at the time were similarly engrossed in their own activities. Still her father blamed Ethel. 'Didn't look, didn't think, didn't care,' he thundered. His own negligence, or that of the elder brothers or servants, was not under consideration. The assumption was that she, as the next eldest capable girl, should automatically have become her mother's substitute, and from that unhappy moment in time Ethel took on her new role. Her preferred activities had to be sacrificed so that she could attend to her new duties.

In order to be able to develop the skills necessary for her future role as a woman, wife or mother, any young girl had to learn the rudimentary lesson that a quintessential part of her role and duty was

---

[19] Rosa Nouchette Carey
[20] Charlotte Yonge, *The Daisy Chain*, 1856

the willing acceptance of being useful to others. I recently acquired a wonderful little book, supposedly written for girls of about seven. It was written by the Rev W.K. Tweedie and it is a beautiful little book, heavily embossed with gold markings on the cover, and with intricate engravings illustrating many of the pages, but there is no misunderstanding the fundamental message it contained regarding the position of the female sex. *Daily Duty, a Book for the Nursery, Fireside and School* was published in 1855 and clearly reinforced their traditional role. Almost at the outset, in quite a gentle manner, it stated:

> *You are not a queen or a princess, and therefore you must expect to do some work… I advise you to begin as early as possible to be your mother's helper in every part of useful affairs. Take as much off her hands as you can.*

The same message became more forceful in a later chapter:

> *You were not sent in to the world for yourself, but to care for others and be useful. Sometimes it will cost you a sacrifice to do so, but you will be all the happier for making this sacrifice. It is the privilege of your sex to forget self, and scatter blessings upon others… Begin with those who are nearest you, those who live in the same house as you. It will soon be found out by all around you that you like to be employed in their service. If a little piece of work will oblige anyone, do it at once… Such conduct sheds a sort of sunshine over a whole company.*

This was preparation for life as a woman, where her daily task would be anticipating the needs of others and meeting those needs before any consideration of self could take place. It was one thing, however, to 'scatter blessings' and shed 'sunshine' by helping people, it was quite another when everyone felt you were 'in their service'. It could so easily be an unending occupation and be taken for granted, and abused, by others. Harriet Martineau's *Household Education*, affirmed that children learn from the mother that 'it is an honour to be useful, as well as a comfort to be neat and industrious'.[21] Sarah Ellis summarised

---

[21] Harriet Martineau, *Household Education*, 1849

the task ahead: 'To know everything which can properly come within a woman's sphere of duty ought to be the ambition of every female mind.' [22]

Part of the conditioning of a young girl, therefore, was getting her to accept that being feminine was not just being one of the 'gentle sex'; it could also mean accepting a degree of servility. To put oneself first, to be pushy, to draw attention to oneself were also not considered to be feminine attributes.

> *To be able to do a great many things tolerably well is of infinitely more value to a woman, than to be able to excel in one. By the former she may render herself generally useful; by the latter she may dazzle for an hour... The Daughters of England must feel within themselves that a higher and nobler destiny is theirs.* [23]

It is not difficult to see how such instructions would help prepare girls for a traditional marriage; I have no doubt that they formed part of many a young girl's general education. Indeed, many novels of the period contain tiny snippets of conversation, or simple observations, that reflect the acceptance of the role from a very early age. In *Scenes and Characters* the older boys have returned from their boarding school. One sister, Jane, immediately went off to find a particular volume of the encyclopaedia for Maurice, while Phyllis was sent upstairs to bring Reginald his slippers and 'away went Phyllis well pleased to be her brother's fag'. [24] This was very similar to, 'she was ready to do anything one asks her, just as if doing it was the very best thing she liked in the world'. [25] Sarah Ellis had commented earlier, 'There is no sensation more cheering and delightful than the conviction of having been useful; and I have generally found young people particularly susceptible of this pleasure'. [26]

From a twenty-first-century perspective it may grate a little to see how only the girls were expected to become what appear to be

[22] Sarah Stickney Ellis, *The Daughters of England*, 1842
[23] Ibid
[24] Charlotte Yonge, *Scenes and Characters*, 1847
[25] Elizabeth Gaskell, *Wives and Daughters*, 1864
[26] Sarah Stickney Ellis, *The Mothers of England*, 1844

extra servants, but there does seem to have been a genuine pleasure in fulfilling at least some of the tasks. Such comments as 'I am quite ready to help you, Margaret, you know there is nothing I enjoy more than making myself useful' [27] could be found in girls' stories throughout the century. There was, though, an interesting variation on the theme in another story, a few years later, when a young girl called Nan explained the reason behind the enthusiasm: 'It gives one such a lovely warm, glowey feeling to help other people'.[28]

The girls' willingness to do tasks may not just have been a question of physically enjoying the tasks in themselves, or feeling virtuous helping others; there could have been more to it than that. Nan could genuinely have been on to something. Just as a little aside, I wonder if you have been following some modern scientific research regarding the personal chemistry of helping other people. Apparently endorphins, oxytocin and possibly even drapamine are released in the brain when we willingly do good things for others, and these natural chemicals have the effect of making us feel happier and better about ourselves. So rather than considering it a bit sickly sweet to refer to a 'warm glowey feeling' when running around as a voluntary servant within the family, it may have been an accurate description of their physical feelings at the time. This could perhaps help to explain why women (and girls) in Victorian times could sometimes appear so smug and self-satisfied when performing their duties, however unpleasant. It may not just have been a religious sense of deferred gratification as previously suggested – i.e. performing difficult or unpleasant tasks in this world with the hope of salvation in the next – the reward could have been much more immediate.

Being constantly ready to attend to the needs of others could have other consequences for a girl, in terms of her own personal development and the growth of her self-esteem. In effect, her time was not her own; any task that she was employed in could be interrupted if her attention was required elsewhere. Purely considering her own wishes would be taken as a sign of selfishness – a serious moral fault that would need to be corrected. Florence Nightingale made the comment:

[27] Rosa Nouchette Carey, *For Lilias*
[28] Mrs George de Horne Vaizey, *A Houseful of Girls*, 1902

Women never have half an hour in their own lives (excepting before or after anybody is up in the house) that they can call their own, without fear of offending or hurting somebody. Why do people sit up so late, or more rarely, get up so early? Not because the day is not long enough, but because they have no time in the day to themselves... A married woman was heard to wish that she could break a limb that she might have a little time to herself.[29]

This comment is particularly apposite in that much of Florence's subsequent life as an adult was spent as an invalid, not with broken limbs but still bedridden, and from that position she was thus ideally placed to avoid the time-consuming domestic chores normally considered appropriate for women, and she became free to contribute so much to the development of nursing and general health reforms in this country.

Female writers frequently mentioned this lack of time that girls and women could call their own during both the eighteenth and nineteenth centuries. In *The Daisy Chain,* for example, when a young friend of the family had to take over domestic duties in her own household she was asked:

"But what becomes of your business?"

"I get time one way or another. There is the evening very often when I have sung both [my brother] and papa to sleep. I had two hours, all to myself, yesterday night," said Meta with a look of congratulation.[30]

Even when girls from real life remember a happy childhood with loving parents, the role of the daughter as servant substitute can be quite obvious. In her autobiography Molly Hughes recalled, 'I came last in all distribution at table, treats of sweets and so on. I was expected to wait on the boys, run messages, fetch things left upstairs and never grumble, let alone refuse.' Yet she accepted all of this, and in her own childish way she had rationalised it, believing her mother did not want her to be 'spoilt' by her elder brothers, so had made her come last in all things, and anyway she 'loved running about'[31].

---

[29] Florence Nightingale, *Cassandra*, 1854
[30] Charlotte Yonge
[31] © Molly Vivien Hughes, *A London Child of the 1870's*, 1934, p6-7

If we look back to our own childhoods, although we may have forgotten much of the everyday detail, some events still linger that have left a particularly strong impression upon us. Trivial events, though, which may seem minor and insignificant in themselves, could easily become part of a broader pattern and, over time, these too may have influenced the subsequent development of our own attitudes and ideas. Nowadays we are very aware of how a child's self-image can be influenced and developed by the behaviour and attitudes of its parents. For a girl growing up in the Victorian period it was no different. If she was a loved child, even though her parents may have had very traditional, limited views of the role of women, she could still grow up feeling very positive about herself and the future role she may play as a wife, or mother, and the increasing contributions she would be able to make to the world around her. Some may not have been so fortunate.

Girls could easily develop low self-esteem if they were reared in homes where the male was dominant and the mother considered inferior. Consider what everlasting damage would be done to girls if they were constantly told:

> *You are not of the least importance. What are you? A creature of no account. A lass that has to obey her father until she gets a man. And then to obey him.*[32]

A father who treated his wife and daughters as inferiors would also be teaching a dangerous lesson to his sons, as Frances Power Cobbe put it:

> *How is a lad to learn to reverence a woman who he sees daily scoffed at, beaten and abused, and when he knows the laws of his country forbid her, ever and under any circumstances, to exercise the rights of citizenship; nay, which deny to her the guardianship of himself – of the very child of her bosom – should her husband choose to hand him over to her rival out of the street?*[33]

---

[32] Margaret Oliphant, *Kirsteen*, 1890
[33] Frances Power Cobbe, 'Wife Torture in England', *Contemporary Review*, April 1878

From both adult and children's literature it is possible to find an abundance of examples of belittling comments about the female sex from small boys through to old men. In *The Making of a Schoolgirl*, one boy, for example, was prepared to admit he 'had no definite opinions at all but merely regarded the whole sex vaguely as inferior and not worth troubling about'.[34] From the same book, being subjected to such dismissive comparisons as 'just like a girl' or receiving direct put-downs like 'you are only a girl' from male siblings might be considered trivial childhood incidents, but they take on a somewhat different perspective when you get the other side of the picture. The younger sister concerned had already experienced sufficient negative incidents to find herself having to acknowledge that, regarding such comments, 'I had to own sorrowfully that this was the case'.[35]

Another reason girls could feel disadvantaged was with regard to money. From my earlier research I had discovered that girls in eighteenth-century writings were very aware of being financial burdens to their parents; their daughter's marriage was often an economic necessity. With some exceptions amongst the wealthier population, male offspring would be expected to contribute to the household budget, to make their own way in life and possibly even support additional members of the family, not just the aged parents. This often meant that they needed a good education, and education had to be paid for. Girls would be less able to give financial support to their families – having other duties to perform at home – and as a rule had far less spent on their education. This difference in financial capability could result in preferential treatment within the family setting. In her autobiographical novel Flora Thompson said that girls were made to feel 'one too many in an overcrowded room, while her brothers when they left school and began to bring home a few shillings weekly were treated with a new consideration and made much of '.[36]

It was not uncommon for mothers and daughters to go without, for the benefit of their sons, particularly boys or young men away at school or college, who may not have been either aware of, or bothered about, the sacrifices made by those at home in order to fill their flowing purses – funds that may then have been frittered away on

---

[34] © Evelyn Sharp, *The Making of a Schoolgirl*, 1989 pp. 33
[35] © Evelyn Sharp, *The Making of a Schoolgirl*, 1989, pp. 92, 41, 28
[36] © Flora Thompson, *Lark Rise to Candleford*, (2011 edition), p148-149

merely frivolous pursuits. Not every father was like 'Mr Douglas [who] felt that every farthing spent on the female portion of his household was so much taken from his boys',[37] but there is not only an abundance of examples of girls who had to make some such sacrifice, there is also increasing evidence of the resentment it could cause.

The girl, beloved as she was, must always be prepared to make sacrifices for her brothers. In order that they should have a college education and every social advantage, Viola had to go almost without any education at all.[38]

Molly Hughes referred to another basic financial difference within her own childhood home. Her father made a point of giving his sons weekly pocket money, but as a girl she had to find a way to persuade her father to give her any *whenever* she had set her heart on a particular something.[39]

This lack of earning potential and their often total economic dependence on their fathers was another factor that could lead girls to accept their dutiful role as daughters, one that could easily be extended into their role as dutiful wives. Without their male providers, women could come to believe that they were worth nothing as individuals and so accepted the limitations of their lives that gender could bring. It would be easy therefore to assume that girls in the past did not pay particular attention to the differences in the way their male siblings were treated, particularly if they came from happy families, but it would be wrong to make such assumptions.

Although girls tended to accept their domestic role dutifully, perhaps without question, there is evidence that at times they did consider they had a rougher deal than their own brothers. Little comments are interspersed in the narratives that reflect not just the observations, but also the occasional bitterness of the writers themselves. In her autobiography novelist Elizabeth Missing Sewell commented, 'I always felt myself rather a black sheep in the family, though I am sure I had longings for something better, and vague dreams of distinction, kept under from the sense of being a girl.' [40]

---

[37] Margaret Oliphant, *Kirsteen*
[38] Mona Caird, *Wing of Azrael*, 1889
[39] *A London Child of the 1870's*
[40] Elizabeth Missing Sewell, *The Autobiography of Elizabeth M. Sewell, edited by her niece, Eleanor L. Sewell*, 1907

There was a more specific example, from Margaret Oliphant, which, although it may not have been based on her own family experience, was certainly based on observations she had made elsewhere. The setting was a domestic one, the two girls Ursula and Janey were engaged in doing the family mending, balanced awkwardly on their laps. Their brother Reginald had sole use of the table in the room, although 'what Reginald was doing at the writing table was probably a great deal less useful, but the girls respected his occupation as no one ever thought of respecting theirs', followed by the short summation 'and in everything the boys had so much the best of it'.[41]

There were other aspects of this type of situation, again bringing up the issue of lack of personal time, where women writers refer to the fact that as girls they were expected to work on sewing/mending/ other domestic tasks in any free time they may have otherwise gained, while the brothers whom they sewed/worked for were left free to pursue their own chosen leisure activities.

Not surprisingly the girls occasionally made comments regarding the very clothes themselves:

> By-and-by I pick up sufficient spirit to put on the despised female garments that I hate so thoroughly. How cumbrous, and useless and ridiculous they are! How my gowns, petticoats, crinoline, ribbons, ties, cloaks, hats, bonnets, gloves, tapes, hooks, eyes, buttons, and the one hundred and one et ceteras that make up a girl's costume, chafe and irritate me! What would I not give to be able to leave them all in a heap, and step into Jack's cool, comfortable, easy grey garments?[42]

Until mid-century at least there seemed to be little change in the overall acceptance of the idea that, perhaps with the exception of those in the upper classes, most girls at home would spend time 'being useful' during their daily activities, even if they had been allowed to play more when they were small. Over time, though, attitudes were to change, and there is a delightful comment in the book *The Making of a Schoolgirl* that reflects this. A serious education for girls was gradually being considered more important, and that education would take

[41] Margaret Oliphant, *Phoebe Junior*, 1876
[42] Helen Mathers, *Comin' Thro' the Rye*, 1875

place outside the girls' own homes. This meant that for a while, at least, girls would be exposed to other influences than their own parents and family, no matter how carefully the school had been selected. Here the schoolboy brother Jack was talking about one of his school friends, and the disturbing lesson he had learned from him:

"Wilkins Minor says his sister won't do a thing for him since she went to school, girls are never any more good, he says, when they've once been to school; it makes them so independent, he says. And Wilkins Minor knows." [43]

The move away from the accomplishments, so favoured for girls in the eighteenth century, towards a more academic diet took many decades to achieve and the arguments in favour of both types were made to sound convincing. Boys' education, though, was still considered to be of a far superior standard than anything a girls' institution could offer. From the same book Jack gave his derisory opinion regarding his sister's future establishment:

"You don't call a girls' school school, do you?... How poor! ... I know what girls' schools are,- no studies of their own, no fags, no gyms, no anything... Where does your rubbishy school hang out, Becky?"
    When told it was only the other side of London he scoffed more than ever.
    "Then you won't even go by train?... And you won't even have a river, or a bath, or a five's court? It's going to be a rotten show anyway, and I am jolly glad I'm not a girl." [44]

Within education one of the specific points of contention regarded the traditional male preserve of the classics. As the boys were to be the financial providers, it was necessary that they should receive an appropriate education, which may have included private tutors, schools and university. I had learned that in the eighteenth century, as a child, Sarah Fielding, the future novelist, had been encouraged by her brother, Henry, in her learning of the classics, particularly while he was the more

[43] © Evelyn Sharp, *The Making of a Schoolgirl*, 1989, p41
[44] © Evelyn Sharp, *The Making of a Schoolgirl*, 1989, p25-6

advanced scholar – but he had resented it bitterly when she outpaced him. I have come across similar references in both Victorian autobiographical and fictional works regarding girls who were learning Latin and Greek, which were still not generally considered appropriate for girls to study. Girls might be encouraged to do so if they had a particular bent for it, but *only* if it were to be useful to others, for example, in helping a brother do well in his exams, as Mary Martha Sherwood (a future children's author) had done. To study it for their own benefit was far less acceptable for girls; to be publicly proven better than one's male relatives was definitely not good form.

The novel *The Daisy Chain*, mentioned earlier, was a particular favourite for young readers and provides a key illustration of many of the issues involved here, so I think it may be useful to refer to it in detail. One of the daughters Ethel loved learning, particularly the classics, yet at times her focus on it led her into trouble elsewhere. Although her brother Norman needed her help in order to pass an examination, he felt perfectly justified in agreeing with his father that such activities took too much of her own useful time that could be spent on others. She was told by her father it was 'not desirable for her' to keep pace with Norman in his studies as 'it will tell on her by and bye ... she does not attend to anything properly, and her hair and dress are less tidy ... and she did her work too quickly'. Ethel's mistake was obviously in not showing that she was capable of doing both her classical studies and her domestic activities equally well. Her invalid elder sister, Margaret, went in for pure emotional blackmail:

> For your love of classics and keeping up with Norman you would give up being a useful, steady daughter and sister at home? The sort of woman that dear mama [now deceased] wished to make you, and a comfort to papa?[45]

Even though her brother did concede that 'all my best ideas are stolen from you', in spite of her own protests, to the mutual satisfaction of both brother and father, Ethel was forced to concede the point:

---

[45] Charlotte Yonge

'I suppose it is a wrong sort of ambition to want to learn more, in one's own way, when one is told it is not good for one. I was just going to say I hated being a woman and having these tiresome little trifles – my duty – instead of learning, which is yours, Norman.'

'I am glad you did not, for it would have been very silly of you, it is really time for you to stop, or you would get into being a regular learned lady, and be good for nothing. I don't mean that knowing more than other people would make you so, but minding nothing else would.' [46]

It was not uncommon to find that girls were, in general, very fond of their brothers regardless of the different treatment they may have received within the family. If boys were to become wage earners, or take on a significant role in society, they were the ones who needed encouragement and education to go forwards in the world. While the boys and young men were away at school, college or even work, the girls at home would look forward to their return, eagerly anticipating the exciting stories they would hear about their adventures, their expanding world and their knowledge. Their arrival home was a time of great excitement, celebration and family festivity. Fictional writings and autobiographies alike reflect this. George Eliot even referred to it in one of her sonnets:

His sorrow was my sorrow, and his joy
Sent little leaps and laughs through all my frame;
My doll seemed lifeless and no girlish toy
Had any reason when my brother came. [47]

Boys were looked up to and respected; they could even be worshipped, as did the young Mattie regarding her brother Archie in *Not Like Other Girls:*

Was he not the pride and ornament of the family – the domestic Pope, who issued his Bulls without possibility of contradiction? Whatever Archie did must be right. Was not that their domestic creed? A little slavish perhaps, but still so exquisitely feminine. [48]

---

[46]   Ibid
[47]   Marian Lewes, *Brother and Sister Sonnets*, 1869
[48]   Rosa Nouchette Carey

Every struggle that he faced in the world outside would be felt by those at home and every achievement shared. 'From a boy she had watched his career with dazzled eyes, rejoicing in every stroke of success that came to him as though it were her own'.[49]

This element of hero worship could easily be reinforced if on occasions the brothers showed special kindness or thoughtfulness towards their younger female siblings, perhaps sharing some of the privileges they so freely indulged in, which were forbidden to her. In her autobiography, Molly Hughes showed clearly the rush of excitement as her brother prepared to sneak her out of the house to have a forbidden adventure all of her own:

My father's slogan was that boys should go everywhere, and know everything, and that a girl should stay at home and know nothing. Often the boys must have been sorry for me, and one day when I exclaimed, 'How lovely it must be to go on the top of a bus!', Dym first laughed at the idea, and then suddenly said, 'I say, Barney, let's take her.' Barnholt, of course, was only too ready, and I rushed to get my things on before something could happen to stop us. If I had been asked to a royal ball I couldn't have been more excited.[50]

Bringing home new knowledge and sharing it, whether in the form of books, telling wonderful new stories, or simply passing on newly learned information could also help to foster the same hero worship, particularly when imparted to a younger sister confined at home. I can still remember the feelings of admiration and, yes, privilege when my own elder brother came home from boarding school in the late 1950s and allowed me, his very young sister, to watch his secret pyrotechnics at the bottom of the garden, well hidden from adult view. He was only nine years older, but that moment, that sense of awe, has never left me.

Returning, though, to the Victorian scene, as a child, a girl then may have learned to look up to her brothers, to respect them, to admire them, even to be jealous of them. She would also witness the way males in general were treated and how they, in turn, treated girls and

---

[49] Ibid
[50] © Molly Vivian Hughes, *A London Child of the 1870s*, 1934, p38

41

women within and, perhaps, without the family. But what specifically did she learn of her future role as a wife – how was she actually prepared for that, what were the lessons she learned not necessarily at her mother's knee, but more likely at her mother's side?

If you read widely across the eighteenth and up to the mid-nineteenth century, girls from the higher classes to the middle and, to a lesser extent, down to the lower classes learned about the importance of marriage. In many different forms and situations we read marriage 'gives such meaning to one's life'.[51] The situation had been explained fully in the novel *Married or Single*:

> *We are taught by books, by all the talk we hear from old and young, married and single, that marriage is not only the felicity of women but that her dignity, her attractiveness, her usefulness depends on it; that in short it is a sine qua non – the choice of the alternative is never to be thought of.*[52]

It made marriage sound like guaranteed life fulfilment, although, inevitably, there would be times when it failed to meet some of the expectations. However, there was an implicit negative assumption within the lesson: without marriage, without the existence of a husband and family, a woman was of no importance, she had no value.

> *And pray what do you think would be the use of you if you didn't marry? What can you do but loaf dismally about the place and serve as a wet blanket to everyone's enjoyment? What's the good of a woman but to marry and look after her husband and children? What can she do else?*[53]

It was this very lack of purpose that was acknowledged, by some at least, as the key reason why a young unmarried woman could feel so discontented; a state that would change as soon as she gained a ring on her finger. This was even included in novels for young readers; for example:

> *I think that what makes home life so trying and unsatisfying to so many unmarried women is the want of responsibility, the not feeling it*

---

[51] Rosa Nouchette Carey, *Not Like Other Girls*

[52] Catharine Maria Sedgwick, *Married or Single*, 1857

[53] Mona Caird, *The Wing of Azrael*

really matters, except for themselves, whether they are frivolous or not.
It is that sense of responsibility, which makes even a dull commonplace
married life attractive. The wife feels herself a somebody, a centre.[54]

For all the joys and excitement of a wedding to come, with all the
fun of purchases for trousseau and household, the delights of receiving
presents, congratulations and messages of love from friends and family,
there was a potentially very serious side of marriage – that some were
not to learn until well after they had taken the vows to love, honour and
obey during the marriage service in church. However 'noble', however
'beautiful' the position of a wife was, however much she accepted her
lot as 'different to a man', a wife was honour bound to *obey* her husband,
who remained legally responsible for her in law until the late nineteenth
century. There is a lovely quotation by Mona Caird, 'If only one could
be married without a husband. He is the drawback.'[55] Similar comments
can be found throughout Victorian fiction.

Those simple words of 'love', 'honour' and 'obey' carried far
greater significance than many girls were to realise at the outset of
their journey together. Women were to learn the truth of their own
situation, as wives, once they experienced the reality of being married.
They may have been wooed in splendour, treated as princesses, even
queens or goddesses, but over time the magic could fade. Romantic
wishes and daydreams are a far cry from daily chores and everyday
routine; we all can be guilty of expecting a little too much from our
partners. A wise mother would at least advise her daughter that she
must expect a change in her partner's behaviour after the exciting
engagement, wedding and honeymoon had taken place. As George
Paston wrote:

> *When the two are tied together by the law, and ordered to love each*
> *other by the Holy Church, why then there is no question of compliment*
> *or flattery or pretty little cadeaux in the form of hearts, nothing but*
> *prosaic commonplace duty. Then vanity, which had been masquerading*
> *in the habit of love, throws off its disguise, and turns sour and pettish*
> *and disappointed. And lo the honeymoon is over.*[56]

---

[54] Mrs Molesworth, *White Turrets*, 1896
[55] *The Wing of Azrael*
[56] *A Writer of Books*

Mona Caird was to make the point that it was not just the reality of married life that had struck home, in that the romance may have faded, but a woman could herself change when she became a wife:

> *Marriage changed the colour of things to the feminine mind; what was black suddenly became white. Duty, religion, convenience all came trooping to the front after the wedding ring was firmly on; a man ran no risk by marrying a woman of the dutiful kind.*[57]

Again it was the question of duty. Just as little girls had to learn their duty with regard to respecting their parents, and particularly their fathers, so too did wives have to learn that their duty towards their husbands had some clear definitions too. They would learn this from their mother, their reading, from their religion, even their husband; multiple sources. At this point I am not referring to any purely sexual matters – though that was one of the 'duties' that young women frequently discovered *after* their marriage and I will come to that again in a later chapter. Put in more basic terms one could say, 'The first duty of woman [is] a gentle and undeviating compliance with the wishes and will of your husband'.[58] If a wife did go against the wishes of her husband, it could lead to some very unpleasant situations. In the novel *On Circumstantial Evidence* the wife had dared to do so, but was very taken aback by her husband's hostile and blunt reaction:

> *'You will do no such thing,' he thundered. 'You will be good enough to remember that you are my wife and that your duty is to do as you are told.'*[59]

Young women were told that once married they had to put up with their situation – separation was unthinkable and divorce was generally out of the question until the late 1850s onwards. No matter how unsatisfactory the reality was, it was necessary for a woman to make the best of it, or suffer the consequences. Caroline Norton, who was to be so instrumental in some of the fundamental changes in the institution of marriage that will be covered in this work, once described the situation as it had been for so long:

---

57 Mona Caird, *The Wing of Azrael*
58 Frances Trollope, *One Fault*, 1840
59 Florence Marryat, *On Circumstantial Evidence*, 1889

The die is cast, whatever this man's faults... you cannot disentangle yourself... bear with them. It would be expedient to do this even if it were not your duty, but it is your duty.[60]

When girls had learned to obey their fathers and, in time, their brothers and when they performed household chores, they were known to be preparing for the normal routine of married and family life. It was all part of the conditioning process – but even amongst the older girls it was not to be without challenge. Teenage girls did sometimes query the obligation of having to obey their husbands without question. In *The Ladies Lindores* one girl, Nora, said it is a woman's duty to agree with her husband, and her sister replied:

It is in the Bible... one cannot deny that; still there must be distinctions. A woman who is grown up, and a reasonable creature, cannot obey like a slave. It is still more distinct that a child should obey its parents, but at my age it is not possible that I could just do everything I am told like a little girl.[61]

Looking back at her own experiences in late Victorian times, the writer Vera Brittain gave a fictional example of how mothers helped pass on their own conditioned responses. When one daughter asked why women don't stand up for themselves she was told:

It wouldn't do any good, darling. Men are the lords of creation; they've got nearly all the money in the world, and they learn all kinds of things women aren't clever enough to know about. It's just the way we are made. You'll understand when you are older.[62]

Similarly, other girls were told that if women did stand up for themselves, they were not actually being 'nice' or 'true' women. Mona Caird linked this back to the traditional religious perspective too, for in *The Wing of Azrael* Viola was still being told 'that all things were wisely ordered and that we must not permit a questioning spirit to grow up in us, as that would lead to doubt and sin'.

---

[60] *Stuart of Dunleath*
[61] Margaret Oliphant, *The Ladies Lindores*, 1883
[62] Vera Brittain, *Honourable Estate*, 1936

It was also necessary for girls to learn that, when all else failed, the all-important lesson of duty, which could at times be such a heavy burden, could also provide a vital prop on which to lean and, as such, be of great comfort. There are many references to this by women, and for women, in literature and I think it worth giving a few examples. Elizabeth Missing Sewell made the point succinctly:

> *But there is a strength in duty; it is like nothing else when troubles like quicksands are all around one, it is the firm spot on which to tread, and there is nothing so supportive to oneself as seeing others plant their feet upon it and stand up boldly.*[63]

Similarly, from Florence Marryat, 'Duty is a hard task master but the only one that brings us comfort in the end'[64], and Mrs J.H. Riddell, '[she] tried to do her duty and as a reward the road of duty was smoother to her feet'.[65] In his novel *The Red Spider*, Sabine Baring Gould commented, after the death of the mother, that the eldest daughter 'saw her way chalked for her... the line of duty lay clear before her as a white road in summer heat and she had not even the wish to desert it'.[66]

There could be a sense of reassurance in knowing what you 'should' do in a particular situation, even if you did not necessarily 'want' to do it, and it would, at least, be the path of least resistance as far as other people and their criticisms were concerned, and could even be a means of gaining vital support from them.

Although during the nineteenth century women were to work on raising their position in society in a variety of ways – through education, in employment, within marriage and so on – by doing her duty, by being prepared for submission and self-sacrifice in the interest of others, women were already seen to be leading the way in moral terms. Man was out in the wild world, the cut-throat world of business, while the women protected the home and those within it. Her home influence, at least according to some, was to create improved moral

---

[63] Elizabeth Missing Sewell, *Ursula*, 1858
[64] Florence Marryat, *The Nobler Sex*, 1892
[65] Mrs J.H.Riddell, *Too Much Alone*, 1860
[66] Sabine Baring Gould, *The Red Spider*, 1887

and behavioural standards that could ultimately change the world. Duty was to become a badge of honour not a burden of drudgery. Gladstone himself believed that woman's submission was her strength. Not all women were to agree with him, but, making a woman's submission into a virtue, a moral strength, meant the conditioning process was not considered in a negative way; indeed, it was another lesson a mother had to teach her daughter and this goes some way to explain, in part, why there was often so much resistance to change.

There were other ways to sweeten the lesson of submission too. Long before they became wives and mothers, girls could learn that their virtuous behaviour was already having an effect on their male acquaintances. Charles Dickens had referred to this briefly in *David Copperfield*, for David openly acknowledged, 'Whenever I have not had you, Agnes, to advise and approve me in the beginning, I have seemed to go wild and get into all sorts of difficulty.'[67] In *The Daisy Chain* when Ellen had admitted she could be selfish sometimes, her cousin Percy was swift in his response:

> *You selfish, Ellen! I wish you were a little more so; you are the most patient, devoted little creature that ever took woman's form. You have made me reproach myself enough, I can tell you and I owe you a grudge for doing so... Last time I was home I was blind and cruel and added to your sufferings by my uncalled for harshness, and never had an opportunity till this moment to say how grieved I was, when the truth was known.*[68]

Rosa Nouchette Carey used a similar device when a young man was telling his fiancée (much to her embarrassment) why she was so good for him:

> *I am well enough in my own way, and compared with other men I am not so bad... but as to coming up to you, Nan, by a long way, the thing is impossible. But I tell you this, it helps a fellow to keep right and steady when he believes in the goodness of the girl belonging to him... You have kept me right all my life. How could*

---

[67] Charles Dickens, *David Copperfield*, 1850
[68] Charlotte Yonge

I ever do a mean or shabby action to make you ashamed of me?
When I was tempted once or twice – for idle young fellows will be
tempted – I used to say to myself, no, Nan would not approve if
she knew it. And I held tight to this thought, and I am glad now
that I can look in your dear face and tell you this. It makes me
feel so happy.[69]

Girls only had to aim high:

That is the kind of wife I want... someone to guide me, to teach me.
Ah if women only understood their mission. That girl looked as I can
imagine guardian angels look – I wish she would be mine.[70]

It is easy to look back and review the past with the benefit of hindsight;
it seems all too obvious now that conditioning was one of the key
factors or influences that affected a woman's perceptions of the world
and her own place within it. In the classic novel *The Story of an African
Farm* this process was described in great detail:

They begin to shape us to our cursed end... when we are tiny
things in shoes and socks. We sit with our little feet tucked up
under us at the window, and look out at the boys in their happy
play. We want to go. Then a loving hand is laid on us, 'Little one,
you cannot go,' they say, 'your face will burn and your nice little
white dress will be spoiled'... It finishes its work when we are
grown women, who no more look out wistfully at a more healthy
life; we are contented. We fit our sphere as a Chinese woman's foot
fits her shoe, exactly, as though God had made both – and yet he
knows nothing of either.[71]

Women from as far back as 1700 had been questioning the way they,
as girls, were brought up and how they were expected to behave as
women. Writing in the early twentieth century, the barrister and
lecturer Walter Lyon Blease wrote:

---

[69] *Not Like Other Girls*
[70] C.M.Braeme, *Dora Thorne*
[71] Olive Schreiner

Men have been brought up to regard women as of less importance than themselves and that their desires, feelings and liberty were not to be recognised if they didn't coincide with men... Also from first to last [women] were impressed with the sense of dependence on the superior wisdom of others and of the absence of need for any reliance on themselves.[72]

With the emphasis on duty and servility, and dependence on both the financial and knowledgeable strengths of men, it is not difficult to see how the conditioning process helped prepare the girls as future players in the traditional marriage game. But was it fair to condemn conditioning as the only influencing factor whereby girls remained subjected to the rule of man? Were all girls affected by it to the same degree anyway? And is it fair to blame everyone but the women themselves? Of course not. What I have tried to show in this chapter is some of the ways that girls were subjected to influences that would affect their behaviour and understanding as children, and shown that they may have either grown to question these ideas as they got older or, alternatively, in time, just accepted them.

We have to consider the children themselves as individuals; the classic arguments of nature versus nurture were still valid. Both undoubtedly had a part to play and according to Helen H. Gardener at least, 'both are sadly and awfully awry, largely because too many people, in too many ways, pay to impudent authority the tribute of a thoughtless yes'.[73] Summarising the childhood experience of a mother who had given the 'thoughtless yes', Helen wrote, 'She was taught to obey without question and to believe without thought.' Unless the individual female actually did question her upbringing, and then made a conscious effort to change the process, her own limited beliefs could in turn be passed on to future generations.

I have previously mentioned Florence Nightingale. She and her sister Parthenope provide classic examples of how same sex children, raised within the same family, can become very different people. Florence Nightingale and her sister were brought up by conservative parents who expected their daughters to lead restricted lives and marry

---

[72] Walter Lyon Blease, *The Emancipation of English Women*, 1910
[73] Helen H. Gardener, *A Thoughtless Yes*, 1890

suitable husbands. Unlike her sister, Florence was bored and resentful. She did not want to be submissive to a man; she did not want to waste her intelligence or her life. It took years before she was able to become independent of her parents' influence and make her own pathway, but she and her sister had received the same upbringing.

The 'thoughtless yes' had been accepted by countless wives and mothers, but by their very acceptance, or apparent acceptance, of a submissive and subservient role in life, women, wives and mothers played a negative part in the conditioning process of their own children − even if they failed to realise it. As Sarah Grand put it, 'The mother was oblivious entirely of the natural results of a system which she herself spent her time in promoting and keeping alive.'[74]

There was nothing new in this idea. Such radical authors as Mary Wollstonecraft and Mary Robinson had already pointed it out in the eighteenth century, and Victorian writers took their point. If women, as wives and mothers, failed to teach their daughters their own self-worth as individuals, if they taught them to accept a submissive or subservient role and all the duties that accompanied it, then indeed women were themselves guilty of perpetuating a system that worked against the future development of women and their possible roles in life. If we accept that a conditioning process was taking place, we have to accept that women were as much of a *part* of the process, as they were *victims* of it.

Unfortunately, because of their role as primary carers for children, any 'thoughtless yes' was not just fulfilling a private, religious or devotional intention; other people would be affected by it, and could easily take advantage of it. Sarah Ellis repeatedly referred to the selfishness of men in her series *The Women of England*. In a similar vein an article in the *Girl's Own Paper* of 1893 was to give a warning to all young women:

> *Man, there is no doubt about it, is more or less selfish, he cannot well help himself, it is a fault which to a certain extent is compatible with his position as the 'lord of creation'... the temptation to real selfishness is great.*[75]

---

[74] Sarah Grand, *The Beth Book*, 1897
[75] Countess De Boerio 'Some Marriage Thorns and How to Avoid them', *Girls Own Paper* vol 14, 1893

But who had encouraged this selfishness, who was at least partly responsible for not correcting it? There could be a disturbing dawn of realisation when a woman looked at her son in a newly critical light and asked, 'Am I responsible for this?' One such example came from Margaret Oliphant:

> *There was a poignant sting of injured pride too, in the sensation with which she listened to him. This from the boy she had trained, to whom she must have given his first conception of life, of women and their ways. Had it been her example, against her will, unconscious of any such possibility, that had taught him to despise her?*[76]

The problem was that by women taking on a self-sacrificing role, however good their intentions of love, kindness or devotion, there was a danger that it encouraged any selfish trait men may possess. Indeed, as L.T. Meade noted, 'It is quite possible for an unselfish woman to make a selfish man'.[77] Matilda M. Hays would have agreed, for she asked:

> *Why should women foster in men the selfishness, which none but the highest and the noblest endowed can altogether escape under the conditions in which they grow up, the wife adding fuel and fire to what the mother begins, and the laws of society countenance?*[78]

In the early days of change it must have taken tremendous courage to stand out against the crowd. And those who did were certainly aware of the effects of the conditioning girls received and how they could influence the future, even by starting at home. We can still gain a real sense of awakening, a feeling of the penny freshly dropping for some of the writers concerned, as well as their realisation that there were other parts of the jigsaw that had to be placed, other problems that had to be identified and redressed before any long-term change could take place.

Before we consider these, it is time to shift the focus a little and now look at the boys, and the men, to see what factors were important

---

[76] Margaret Oliphant, *The Ladies Lindores*
[77] *Bel Marjory*
[78] Matilda M. Hays, *Adrienne Hope, The Story of a Life*, 1865

in their perception of adult life, as future players in the marriage game, and how their earlier experiences provided the training ground for some of the conventions and laws of society, which would then be only too easy to accept.

Chapter Three
Power and Control

It was a truth almost universally acknowledged (by most men at least) that to be male was to be superior, and by logical deduction a husband was thus superior to his wife. He had status, power and authority and his position was reinforced by both religion and law. It was even asserted that the key to the general stability of the country was through the man, as a husband, holding power and authority over his wife and family, and her willingness to accept it. If we are considering any changes that occurred regarding marriage in Victorian times, it is important that we look at the processes by which he acquired that personal status and power. It was not just a question of when a boy became a man but how he became one.

In his work *The Subjection of Women* John Stuart Mill made what, to him, seemed a very astute observation:

> *People are little aware... how early the notion of his inherent superiority to a girl arises in mind, how it grows with his growth and strengthens with his strength, how it is inoculated by one schoolboy upon another; how early the youth thinks himself superior to his mother, and how sublime and sultan like a sense of superiority he feels, above all, over the woman whom he honours by admitting her to a partnership of his life.* [1]

Unbeknown to him many women writers had actually been aware of this for some considerable time, and wanted to do something about it.

In order to truly understand and appreciate *how* this state of mind came to be accepted so easily, and from such a young age, we need to focus on the actual process of growing up, as a boy, that many

---

[1]   John Stuart Mill, *The Subjection of Women*, 1869

were to experience and, while doing so, I would like to pose a few critical questions. What did a growing boy learn of family gender roles, about women, his duty or responsibilities towards them? How did the females in his life, even from a tender age, actually contribute to his own self-image as a developing male? What were his own expectations as a boy or young man, and how did they fit into the world that he found as an adult, a husband or father himself? And what, after all, were the attributes of a successful man?

You may previously have heard the old adage 'give me a boy until the age of seven and I will give you a man'. I am not sure who actually said it. Some say it may have been St Francis Xavier and at the time he, personally, may well have been right. However, when boys were very young, during the eighteenth and nineteenth centuries, they were reared primarily by females – their mothers, perhaps their governesses, nursery maids and so on – and the foundations of any future development began with them. But much as a nineteenth-century mother may have been attached to her son, there were certain limitations regarding the education she could provide for him. While it may seem unfair to the modern female that boys in the past were the ones who were generally given a serious education, times were different then. For all the judgements we make in retrospect now, men were the ones who held the positions of authority at the time; their needs and duties were seen to be different and so they had to be educated accordingly. In all fairness, what could an ill-educated woman teach a boy about the skills and knowledge he would need to survive, let alone thrive, in the world outside her own home, with the exception of some sound Christian principles, which she could hope would offer him some guidance and protection against the unknown?

Through the minute details of their daily lives, boys, as well as girls, would learn patterns of behaviour that would affect their own lives in the future, and here the influence of the mother was known to be particularly significant. Samuel Smiles, author of the highly successful volume *Self Help*, was one of many famous men who were to acknowledge it. He had been particularly impressed by the selfless dedication of his own mother in raising her eleven surviving children under difficult circumstances, and mentioned many other important and famous men in his book, including Napoleon, who were similarly affected by their own mother's devotion.

A mother's responsibilities were immense for just as she could be the first to spot and encourage a child's developing talents, she could equally, in his eyes at least, be blamed for man's future failings. Much of her work had to be completed in the formative years before her son left her close guardianship within the home, and before he became open to the ideas and influence of others. Smiles stated:

Between childhood and manhood how incalculable is the mischief which ignorance in the home has the power to cause! Between the drawing of the first breath and the last, how vast is the moral suffering and disease occasioned by incompetent mothers and nurses. Commit a child to the care of a worthless and ignorant woman and no culture in after-life will remedy the evil you have done… The influence of the woman is everywhere. Her condition influences the morals, manners and character of the people in all countries… In short the influence of woman more or less affects for good or evil the entire destinies of man.[2]

As we saw in Chapter Two John Ruskin had a similar belief. Although both men conveniently ignored the responsibilities a boy/man may have in making his own future decisions, they did have a point. A mother could, for example, cause serious problems by spoiling her son through over-kindness, a common habit that could last well beyond the years of childhood. Thus 'we train the men to be selfish by spoiling them and doing too many of the little tasks we do out of love, which they then don't expect to do for themselves'.[3] Anne Brontë shared this belief and, in *The Tenant of Wildfell Hall*, she commented on the imprudence of a mother who indulged her son 'to the top of his bent … [doing] her utmost to encourage those germs of folly and vice it was her duty to suppress'.[4]

However, there were more serious issues at stake if mothers actually failed to discipline their young boys, with far greater implications for any weaker creature, and that included the women themselves. Let us take a look at a very specific example. Imagine a small boy at play, watched and encouraged by his mother. A boy keen on playing happily with inanimate toy soldiers may well have chosen to take up a

---

[2] Samuel Smiles, *Self Help*, 1855
[3] William Makepeace Thackeray, *Pendennis*, 1849
[4] Anne Brontë, *The Tenant of Wildfell Hall*, 1848

military career as he grew older, engaging in violence in the service of his country, but the child's game, even when playing with another boy, was not necessarily an act of deliberate cruelty. There were children, however, who took great pleasure in cruel or aggressive activities from an early age. I found this example in a volume entitled *The Mother's Friend*, published in 1864:

> *It has also been noticed, that tyrants and bloodthirsty men were once children who delighted in petty acts of cruelty... However small or insignificant an act of cruelty may appear, which the mother observes in her darling boy, it should be instantly reproved.*[5]

It was always better to teach by example, but sometimes direct intervention was necessary. When this author's own 'merry little four year old' proceeded to take great delight catching flies at the window, pulling their wings off and then 'laughing most heartily at the sufferings and pain of these poor mangled creatures, as they struggled on the window bench, and kicked and writhed in the agonies he had inflicted on them', his mother took appropriate action.

> *His astonished mother called the little butcher to her side, told him weeping, that flies, and every other living creature, were made by God, and that they as well as he had feelings, and that cruelty to God's creatures was a great sin.*[6]

This was from an actual advice book for mothers, a work of Christian reference, and it is not difficult for us to imagine what dangers could lie ahead if such behaviour had been left without reproof.

George Eliot was to point out in *The Mill on the Floss* that taking pleasure in inflicting cruelty in small ways could easily be extended towards other creatures: 'From a very young age Tom showed a desire for mastery over the inferior animals, wild and domestic, including cockchafers, neighbours, dogs and small sisters'.[7] It was clearly the mother's moral duty to correct such behaviour.

At this point you may be reminded of a quotation I used in my

5 Ann Jane Morgan (ed.). *The Mother's Friend*, 1864
6 Ibid
7 George Eliot, *The Mill on The Floss*, 1860

first book, by Samuel Richardson: 'We begin as boys with birds, when grown up we go onto women'.[8] If uncorrected, similar unpleasant actions could later be inflicted on sisters or wives, as the boys grew up into cruel and heartless men. So it was very important that a woman should teach her son that part of his growing duty, to God, to her, and for himself, was to develop a healthy respect for the female sex and take care of females in his own family, and later beyond it. If she merely taught him that males only were of any consequence in the world, and allowed him to learn and accept that she and his sisters were there only to serve his father and himself, then she was encouraging him to believe in the inferiority of women and to act upon those beliefs as he grew up.

Women were generally taking their other parenting responsibilities very seriously, making sure they helped to instil some form of work ethic, accept and pass on their Christian duty, inculcate a respect for authority figures and so on. I have come across several references to real factory owners who looked to the good nature of the mother when assessing the worth of a future local worker before they were prepared to offer him employment, and this brings us back neatly to the maxim 'give me a boy until the age of seven…' However, a mother's influence over her children is not the only factor we have to consider regarding a boy's development.

Until they were about four or five, small boys used to wear dresses – just like their sisters. You may have seen old Victorian photographs of them that seem a little strange to us now. Once they reached that age, though, the boys were taken out of their dresses and put into breeches. They began to be treated as boys, and boys were undoubtedly different. As Julia Ewing described, in her book *Jackanapes* 'You are a good boy, an obedient boy, an honourable boy and a kind boy. But you are – in short, you are a boy.'[9]

From his father a boy would have learned patterns of behaviour associated with manhood. He would learn that the male role was as a doer and provider, whether as an estate owner or as a professional or working man, and he would learn that, in time, he too would go out to take his place in the world. Once he was old enough to be

---

[8]   Samuel Richardson, *Clarissa*, 1748
[9]   Julia Ewing, *Jackanapes*, 1884

recognised as a boy, as opposed to an infant, his separation from the world of the female had begun. In time he would learn to identify himself with his father, with manly sports and activities, perhaps joining him on his walks or trips to work, or accompanying him on journeys further afield. Gradually he would learn to develop his own interests and abilities, which again would have more in common with his father than his mother and sisters, and thus continued to help distance himself from them.

Sarah Ellis, frequently quoted in Chapter Two, had this to say on the subject:

> *From their early childhood girls are accustomed to fill an inferior place, to give up, to fall back; while boys, on the other hand, have to suffer all the disadvantages in after life, of having their precocious selfishness encouraged, from the time when they first began to feel the dignity of superior power and the triumph of occupying a superior place.*[10]

We gain a very direct and personal image in this early contrast between the sexes from George Eliot, in *The Mill on the Floss*, for Tom had knowledge that his sister Maggie thought was wonderful and she:

> *...was rather in awe of Tom's superiority... [whereas] Tom indeed was of the opinion that Maggie was a silly little thing – all girls were silly – they couldn't throw a stone so as to hit anything, couldn't do anything with a pocket knife and were frightened of frogs. Still he was very fond of his sister and meant always to take care of her, make her his housekeeper, and punish her when she did wrong.*

At some point boys became aware of their differences and they began to challenge their early supervisors – in their learning, in their pastimes, in their desire for freedom and autonomy. The fictional legend Tom Brown 'began the struggle against the yoke and authority of his nurse' when he was aged only four. 'His battles... are wars of independence'.[11]

I found a rather delightful illustration of a boy challenging the will of his father in the autobiographical work, *Father and Son* by Edmund

10 Sarah Ellis, *The Wives of England*, 1843
11 Thomas Hughes, *Tom Brown's Schooldays*, 1857

Gosse. Edmund was raised by his very religious father and whenever he asked permission to do something that the father wished to forbid, his father would kneel and apparently pray. The father would then say that he had prayed to God about it and God had said 'No'. One day Edmund wanted to attend a tea party and told his father about it, but, before his father could intervene, Edmund told him he had already prayed about it and this time God had said 'Yes'. Edmund went to the party.[12]

There were other more traditional ways for a child to get his own way; in *Pendennis* a young Master Clavering was thus described:

> *He became too strong for the authority of his fond parents and governess, and rather governed them than permitted himself to be led by their orders. With his papa he was silent and sulky; with his mamma he roared and fought when any contest between them arose as to the gratification of his appetite or other wish of the heart; and in his disputes with his governess over his book, he kicked that quiet creature's shins so fiercely that she was entirely overmastered and subdued by him.*[13]

I have found evidence for this rising challenge in both male and female literature – but neither of which have been very complimentary to the female carers concerned. Put simply in the classic *Eric, or Little By Little*, 'Beyond a certain age, no boy of spirit can be safely guided by a woman's hand alone. Eric Williams was now twelve years old.'[14] A more vivid example of what it felt like to be the woman concerned was shown by the governess in *Chantry House* where:

> *… Griff grew beyond her management, and was taunted by 'fellows in the square' into assertions of manliness.*

That, however, was not the only thing that was disturbing her, for:

> *…she owned with tears she could not conscientiously be responsible any longer for Griffiths – who not only openly denied her authority, but had found out how little she knew and laughed at her.*[15]

---

[12] Edmund Gosse, *Father and Son*, 1907
[13] William Makepeace Thackeray
[14] Frederic W. Farrar, *Eric, or Little by Little*, 1858
[15] Charlotte Yonge, *Chantry House*, 1886

A woman in such an inferior position, whether governess or even mother, could not be entrusted to take on the proper education of a boy. He had to learn what masculinity was all about – what it meant to be a man, what was required of him in the world and what skills and knowledge he would need to succeed in it. He would do this by watching and listening to his father and other male relatives, from tutors and teachers and men at work in the world. Woman, for all her proclaimed moral virtues, just did not have what it took, although her early moral teachings would hopefully remain with him for the rest of his life. Many novels written by both male and female authors contained parting scenes where a young boy left home for the first time, generally to attend school, and the most common piece of advice given to him was 'never do anything that you could not tell to your mother'. Needless to say the boys did plenty that their mothers never got to hear about, and as they got older they did not necessarily continue to value the earlier moral advice they had received:

> *Even your admirable advice may be a bore sometimes. You are faultless; but it does not follow that everybody in the family is to think exactly like yourself.*[16]

It was not uncommon for a young boy to go to a local schoolmaster, or to start to have masters visit him at home for tuition in the subjects he would need at school. Already he was being treated in a special way, apart from his female siblings, and his activities and his learning were seen as being of greater importance than theirs. His position was changing and he could already be feeling superior to his female siblings because of the knowledge he was acquiring and the freedoms and privileges he had gained.

One thing that becomes clear very quickly on reading literature about boys' schools is how necessary it was for the newly arrived boys to distance themselves from their homes and the feminine influence there. Boys who failed to notice the importance of this could easily find themselves open to teasing and bullying. We are already familiar with comments like 'You are only a girl' within the home environment, but the issue became far more serious away from home.

---

[16] William Makepeace Thackeray, *Pendennis*

A boy who showed too much emotional response to the separation from his mother and home could find that at the very least he would gain labels in the form of nicknames that could be hard to shake off. The names Sarah, Betty, Molly or Jenny were used in a derogatory way instead of his own name; comments could be made on the state of his hair or the frequency with which he paid attention to it; spiteful comments could be directed at the over-embroidery on the shirts and collars that he had taken to school (so lovingly sewn by mother and sisters); even taunting nursery rhymes could be sung around him to remind him of his immaturity. All of these taunts could be very sharp weapons used against a new boy until he learned to look beyond them and join in the fraternity of the boys' school by adopting the language and behaviour of the boys within it.

In *Tom Brown's Schooldays,* it befell Tom to coach another, weaker boy, called Arthur, and he gave him the following advice: 'Speak straight up and don't be afraid or you will get bullied. Don't say you can sing, don't talk about home, mothers or sisters,' and he warned Arthur about the teasing he could expect if he showed any signs of being homesick, or if he was seen as 'mamma's-darling'.[17] The idea of the indignity and humiliation a boy could be made to feel if teased about being a girl can readily be imagined in *Tom, Dick and Harry*, where this Tom was made to attend a girls' school for his Latin lessons after he had had to leave his previous boys' school. He contemplated the consequences with horror:

> *The idea that any of his fellows should find out that I, a 13 year old boy, was going to attend a girl's school and be taught Latin and sums by a female, was enough to make my hair stand on end. How they would laugh and wax merry at my expense. How they would draw pictures of me in the book covers with long curls and petticoats. How they would address me as Jemima, and talk to one another in a high falsetto voice! How they would fall into hysterics when they met me and weep copiously and ask me to lend them hairpins and parasols. I knew what it would be like only too well and quaked as I imagined it.*[18]

---

[17] Thomas Hughes
[18] Talbot Baines Reed, *Tom, Dick and Harry*, 1894

Even if an older schoolboy had a younger brother starting at the school, he too could be teased if his brother was over-emotional; it was thus not unknown for an older boy to distance himself from his sibling – until the younger boy had at least had a chance to earn the attention. In *The Crofton Boys* Philip explained why he did not support his brother Hugh: 'The boys were all ready to laugh at me about a little brother that was scarcely better than a girl'.[19] The arrival of any new boy not only provided opportunities for such teasing but, for those who joined in, it also provided opportunities to reinforce their own superiority as older boys, who were more experienced and who had successfully distanced themselves from the female-centred domestic world.

Some schools ran initiation ceremonies – *Tom Brown's Schooldays* referred to having to sing in public or being made to drink quantities of saltwater. *Chantry House* described boys being hung out of a third-storey window or having to grasp the hot bars of a fire grate bare-handed. Unpleasant though some of the experiences may have been, such initiations marked a significant point in a boy's development, separating him from the sheltered and mainly feminine society in which he had previously been confined. After successfully completing one of these initiation ceremonies, there was a feeling of satisfaction: 'There he lay, half doubtful as to where in the universe he was, but conscious that he had made a step in life which he was anxious to take'.[20]

Many male writers wrote about life in a boys' school, with authors such as Charles Dickens and William Makepeace Thackeray confining themselves to a few chapters, while others like Thomas Hughes and Talbot Baines Reed were to focus more substantially on the subject. These male writers were obviously able to write from their own personal experience or knowledge, but female writers could still write in a similar vein because of the learned experience of brothers or other family members or friends. One exception to this was Harriet Martineau, who gained an interesting but unusual perspective on boys' schools. She actually attended one, and some of her own personal experiences there are included in her story

---

[19] Harriet Martineau, *The Crofton Boys*, 1841
[20] Thomas Hughes, *Tom Brown's Schooldays*

The Crofton Boys. The reason she attended a boys' school was that in response to its falling numbers the foresighted headmaster opened the doors to some girls in order to save his school. Harriet thus gained a female perspective regarding boys' behaviour, amongst their peers, that other female writers were not necessarily exposed to. She described the early experiences of boys in school very simply: 'Little boys are looked on as little girls in school until they show that they are little men.'

So part of the school experience for boys was their separation from the world of women and their assumed status change in doing so. They had entered the world of boys, of men, and there was much to learn. For a start what did it mean to be a man? Although there was often some common ground, people had different such views on the subject. Later in the century one clergyman, Henry Downton, wrote a poem for the benefit of young men, offering them a general code of behaviour:

> *Whatever you are, be brave, boys!*
> *The liar's a coward and slave, boys;*
> *Tho' clever at ruses*
> *And sharp at excuses*
> *He's a sneaking and pitiful knave, boys.*
>
> *Whatever you are, be frank, boys!*
> *'Tis better than money and rank, boys;*
> *Still cleave to the right;*
> *Be lovers of light;*
> *Be open, be above board, be frank, boys.*
>
> *Whatever you are, be kind, boys,*
> *Be gentle in manners and mind, boys,*
> *The man gentle in mien,*
> *Words, and temper, I ween,*
> *Is the gentleman truly refined, boys.*
>
> *But whatever you are be true, boys,*
> *Be visible through and through, boys,*
> *Leave to the others the shamming,*

The 'greening' and 'cramming'
In fun and in earnest, be true, boys.[21]

For a mother preparing her son for school, being a man probably meant being a gentleman, a man worthy of respect, perhaps worthy of his father's name. For a boy it could mean being a man of the world, one who smoked and drank, who rode horses and had all sorts of adventures away from home. It meant he had to learn new forms of acceptable behaviour and attitudes, and it meant that, for a while at least, he may have to turn his back on some of the precepts he had previously been taught. In 1858 Frederick W. Farrar published what was to become a major classic in the world of boys' stories: *Eric, or Little by Little*. His preface neatly parallels the moral premise of conduct literature for girls that I have referred to in Chapter Two, as well as in my previous book:

> *The story of Eric was written but with one single object – the vivid inculcation of inward purity and moral purpose, by the history of a boy, who in spite of the inherent nobility of his disposition, falls into all folly and wickedness until he has learned to seek help from above. I am deeply thankful to know – from testimony public and private, anonymous and acknowledged – that this object has, by God's blessing, been fulfilled.*

Eric fell by the wayside; he preferred the company of the wrong crowd, he gave up his work ethic and even cheated, he went out of bounds, he drank and he smoked. Worse than all of these he finally had to acknowledge, in true Victorian melodramatic fashion, that the grief that he personally had inflicted on his mother had ultimately caused her death. His tutor showed clearly where he went wrong:

> *The true preparation for life, the true basis of a manly character, is not to have been ignorant of evil, but to have known it and avoided it; not to have been sheltered from temptation, but to have passed through it, and overcome it by God's help.*

---

[21] quoted in Mrs Charles Bray, *Elements of Morality in Essay Lessons, for Home and School Teaching*, 1897

Only on his deathbed did Eric find reconciliation for his misdeeds, when he finally turned to God, and was also reunited with his mother, just in the nick of time.

It is difficult to know where to put a section on the importance of religion in the upbringing of boys and young men. Religion pervaded all aspects of people's lives; with a Christian upbringing at home, then having a tutor or teacher who was raised on Christian principles – frequently indeed a man of the cloth – and later listening to a school headmaster who regularly thundered his sermons at his scholarly flock (like Thomas Arnold at Rugby), all stressed the importance of a young man developing the attributes of a Christian man. The guidance of his tutors provided continuity for the lessons given out in church, and were to re-emphasise those taught at home. In the Bible, Genesis talked of the creation of man from woman and the God-given authority of man over woman. St Paul was particularly strong on giving advice on the silence of women and the need for wives to obey their husbands, as well as for children to obey their parents, and clerics in abundance stressed the dire consequences of those who did not. Eric, of course, was one such boy.

Rather than virtuously avoiding all the pitfalls of life, or suffering the dreadful consequences if you succumbed, a more realistic view was that exposure to temptations, of all kinds, would inevitably happen, but that each boy had to go through a process – perhaps even trying out some of the dreaded evils of smoking, drinking, gambling or worse – and ultimately make his own decision against at least some of them. *The Fifth Form Boys at St Dominic's* were very human:

> *Neither angels nor monstrosities, but for the most part ardent, impulsive, out and out workaday lads, with the faults and failings of inexperience and impetuosity no doubt, but also with that moral grit and downright honesty of purpose that are still, we believe, the distinguishing mark of the true British public school boy… Our heroes had their full share of trouble – what real life hero has not? – but they come out of the ordeal purified and strengthened with nobler aspirations after duty, and tender thoughts of helpfulness, towards those needing, if far from seeking, their succouring arm.*[22]

---

[22] Talbot Baines Reed, *The Fifth Form at St Dominic's*, 1881

Although I do not intend to look too deeply into the curriculum studied by boys at school, until at least the mid-nineteenth century the actual content was generally very different to that studied by girls. Girls tended to be told what to say, to do and to think. The emphasis on learning classics, mathematics and so on, for boys, was a very different discipline that required logic and reasoning, and would encourage independent thought. At school the boys were to learn the strengths of independence, courage and fortitude, which would undoubtedly help them in the outside world of commerce and business, but they were also to learn much about team spirit, group identity and the pleasure and prowess of engaging in manly sporting activities. They would learn the importance of being a member of a group or a club, of loyalty and not telling tales, of taking responsibility for their own actions, and accepting punishments – even if unfairly given and, when necessary, helping those less able within the group. The positions of prefect and head boy were much respected, particularly after the reforms instigated by Thomas Arnold at Rugby, and many younger boys aspired to reach those giddy heights. By being a part of such an institution, a boy learned to appreciate and admire what the older boys exhibited as manly behaviours, and tried to emulate them.

Even engaging in, or standing up to, such unpleasant practices as bullying could be seen as part of that process, and that could include learning an alternative approach to women. Sarah Ellis, who contributed so much to the theory of how females should behave in the nineteenth century, had a very strong opinion regarding boys' education. Just as she saw the dangers of foolish and indulgent mothers causing problems by spoiling the boys, she was highly critical of the culture of public schools where, in her opinion, 'the influence, the character and the very name of woman was a by word of contempt'.[23]

It will be hard to actually assess what *direct* influence a school had on a young boy's behaviour regarding women. Although I have already shown some of the evidence we have of the way boys would need to distance themselves from home when they attended school, in order to reinforce their own masculine status there, the same sources show that how a young man or boy behaved when he returned to

---

[23] *The Wives of England*

the family home, or when he encountered females in a social setting, differed according to both his own family relationships and his own personal development.

Girls looked up to their brothers, and we have seen how eager they could be to please them on their return home. Although Harriet Martineau had attended a boys' school, she had seen both sides of the fence, and described what it was like to be the girl left behind when the brothers went off to school, and how inferior one could feel when the boys returned. Thus Agnes had definitely felt out of place:

> ...as she always did when any of the Crofton boys came. They had so much to say to each other of things she did not understand and so very little to say to her, that she felt continuously as if she was in the way.[24]

As this text was primarily written for boys, it is not surprising that Harriet encouraged them to be more thoughtful in their behaviour towards those left behind. It is to be hoped that some of her readers took the hint.

When he did come home the image that a son presented to his mother could be very different to the one seen by his schoolmates. Denied some of the knowledge of her son's school activities, a mother may have considered her son as innocent as the day he had left her. Thackeray provided a bit of an eye-opener on this one, even warning mothers what they should expect, as this next quotation aptly illustrates:

> And by the way, ye tender mothers and sober fathers of Christian families, a prodigious thing that theory of life is as orally learned at a great public school. Why, if you could hear those boys of fourteen who blush before mothers, and sneak off in silence in the presence of their daughters, talking among each other – it would be the women's turn to blush then. Before he was twelve years old, and while his mother fancied him an angel of candour, little Pen had heard enough talk to make him quite awfully wise on certain points – and so, Madam, has your pretty little rosy-cheeked son, who is coming home from school for the ensuing Christmas holidays.[25]

---

24 *The Crofton Boys*
25 William Makepeace Thackeray, *Pendennis*

What the boys had also learned, by then, was that they *were* different – they had greater access to learning and the world outside – and that their own place would be within that world, not merely restricted to the domestic hearth. Regardless of whether a boy attended a local school or was sent far away, he knew that his future place was as a man *of* the world, and that women did not hold a significant position there. Schools may or may not have openly encouraged women to be treated with contempt, but they certainly promoted the superiority of the male sex.

For any boy leaving the confines of home or school, the world was an exciting place. It is not difficult to imagine the feelings of nervousness combined with the pleasurable anticipations of new experiences. Reading classics by Thackeray and Dickens certainly help you to appreciate those. We learn of young lads, for example, wishing to cover their inexperience at travelling alone for the first time, knowing what food to order in an inn, trying to appear taller or making their voice sound deeper and even wishing their facial hair would start growing so they could ask the maid for shaving water! And beyond these early difficulties, as Pendennis was only too aware, 'there were such manly pleasures and enjoyments' to look forward to.

Similarly, as he left school for the last time David Copperfield reflected:

> *I had been very happy there… and I was eminent and distinguished in that little world. For these reasons I was sorry to go; but for other reasons, unsubstantial enough, I was glad. Misty ideas of being a young man at my own disposal, of the importance attaching to a young man at his own disposal, of the wonderful things to be seen and done by that magnificent animal, and the wonderful effects he could not fail to have upon society, lured me away.*[26]

While he had been a child at home a boy was financially dependent, generally upon his father, and he was also used to having most of the major decisions of his life made for him and that dependence continued if he attended school or college. However, the time for change would come. He may have been prepared for some of the challenges he would face when he finally left home, his father may

---

[26] Charles Dickens, *David Copperfield, 1850*

have given him some indication of the need for emotional resilience and explaining the need to work for a living, but there was nothing like experiencing real life to facilitate his learning curve. Just as there were many advice books for girls and young women, so too were there such publications for young men. There were volumes to assist during the process of leaving home, attending university for the first time, even joining the army or navy.

Once the matter of finding initial employment had been dealt with there were so many choices to be made: where to live, how to live, what to have for breakfast/dinner tonight and, that wonderful choice, how to spend the first wage. There was so much pleasure in being able to decide how to spend one's own earnings – regardless of how large or small the amount. It would be necessary to learn to budget – or face the consequences of falling into debt. Money undoubtedly gave you power – and that was a lesson young men learned very quickly. It gave them the right to be a decision maker, the status of ownership, the power of control over others, and that could be a very positive and addictive feeling:

> *As for Arthur Pendennis, after that awful shock which the sight of his dead father must have produced on him, and the pity and feeling which such an event no doubt occasioned, I am not sure that in the very moment of the grief, and as he embraced his mother, and tenderly consoled her, and promised to love her forever, there was not springing up in his breast a feeling of secret triumph and exultation. He was the chief now and lord. He was Pendennis, and all around him were his servants and handmaids.*[27]

It was also important that from the outset young men had to learn to take care of themselves – in matters of nourishment, personal grooming, dress and so on. At home 'someone else' had organised the practical considerations of life – the food in the pantry, the linen on the bed, having suitable clothes to wear, etc. – and 'someone else' paid for them. It was very easy to take such services for granted, and realise only later, as Pendennis did at university, just how much you missed them. 'It was not til long, long after he was gone, that Pen remembered how constant and tender the affection of these women had been, and how selfish his own conduct was'.

---

[27] William Makepeace Thackeray, *Pendennis*

Being at work, or at least being out in the world of men, taught you other things: women frequently acted in a serving capacity – the laundress, the cook, the barmaid or maid of all work; all were used to taking their orders from men and it was very easy to learn how to give those orders, and how to expect the services to be delivered. I have come across various references to how female siblings noticed a change in the general behaviour of a son returning to visit his family home, and it was not always for the better, no matter how respectfully he may have continued to behave towards his own mother.

Going to work had reinforced his masculine status, away from home, away from the comforts and support it provided, standing alone in the society of men and boys. It gave him purpose and his own place in the world, and it was the scene of the achievement of his ambitions in life. Earning money had given him independence, status and position. Hopefully he had become respectable and responsible. It is not difficult to imagine the scenario of such a young man visiting home for the first time, taking delight in showing off his new hat, waistcoat or overcoat to his devoted sister or mother as outward signs of a successful working man.

We also need to consider what made him identify himself as a man, in his own eyes as well as in the eyes of others. There were many views on the subject. Betsey Trotwood had told her young nephew, David Copperfield:

> ...what I want you to be... is a firm fellow with a will of your own, with resolution, with determination, with character, Trot – with strength of character that is not to be influenced, except on good reason, by anybody or by anything.[28]

Later in life David talked of his own adopted habits of punctuality, order and diligence and his determination to succeed. 'Whatever I have tried to do in life I have tried with my whole heart to do well ... there is not substitute for thorough going, ardent, and radical, sincere earnestness'.

The popular Baptist writer William Landels was very clear on the subject; in his view being a man was not just a question of wearing certain clothes or his physical prowess – it was much more to do with his inner nature, his morals, his attitudes and his general behaviour:

---

[28] Charles Dickens, *David Copperfield*

Of men I would speak… men who can think soundly, feel generously, act nobly; good, true and noble men; competent men withal, who be their sphere wide or narrow, prominent or obscure, according to their opportunities, leave their impress upon the world and make the world their debtors; in a word, and using the term in its truest and highest sense, what we would call manly men. [29]

For Landels the real examples of manliness came from those who were men of religion:

Men whose religion is not talk but a principle of action – a principle lodged deep into the heart, and running out into all they do, whether it be working, fighting, planning or praying, purifying all, beautifying all, ennobling it. [30]

Samuel Smiles in his book *Self Help* reaffirmed that a man's happiness and well-being depended upon:

…diligent self culture, self discipline and self control, and above all on that honest and upright performance of that individual duty which is the glory of manly character… Riches and rank have no necessary connection with genuine gentlemanly qualities.

The connection between manliness and being a gentleman was one to be much discussed in Victorian times and, of course, it could depend upon one's class and social position. One may have all the characteristics of a man – but that did not necessarily mean one was a gentleman, and it was very easy to be judgemental. Using our example of a now educated young man, he had proved himself, he had money, he wore decent clothes, and he was independent, and ready to set up his own household, with servants to look after his domestic needs. What else did he need? At that point he may well have felt ready to face responsibility for at least one other dependent; he was getting ready to take on the responsibility of a wife and a family. These were additional accessories that were generally

---

[29] William Landels, *How Men Are Made*, 1859
[30] Ibid

recognised by other men, and women, that he was a man who was indeed well established.

We have moved a long way from our image of a small boy, arriving at school and learning that it was necessary to separate himself from the world of females, who had previously been in charge of him and feeling, to some extent, disdainful towards them. I do not intend to spend much time considering the transition from this position to one where he found females to be desirable companions – in whatever form – but gradually he may have learned to see young women, at least, in a different light. E. F. Benson noted this change in his autobiographical novel, while having a conversation with a friend:

'Tisn't as if I was a little boy any longer… When a fellow is close on seventeen, as you and I are, it's time he began to realise he's grown up…'
'But do you propose to marry at seventeen?… It's not much more than a fortnight or so that you thought all girls were rotten… Well, it seems so queer of you… It's rot if you are going to think about, and talk about, nothing else than a female girl. Besides she must be frightfully old. I shouldn't wonder if she was twenty…'
Then, part of his growth, had come this violent adoration of Violet Gray, as natural as the strutting of a young male bird, when first it is conscious of another sex than his. David had suddenly perceived that though in many things girls are 'rotters', there was something about them that made it necessary to wear button-holes.[31]

There was a world of difference between being critical of someone who was 'just a girl' and actually admiring a young woman, and there was much our young man could do to impress the female of his choice.

By virtue of his greater access to learning, by his own knowledge and application of such skills as logic and deduction, a man could justifiably claim that he had a superior education and, by extension, that he was intellectually superior to any woman. Some men took great delight in exhibiting their superior knowledge in public. Rosina Bulwer Lytton observed the habit men had of standing at one end of a room, talking away from the women, as 'being alone capable of

---

[31] E.F.Benson, *David Blaize*, 1916

understanding or appreciating the wonders of masculine intellect'. From her own experiences she knew that some of these men gained great satisfaction 'from the pleasure and superiority [they] felt in talking before ladies of what they could possibly know nothing about'.[32]

According to his own personal beliefs our young man may have been prepared to treat the young woman with respect and kindness, even love, but that was not necessarily the case. He was physically and educationally superior, and he could now financially support her. His position could also make it very easy to make value judgements about women regarding not just their actual level of learning and experience, but also their total capabilities. He could believe that as women had very little learning they were therefore capable of learning very little, and because they were not capable in the same way as men, it was absolutely necessary for men to decision-make on their behalf and to offer them protection from the world.

By the time a bride was ready to take her vows at the altar, her husband-to-be had already had a lifetime of experiences that had prepared him for the role of head of the household. When you add to this the religious authority that a husband was given over his wife (more about this shortly), it made his position of superiority very secure, and the laws for much of the Victorian period would firmly reinforce it. A leading member of the Plymouth Brethren William Kelly acknowledged that some husbands may have been difficult to live with, but the husband had still been appointed master, and he commented, 'It is a great thing to be always certain that God is right'.[33]

With the formality of a church setting, using the Service of Matrimony from the *Book of Common Prayer*, first printed in 1662, vowing before God and the entire congregation, the bride would promise 'to obey and serve, love, honour, and keep' her husband. In that first vow the key word was 'obey', and by accepting her fiancé's proposal, a woman indicated she had accepted the terms. How the husband would receive this obeisance, how he would construe his right to demand it, was a matter of his interpretation and personal belief. The Bible gave clear guidance in both the Old and New Testaments.

---

[32] Rosina Bulwer Lytton, *Cheveley: or The Man of Honour*, 1839
[33] William Kelly, *Lectures on the Epistle of Paul the Apostle to the Ephesians*, n.d. pre 1906

In Genesis, after the Fall, God told Eve that Adam 'shall rule over thee'. Similarly St Paul clearly stated:

> *For the husband is head of the wife, even as Christ is head of the church: and he is the Saviour of the body. Therefore as the church is subject unto Christ, so let the wives be to their husbands in everything.*[34]

So a wife should obey her husband. Full stop. Such clear instructions were repeated regularly to make sure there was no misunderstanding. According to religious dogma the authority of a husband was absolute, and men for generations were only too happy to justify their behaviour towards their wives by referring to it. There are countless examples of this in literature, both fiction and non-fiction. A good wife was therefore one who did obey, who did respect her husband's authority and would not dream of challenging it. Hence the advice given to Lady Cumnor: 'You must reverence your husband and conform to his opinion in all things. Look up to him as your head and do nothing without consulting him'.[35] Eliza Lynn Linton was being very outspoken earlier when, in her radical novel, she had stated, 'The majority of men make submission and virtue their female synonyms, and endorse that woman alone as loveable who takes such hue as they bestow, and speak such words as they indite'.[36]

This particular book had not been well received – her words were too close to the mark for a woman to utter. Yet it was perfectly acceptable for a man like William Landels to state, 'It is the right of the husband to rule and the duty of the wife to obey. And we confess ourselves unable to understand how any sensible woman can wish it to be otherwise'. Yet even he recommended that:

> *If the husband's will prevailed (as it ought to prevail, if it be merely a question of will), it would be so gently asserted, and so readily yielded to, that the thought of being oppressed would never enter the wife's mind.*[37]

---

[34] St Paul, *Letters to the Ephesians*, 5, 23
[35] Elizabeth Gaskell, *Wives and Daughters*, 1864
[36] Eliza Lynn Linton, *Realities*, 1851
[37] Walter Landels, *The Marriage Ring*, 1883

There were several reasons given for the need for the wife's acquiescence – it was not an arbitrary imposition. One of the key justifications for it, and reinforced by religious doctrine, was that there should be peace and harmony in the domestic setting, which was possible only if there was one person clearly in command. That person was to be the husband. When we come to look at the legal changes during the mid to late nineteenth century, this point will be referred to again and again. It was inconceivable that domestic harmony could exist if the wife had a will of her own and was free to exercise it.

Caroline Norton described the situation very clearly:

> *One of the most simple associations in the mind of a man who loves is that of being strong enough to defend and protect the weaker one. He instinctively feels that she is 'the weaker vessel', and the woman who carries into her home the consciousness, real or fancied, of her superiority, carries with her a poison, which will embitter the cup for life.*[38]

A few years earlier William Cobbett, a writer and journalist, had written:

> *There must be a head of every household and an undivided authority. And then it is so clearly just that the authority should rest with him, on whose head rests the whole responsibility, that a woman, when patiently reasoned with, must be a virago in her very nature not to submit with docility to the terms of her marriage vow.*

As he expanded his argument he added:

> *A house divided against itself, or rather in itself, cannot stand, and it is divided against itself if there is a divided authority. The wife ought to be heard and patiently heard; she ought to be reasoned with, and, if possible, convinced, but if after all endeavours in this way, she remain opposed to the husband's opinion, his will must be obeyed or he, at once, becomes nothing; she is, in fact, the master and he is nothing but an insignificant inmate.*[39]

---

[38] Caroline Norton, *The Wife and Woman's Reward*, 1835
[39] William Cobbett, *Advice to Young Men, and Incidentally to Young Women, in the Middle and Higher Ranks of Life*, 1829

Herein lies the crux of the matter. The husband *needed* to be the head of the household. He needed to be the authority – even in the domestic setting, not just because the religious message told him so, but also because the position was seen as a key part of his manhood, a public exhibition of his masculinity. As I have previously indicated, one of the key signs of manhood was the possession of a wife. How she behaved, how she looked, all reflected upon him. It was important that she was seen to act as a wife and obey him. If she did not, she was failing to abide by her marriage vows, and worse than that it was believed she was going against the laws of Christ himself. William Landels asked, 'Where is the wife worthy of the name – the wife who has anything like a due respect for her husband, who would prefer that her own will should govern?'[40]

Having a wife reinforced his own identity as a husband and as a man, and having an obedient and submissive wife made him feel strong and masterful. George Meredith referred to this attitude in one of his works, describing Sir Miles who believed 'not to have mastered a woman ... [was] the meanest confession a man could make', and whose own wife was 'a well drilled, many childed, timid little shadow of a wife'[41]

If a wife failed to submit gracefully, it reflected badly upon her and it reflected badly upon him. In *The Marriage Ring* Landels also asserted that:

> *...such a woman cannot imagine that she is honoured by the degradation of her husband, even though that degradation be voluntary, indeed she will despise him if he weakly allows the sceptre to pass out of his hand.*

So husbands held the authority, as the head of the family, but that did not necessarily mean that wives were considered totally inferior to them. For anyone familiar with the literature of the Victorian period the idea of separate spheres is one of the givens: the men went out into the world and the women stayed at home. Actually such a stark division of placement is somewhat inaccurate. Different social classes, different economic circumstances, different personal beliefs could all

---

[40]   *The Marriage Ring*
[41]   George Meredith, *The Ordeal of Richard Peverel*, 1859

affect the actual role the woman played in the equation, but the picture of such an ideal remained, and the assumption that a woman actually needed, and wanted, a man's protection from the world pervaded many levels of society. How she was regarded within that domestic setting was very much dependent upon the attitudes and beliefs of the man protecting her. It was not uncommon to come across such views as the following:

> *The man in his rough work in the open world must encounter all peril and trial; to him therefore must be the failure, the offence, the inevitable error: often he must be wounded or subdued; often misled and always hardened. But he guards the woman from all this; within his house, as ruled by her, unless she herself has sought it, need enter no danger. This is the true nature of home – it is the place of peace … it is a sacred place, a vestal temple, a temple of the hearth watched over by Household Gods… and wherever a true wife is, this home is always round her.*

This particular quotation is from *Of Queen's Gardens*, by John Ruskin, a classic text of 1865, and shows the reverence that was apparently held by some men, for women, and was an acknowledgement that a wife had a very special place in life, to complement her husband's chivalric role. This had already been much discussed by Sarah Ellis in her conduct books for women:

> *And a sacred ennobling trust it is for woman to have the happiness of such a being committed to her charge – a holy privilege to be the chosen companion of his lot – to come with her helplessness and weakness to find safety under his protection, and to repose her own perturbed and troubled mind beneath the shelter of his love… It would, indeed, be a hard thing to refuse to the husband who returns home from his desk, his counter or the fields, the best seat or choicest food, with any other indulgences his circumstances may afford.*[42]

William Landels, whom I have already mentioned, was very much a supporter of the separate spheres argument, asserting that woman

---

[42] *The Wives of England*

was by no means man's inferior; indeed, if anything, he was actually inferior to her in some ways because of her willingness to sacrifice herself in the service of her husband and family.[43] Landels was also keen to point out that though it may be proven in time that a woman could do many of the tasks achieved by a man, he could not do hers half so well. Domestic attentions; care of the children, the sick and the dying; these needed the benefit of a woman's touch. The home was her sphere of excellence.

Some men, and indeed some women, saw it that way. However, it becomes obvious that many Victorian men did not. For however hard such men as Ruskin may have argued, there were some things that did not fit in with the notion of the home being the woman's sphere, with her queening over it. For the one who reigned supreme over the domestic situation was still the man, *unless* he, as the husband, chose *not* to exercise his rights. And in that supremacy he had not just the basis of religious authority behind him, as we have seen; until well into the Victorian period he had the full support of English law. From all my research in both the realms of fiction and non-fiction, it is perfectly obvious that with very few exceptions men were only too happy to accept the extra powers they had, *within* the domestic sphere, and indeed expected to continue to have them as a matter of right. I am of course referring to the legal rights of a husband and how they extended over property, possessions, wives and children.

Let us go back a little and return to our example of the young lad who has gone through school and become an independent young man. Over time he would have become aware of the personal advantages to be gained from getting married and considered what use he planned to make of them. In literature I have found many examples of young men being advised to marry for financial reasons, or their own determination to do so. Thus Pendennis told his friend Warrington:

I am getting on in life. I have got devilish little money. I want some. I am thinking of getting some and settling in life. I'm thinking of settling. I'm thinking of marrying, old boy... I've rather serious thoughts about settling and marrying. No man can get on in life without some serious money at his back... And as I have not got

---

43 William Landels, *The True Glory of Woman*, 1871

enough capital from my father's, I must get some by my wife, that's all
... if ever I marry it will be a marriage of reason that I make with a
well bred, good tempered, good looking person who has a little money
and so forth, that will cushion our carriage in its course through life. [44]

During the marriage service the groom actually said, 'With all my
worldly goods I thee endow', but that was not strictly true for, as
Margaret Oliphant pointed out, the husband was the one who made
all the gains: 'Everything is his; his own earnings, her earnings, the
property of both. Happy husband, unfortunate wife'.[45]

Although many men had knowledge of the law, through their
education or business dealings, not all women were familiar with the
full extent of the situation regarding the transfer of property rights
after marriage. Any husband was indeed in a fortunate position, for,
unless his wife had had a marriage settlement arranged on her behalf,
once they were married he took control of all her wealth, her money,
her possessions, and her property. It was assumed that because he had
greater knowledge and experience he would make sound decisions
that would be in their best interest. Even if a settlement did exist, there
were ways and means to get round it, so women writers from the
eighteenth century onwards had been trying to forewarn members of
their sex that there could be problems ahead:

> *He flattered himself that he knew the world, and the sex, too well for*
> *any danger to exist that property settled on a wife could fail in one*
> *way or the other to become the property of the husband. He had made*
> *himself familiar in theory at least, both with kissing and cuffing, and*
> *no man could have a more implicit confidence in the law that he had,*
> *in that which says, what belongs to my wife is mine, what belongs to*
> *me is my own.* [46]

In his position as head of the household, and as the more
knowledgeable of the two, a new husband thus gained financial
control of all household affairs, even if he chose to delegate the
day-to-day domestic affairs (including budgeting) to his wife. Such

---

[44] William Makepeace Thackeray, *Pendennis*
[45] Margaret Oliphant, 'The Grievances of Women', *Fraser's Magazine*, May 1880
[46] Frances Trollope, *The Life and Adventures of a Clever Woman*, 1854

a position was thought to promote domestic harmony, but it was a position that could be exploited. I have found frequent references in both eighteenth- and nineteenth-century literature to an additional and somewhat disturbing power over a woman that was to be gained by controlling the purse strings. The renowned early novelist Samuel Richardson had commented on this when he stated that any financial independence a wife had 'destroys love, by putting it out of a man's power to lay any obligation on her that might engage gratitude and kindle affection'.[47] In other words a woman could have to barter her self, her affections, even her body in order to get the things she wanted from her husband. Mary Elizabeth Braddon referred to the same point in one of her novels when a male character stated:

> *I will freely own to you that I do not understand or approve the modern system of making a wife independent of her husband. Dependence is one of woman's sweetest attributes, her most winning charm.*[48]

There were other advantages for a man by being married, for, apart from becoming his financial dependent, his wife was now legally bound to him. It was practically impossible for her to get a divorce if she was unhappy. She was no longer a free person; she needed his permission to do things. She was permanently tied to him, and would be returned to him should she decide to leave. She was also ordered to subject herself to him in all things, and that included sex. There was no such thing as rape in marriage in this country, at least not until 1991. It was rather interesting to discover that one Victorian doctor, who preferred to remain anonymous, was known to comment that if girls were actually made aware of the fact that this sexual obligation was expected, or rather demanded of them, in marriage, then they would have been far less willing to take their marriage vows.

In addition to the obvious advantages a husband had gained, he did take on certain obligations and responsibilities. He became legally responsible for his wife, he had to act as her representative and on her behalf. Ordinary men were able to vote in elections – at least after the Reform Bill of 1832 had expanded the electorate – but she

---

[47] Samuel Richardson, *The Rambler*, No.97, Feb 19th 1751
[48] Mary Elizabeth Braddon, *Taken at the Flood*, 1874

had no political voice. She lost her legal identity as an individual and thus could no longer engage in contracts, sue or be sued. Any debts she ran up became his to deal with. In one way it was necessary for a husband to watch the purse strings, for he would be the one to take the consequences if they were stretched too far. It provided an additional justification for his need to be in control – it all made perfect sense.

At this point it is probably appropriate to mention any children from the marriage. As a father the husband had responsibilities for them and rights over them. He may well have envisaged a son as his heir, to property, to family estate, to his business. Just as his wife was now his dependent, so any children would become his dependents too and as such he was their legal custodian, and could determine who should care for his children in the event of his being unable to do so, or if he died. Having children was another way that he could exert his power and authority over his wife too – for she looked after the children only *if* he approved. Once again it was all to do with his position, supported by religion and law. Just as a wife had to obey, so too did his children. He expected them all to acknowledge his authority and respect him, just as he had been brought up to do.

During this chapter we have seen how men could and did have great confidence in themselves and their abilities, and how as husbands and fathers their belief in God had justified their position of authority. According to Sarah Ellis, 'It is unquestionably the inalienable right of all men, whether ill or well, rich or poor, wise or foolish, to be treated with deference and made much of in their own home'.[49] Any failure to do so could be taken as a dereliction of female duty. With all the romantic notions of courtly love, the chivalric actions of a dedicated lover protecting the feeble and delicate female from the dragons of worldly life, the heroic actions of the physically stronger, and the eternal gratitude and submission of the weaker sex, it really was not difficult to see the apparent logic of the argument and the need for its acceptance and continuance by some, if not all, of the participants themselves.

With the ultimate demonstration of his own masculinity, his apotheosis of manhood, our given exemplary male was now in

---

[49] *The Wives of England*

possession of a wife and family. He was in control of both them and their possessions, and it felt perfectly right and fitting that he should be so. He too had been conditioned to accept his role in the game. There was nothing amiss in the situation from his perspective and a dutifully trained wife would support him by accepting her submissive role in exchange for his protection. That was marriage as it was accepted, at least for the first half of the nineteenth century.

However, in spite of all her exhortations on how women should fulfil their wifely duties, Sarah Ellis had still felt it necessary to warn her readers that 'All women should… be prepared for discovering faults in men, as they are for beholding spots in the sun, or clouds in the summer sky'.[50] Only time would tell.

---

[50] Ibid

PART THREE

TIME FOR CHANGE

Chapter Four
Enough is Enough

You are free to walk about, looking this way and that, critically surveying all, able to make your own choice after mature deliberation, while we may not look around us or seek to judge for ourselves. On the contrary, we must accept the first rose that is offered to us, think it adorable, perfect, fall down before it in worship and look contentedly at it 'til the end of our days… Oh what a bitter hour that must be, when a woman lifts her eyes, and looking at her husband sitting opposite her, realises for the first time that she has made a mistake.[1]

So where did it all go wrong? At what point did the chivalric rhetoric become too much? When did the generous reassurances that the 'interests of women' were protected by law no longer seem convincing, and how did the idea that something had to change shift from being a thought into an action? What indeed took the game to a different level? These are not the sorts of questions that can be given a simple answer.

We now know that women writers throughout the eighteenth century were, in their own way, protesting about the injustices in law and society that affected them personally. Many of the issues raised in my first book, for example the limited educational opportunities for girls and expected submission of the female sex, had been reiterated again and again by individuals who shared some common, and often distressing, experiences, but at least, by now, we should have some greater understanding about why their personal conditioning and circumstances may have inhibited any feelings of rebellion, let alone willingness to directly challenge the status quo.

Although the primary focus of my work is the changing nature of

---

[1]   Helen Mathers, *Comin' Thro' the Rye*, 1875

the relationship between husbands and wives, it has to be acknowledged that not all men failed to respect and care for their partners. While few men spoke out openly against the traditional system, it is true that there were those who believed in the importance of a patriarchal society and yet took on their authoritative role within marriage without feeling the need to exert any force to maintain it. Many women themselves were happy with the system, or were prepared to accept it, even if they privately disagreed with the principle involved. That being said I intend to leave those happy couples to one side, and look more closely at some of the problems that were faced by many women after they had taken their vows.

Let us begin with a newly married bride: eager to please her husband, devoted to his interests and apparently convinced that he is her superior. Life may have continued rosily as they learned to live together, especially if each acted out their role as preconceived by the other, but real, day-to-day experience is a great way for removing those rose-coloured spectacles, those unrealistic preconceptions. At some point something would change. One journalist, Eliza Lynn Linton, described a wife facing the moment of truth in one of her articles:

> *She had been taught to believe in men, and to honour them, and she did not wish to unlearn her lesson... For the first few weeks all went according to the brightness of her belief... She believed as others, ardent and loving, have believed, and she awoke like them, when the bitter fruit of knowledge was between her lips and the dead leaves of her young hopes strewed the ground at her feet.* [2]

Time and again married couples were to discover their partners were not quite as they wished them to be. The husband and the wife did not behave in the same way as the courting lover and the fair maiden. William Makepeace Thackeray had humorously commented that things would be very different if women had seen men in a more realistic light:

> *Let a man pray that none of his womenkind should form a just estimation of him. If your wife knew you as you are, neighbour, she*

---

[2]   Eliza Lynn Linton, '*One of Our Legal Fictions*', Household Words, April 1854

would not grieve much about being your widow, and would let your grave-lamp go out very soon, or perhaps not even take the trouble to light it.[3]

There were many things that women had to learn about married life; for example, they would <u>not</u> necessarily be able to do exactly as they wanted. Numerous brides-to-be had joyfully anticipated greater freedom in marriage than they had received under the jurisdiction of their fathers, but then had subsequently failed to achieve it, much to their obvious dismay. Women writers, often writing semi-autobiographically, referred to this frequently in their novels:

Englishmen seem to think that the nearest approach to perfection in a wife is to be found alone in those women who are the best imitation of automatons.[4]

She became every day and every hour more and more fully aware that she was to live, move and have her being wholly and solely... according to, and dependent on, the will and pleasure of her husband.[5]

He rules over me, though the reins be silken ones, and I don't wish to be ruled.[6]

In December 1868 an article was published in a popular periodical, which summarised the general view of wedlock, as held by many men of the time:

A woman's whole life and being, her soul, body, time, property, thought and care ought to be given to her husband; that nothing short of such absorption in him and his interests makes her a true wife; and that when she is thus absorbed even a very mediocre character and inferior intellect can make a man happy.[7]

---

[3]   *Pendennis*

[4]   Rosina Bulwer Lytton, *Cheveley: Or, The Man of Honour*

[5]   Frances Trollope, *One Fault*, 1840

[6]   Florence Marryat, *At Heart a Rake*, 1895

[7]   Frances Power Cobbe, 'Criminals, Idiots, Women and Minors', *Fraser's Magazine*, December 1868

As we saw in Chapter Three, just as women had been conditioned by their inferior education so too had men been conditioned into believing they *were* the superior species, and they generally did possess far greater knowledge, and did have a much broader experience of the world than the vast majority of women. It is not really surprising, then, that males tended to hold little respect for the intellectual abilities of women, particularly if they had never personally encountered a really intelligent female, or were prepared to regard such a being as truly exceptional.

The combination of this masculine 'superiority' and the expectation of wifely obedience meant that wives may have found it necessary to suppress their real abilities in spite of any personal resentment or distress they may have suffered in the process of doing so. It was not pleasant for an intelligent wife to be considered intellectually inferior, let alone be treated as such; it could be a very demoralising experience. Also any woman who did show genuine intelligence, particularly in the wrong company, could easily find herself labelled 'unfeminine' or 'unnatural' – by either sex. However necessary it was deemed at the time, choosing to play down her own abilities and understanding would, unfortunately, both help to reinforce the husband's/male ego and, at the same time, continue to diminish her own, as well as help reinforce the common image of the female sex.

In one of her novels Florence Marryat was to describe a wife's position where her husband excluded her from any serious activity; many feminists were to later echo her words in the struggle for emancipation:

> *He always thought her too childish to consult about any of his private affairs: he had treated her as a child, without ever taking the trouble to find out whether she was so or not.*[8]

It could also be difficult for a married woman to have the opportunity to fully develop her own intellectual skills, if she wanted to, when she was constantly beset by domestic obligations, while having to support her husband in his more 'important' ones. In addition to the frequent comments on their lack of free time in general, there were to be some

---

[8]   Florence Marryat, *Love's Conflict*, 1865

rather perceptive remarks regarding the success of men's ventures, and the fact that there was, for example, no female equivalent of Shakespeare.

> *How many masculine works we marvel would be suppressed if all the quiet temple chambers, all the silent libraries and unapproachable studies, were shut up and the authors had to scribble in a drawing room, with children, nurses, notes and visitors pouring in and out all day long?[9]*

Sarah Ellis, that conduct book guru of earlier chapters, had been only too clear in *The Wives of England*, in a section entitled 'Trials of Married Life', that if a wife did make the mistake of showing equal or superior skills, the husband would feel threatened, or jealous, and he would certainly try to thwart her. Other women writers were to agree with this: 'A man of ordinary calibre never forgives superiority in a woman'[10] and 'Man did not care much for women whose intellect made him aware of the deficiency of his own'[11] were typical examples. Years later women were apparently still being told:

> *You've got to play the silly fool to a man, then he feels superior... You must know nothing, do nothing, see nothing but just what suits his pleasure and convenience and in order to answer to his requirements you must either be a hypocrite or a blind worm, without eyes or intelligence.[12]*

His feelings of superiority could also make a husband believe himself to be totally infallible. So, having accepted that superior position, the husband could also feel that he had the duty as well as the right to correct his wife, although she may have neither agreed with his opinion nor appreciated the lesson. Frances Trollope was one authoress who frequently made references to this belief in her works, and showed how the wives could be affected by it. A particularly relevant novel here was *One Fault,* published in 1840, and the following three examples were all taken from that. Thus, Mr Wentworth informed his wife:

---

[9]   Frances Power Cobbe, 'The Subjection of Women', *Theological Review*, 1869
[10]   Matilda Hays, *Adrienne Hope*
[11]   Florence Marryat, *On Circumstantial Evidence*, 1889
[12]   Sarah Grand, *The Beth Book*, 1897

And when it happens that I do not perfectly agree with you, it need produce no mortification on your part, as, of course dearest, I shall never scruple to put you right.

An authorial comment clarified the underlying problem:

And as is usual for all men of his temperament, he quite overlooked the possibility of his wife's feelings on the subject being in perfect contrast to his own.

It is easy to see why many have interpreted marriage, as it used to be, as primarily being concerned with power and control. For all the talk of a woman's persuasive power over men, and a wife only having to flatter her husband in order to wheedle out of him whatever she actually wanted, that argument fell down at one basic stumbling block – the husband would accept the flattery and give in to the request only if it actually suited him to do so. Once again although Mr Wentworth allowed his wife to tell him what she wanted, it might have been a pointless concession:

Ask then for everything you wish... I will never abuse the trust you have reposed in me by permitting the slightest thing I don't perfectly approve.

So a wife may have become extremely disgruntled if her husband treated her as an inferior in intellect, status and value within the marriage – even if she had felt it was her duty to put up with it. Complaining or nagging would hardly improve matters, and many women sought refuge in their writing, relieving their feelings by writing privately in diaries or in more public form, but, whatever action a wife chose to take, she could still end up feeling completely stifled and disheartened by it all. In another of her novels Frances summarised the situation:

There must be something very, very deplorable in being perpetually exposed – not to the anger, not to the reprehension, not to the dislike of the being you have selected as your companion for life, but everlastingly to his, or her, contempt.[13]

---

[13] Frances Trollope, *Petticoat Government*, 1852

By degrees wives could lose their individuality, their spirit, their will. It was possible for the wife to become a doormat. This problem could be compounded by another trait that at least some men seemed to show: a total inability to be aware of the feelings of their partners or, at least, to believe those feelings to be unimportant. This was one of the *Trials of Married Life*, mentioned by Sarah Ellis, the husband's 'incapability … of placing himself in idea in the situation of another person, so as to identify his feelings with theirs, and thus to enter in what they suffer and enjoy as if the feeling were his own'.[14] In other words such a husband was generally unable, and unwilling, to stand in his wife's shoes.

It has to be acknowledged that there were some men who believed in the abilities of women, a few of whom were actually willing to put their beliefs into writing. An early pre-Victorian example of this was the joint production between William Thompson and Anna Wheeler (mother of Rosina Bulwer Lytton mentioned earlier) with the long-winded title of *Appeal of One Half of the Human Race, Women, Against the Pretensions of the Other Half, Men, to Retain Them in Political, and Thence in Civil and Domestic Slavery*. It was published in 1825 and is not known to have had any significant effect on society, although it is taken as an indicator of changing views. Another more well-known and key supporter of women was John Stuart Mill whose joint venture with Harriet Taylor resulted in the writing of *The Subjection of Women*, which was eventually published in 1869 some eight years after he had written it up. It is well worth noting that the extended delay was because even he felt it would not have been well received at the time the manuscript was finished. There will be more to say upon this essay in subsequent chapters.

In direct contrast to this, *many* women from 1700 onwards had consistently asserted the capabilities of their own sex, and their works of both fiction and non-fiction continued to prove it. Commenting on 'The Laws Concerning Women', Margaret Oliphant was quite clear on this matter:

> *Let us not enter upon that tender question of mental inferiority. Every individual woman we presume is perfectly easy on her own account that she at least is not remarkably behind her masculine companions.*[15]

---

14 *The Wives of England*
15 Margaret Oliphant, 'The Laws Concerning Women', *Blackwood's Edinburgh Magazine*, 1856

Ten years later she was very clear on what she thought of men's abilities too:

> *Most of them in reality instead of being the free, bright, brave creatures we had dreamed of required a vast deal of propping up and stimulating to keep their front to the world.*[16]

Apart from the assumed superiority that increasingly caused concern to women, there were other fundamental grievances. One underlying complaint, which was a direct result of the conditioning that both boys and girls had received, was the basic selfishness of men. Those who were used to getting what they wanted were at a grave risk of turning into very self-centred individuals:

> *But men always delude themselves by believing what they wish to do is precisely what they ought, and Maurice Stern imagined that the course he was pursuing, because he liked it himself, was the best possible for his wife and child.*[17]

A common area for contention within marriages (including modern ones) is the question of money. All stages of a man's life then required funds – his education; his experience; his lifestyle; his status – and all could take precedence over his wife at home. We may hear of Victorian women wearing splendid clothes made of extravagant materials so that a man could display his wealth through the exhibition of his wife and family to the outside world, but we also hear of the wives and children, more often the girls, who were left at home to scrimp and save in order to help finance the pursuits and exploits of the self-indulgent men of the family, whose 'future prospects' were often used to justify the current expenditure. Anne Brontë referred to this in her novel *Agnes Grey*, when Lady Ashby commented on her husband's selfishness:

> *And then he must needs have me down in the country to lead the life of a nun, lest I should dishonour him or bring him to ruin; as if he had*

---

[16] Margaret Oliphant, 'The Great Unrepresented', *Blackwood's Edinburgh Magazine*, 1866
[17] Charlotte Riddell, *Too Much Alone*, 1860

not been ten times worse in every way, with his betting book, and his gaming table, and his opera girls and his Lady this and Mrs that – yes and his bottles of wine and glasses of brandy and water too.[18]

It was not just women writers who raised this point. William Makepeace Thackeray too was to comment openly on how men were far happier letting women make sacrifices on their behalf, rather than having to go without themselves. It was one of their basic faults. His novel *Pendennis* was full of such revelations:

A man will lay down his head or peril his life for his honour, but let us be shy how we ask him to give up his ease or his heart's desire. Very few of us can bear that trial... I will not say that a woman will not. They are used to it – we take care to accustom them to sacrifices ... indeed I believe some women would rather actually suffer so than not. They like sacrificing themselves in behalf of the object which their instinct teaches them to love... I hope it may be always so for us all: if we have only Justice to look to, Heaven help us.

By the time women married they had been conditioned to attend to the needs of their husbands, to pre-empt their every desire. Men were used therefore to being the centre of attention and to receiving very special treatment, every day of their lives. For some the arrival of a child, particularly of a male heir, was something to celebrate. Not for all. There is evidence that the arrival of a demanding infant was deeply disturbing to any husband who resented his wife transferring her previously undivided attention away from him. It is a problem many couples have had to adapt to. One such wife was Rosina Bulwer Lytton. She recorded her own feelings of distress after her husband's reaction to the arrival of their first child both within her works of fiction and the prefaces to them:

I desire you may not fool away all your time in that d—d nursery.[19]

Oh Women of England, in your happy homes – Wives, Mothers and

---

[18] Anne Brontë, *Agnes Grey*, 1847
[19] *Cheveley: Or, The Man of Honour*

Daughters, how would you feel? How would you act under similar outrages, if such should befall you? Which God forbid! How would you like to have had your first child turned out of the house the moment it was born, with that summary announcement from your lord and master – that he would rather not have your time and attention taken up with any d—d child?[20]

It hardly needs to be pointed out that there was abundant opportunity for a self-centred husband to be a tyrant within his own home. He could easily choose to exercise his virtually unlimited power over his wife in both physical and mental forms. While she could easily become a mere slave, a drudge to his every whim, there could be other more serious problems; she could be exposed to many different forms of cruelty. It could be her role to 'suffer and be still'.

Yes, yes, a wife's the ticket. Nothing like a wedded wife after all. One can make a servant of her – a body servant – to any extent; it's of no use her grumbling, no use her being offended. She can't go and get another place as did that servant of mine... Servants are so selfish, so ungrateful, I suppose a wife may be selfish and ungrateful too; but then she can't leave one in the lurch without ruining herself. Society happily has a prejudice against runaway wives, and the blame of an out and out quarrel always rests upon them. Ever since Eve ate the apple women have got the worst of it one way or another. Serve 'em right the jades. We can't do without them, but we can keep them in their places, that's one mercy.[21]

As violence and abuse in marriage will be considered in detail in a later chapter, it is sufficient at this stage to say that there were many recorded instances of domestic violence, and they occurred at all levels of society. However, from the above examples it can surely be seen that the conditioning men received could easily lead to extreme unpleasantness or difficulty for any wife who was not prepared to just accept her lot and do her duty, particularly if a husband chose to pay little attention to her own wants and needs. For many a married

---

[20] Rosina Bulwer Lytton, Preface to *Very Successful*, 1856
[21] Emma Worboise, *Husbands and Wives*, 1873

woman the reality of marriage meant that the statements that she had been taught to accept and believe in as a child just did not ring true in real life. She had discovered that some of the following fundamental truths were perhaps, after all, only myths:

- that all men were superior to women;
- that all women were inferior and therefore needed (and wanted) protection;
- that husbands always deserved the authority they held in a marriage;
- that husbands should naturally have control of all finance and property;
- that husbands would always look after the interests of their wives and children;
- that if there was any problem with the marriage it was always the woman's fault.

For whatever reason, there were many men who had failed in their duties and responsibilities, but what could a wife actually do about it? When a husband was dissatisfied with his marriage there were many options open to him. He was a wage earner, or generally had some form of income, and could live independently if he wanted to, so he could just leave. By deserting his wife he could choose to make life very difficult for her. If he was wealthy enough, divorce was an option; although it was a complex and expensive procedure until 1857, it could be arranged, and would leave him free to remarry. Until late in the nineteenth century it was also possible for a husband to have his wife locked up, or do the job himself, and, as a piece of property, he could even choose to sell her.[22] Her situation was very different.

An English wife is in all respects absolutely the property of her husband as any black American slave of its owner. I find it so. The laws of England appointed to regulate the relation of the sexes are so framed that it is all but impossible for a woman to obtain any species of justice from their action, while the lightest demand of man can set the whole crushing machinery at once into motion to overwhelm us into dust.[23]

---

[22] Although this practice was less common in the nineteenth century than previously, it did still occasionally occur, even though it was not a legally recognised practice. The sale of Mrs Trenchard in *The Mayor of Casterbridge*, 1886, was not just a figment of Thomas Hardy's imagination.

[23] Emma Robinson, *Mauleverer's Divorce: A Story of Woman's Wrongs*, 1863

There was actually very little choice for an unhappy woman. A wife was committed for life; it was her duty to stay. She might undertake a little passive resistance, but the chances are she would put up with her situation and consider it her Christian duty to accept the trials and tribulations in this world while looking forward to the benefits of the next. There have also been indications that some women at least preferred to suffer alone rather than share their troubles with family or friends. There are various reasons why this might have been so. The wife had chosen to marry her husband after all and was, in part, protecting her own self-image as well as his; she may have wanted to avoid giving distress to those who cared about her, and she may have had no choice. Very, very few had sufficient wealth and inclination to withstand the scandal and publicity of attempting to openly challenge their husbands, for example, with divorce proceedings, at least during the first half of the nineteenth century, and of course their upbringing and conditioning worked against them. Elizabeth Gaskell explained why such occurrences were rare:

> *The daily life into which people are born, and into which they are absorbed before they are well aware, forms chains which only one in a hundred has moral strength enough to despise, and to break when the right time comes – when an inward necessity for independent action arises, which is superior to all outward conventionalities.*[24]

As I mentioned previously Rosina Bulwer Lytton had felt it necessary to make use of the prefaces to her novels; this was not only to release her own feelings but also to explain and *justify* the actions she had taken in choosing to make personal matters very public. She may not have taken an active part in campaigns on behalf of women; hers was primarily an individual battle where she suffered from physical and mental abuse, violent attacks, financial constraint and deprivation of access to her children. She fought back with words and in 1852, as the hostilities with her husband continued, she threatened that:

> *The odds being cruelly unequal, I shall for the future expose each fresh piece of villainy as it occurs, or if goaded much more, the whole tissue*

---

24 Elizabeth Gaskell, *Ruth*, 1853

*from beginning to end, and it will not be upon my ipse dixit[25] that
the facts I shall lay bare will hang, but on innumerable documents and
hosts of witnesses.[26]*

In 1856 at the beginning of *Very Successful* she warned:

*There is a point of persecution and oppression beyond which even a
woman's legal slave owner is not by the law permitted to go; or if he
does he must expect that even a wife will share the other earthworm's
prerogative and turn when so trampled on.*

Like the vast majority of other women, however, Rosina was not a legal
expert and during her troubled marriage had found her knowledge of
the law sadly wanting. Before I consider the major changes that took
place during the Victorian period and women's role in the achievement
of this, I want to look more closely at the relationship that married
women like Rosina had with the law as Queen Victoria arrived upon
the scene.

In addition to the personal problems outlined above, one of the
fundamental problems for a wife was the legal predisposition to think
of a married woman in terms of a child. This was at the heart of
much legislation concerning them. She therefore was thought to need
protection in much the same way as a child. A father was naturally
responsible for the decision-making for his family, regarding their
welfare, and in turn a husband would take on that responsibility for
his wife. Regardless of how capable or financially independent a
single woman had shown herself to be, the law still transferred that
responsibility for her to her husband. Unless a marriage settlement
had been undertaken on her behalf, he had full legal rights over her
– her property, her income, her body and her children. Even if she
had had any rights as a single woman, she was not considered capable,
let alone desirous, of continuing to exercise those rights as a married
woman. In effect she had been downgraded. This was certainly felt,
and experienced, by women of the time:

---

[25] dfn. A dogmatic and unproven statement, *Concise Oxford English Dictionary*, 2011
[26] Rosina Bulwer Lytton, *School for Husbands*, 1852

But if she unites herself to a man the law immediately steps in and she finds herself legislated for, and her condition of life suddenly and entirely changed. Whatever age she may be of, she is again considered as an infant – she is again under reasonable restraint.[27]

In spite of various publications written by women throughout the eighteenth and nineteenth centuries, clarifying their legal situation, married women generally knew little specific detail regarding the laws that bound them. As a rule it was only when they actually needed support that they turned to the law for assistance and, at that point, they still believed that the law *would* intervene to help them in whatever vulnerable position they found themselves. It was also frequently at that point that they discovered for the first time how few rights they, as married women, actually had.

With all the religious emphasis on marriage in the sight of God, accepting one's duty, and taking public vows in front of family and friends, it is hardly surprising that a woman should make the assumption that marriage was a sacred bond, but she also had made the assumption that it was the same on both sides – in other words:

...a partnership in which each had equal rights, equal responsibilities and did either of them fail in the fulfilment of them, equal powers of self defence against the wrong... [But] she found what many an unfortunate wife, and mother, has found: that according to the Law of England then stood, and with little modification now stands, a married woman has no rights at all.[28]

It is important to remember that although the above extract came from a contemporary novel, this was no fiction. Written specifically in support of the move to extend property rights to all married women, rather than just be granted to those who were separated or divorced, the novel *A Brave Lady* contained far more than just a good story. Originally published between 1869 and 1870 it contained a basic statement of the legal situation for wives during much of Victoria's reign. Like previous women's novels concerning the law it is likely to

[27] Barbara Bodichon, *A Brief Summary in Plain English of the Laws of England Concerning Women*, 1854
[28] Dinah Mulock Craik, *A Brave Lady*, 1870

have reached a far wider female audience than articles in newspapers or legal documents. Once again women were keeping their fellow sisters informed as best they could.

This is what *A Brave Lady* discovered; these genuinely were the rules of play in the marriage game at the date of publication:

> *First… unless there exists an antenuptial settlement, every farthing a wife may have or acquire or earn is not hers but her husband's, to seize and use at his pleasure.*
>
> *Second… that he may personally 'chastise' her – 'confine' her – restrict her to the merest necessities or treat her with every unkindness short of endangering her life – without being punishable.*
>
> *Third – that if she escapes from him he can pursue her and bring her back, forcing her to live with him and share, however unwillingly, the burden and disgrace of his wrong doings, or if he dislikes this he may refuse to maintain her.*
>
> *Then as regards her children. After they are seven years old he can take them from her, denying her even access to them… In fact until they become of age they are as much in his power as his wife is – mere goods and chattels, for whom he is responsible to no-one, so long as he offends society by no open cruelty or crime.*

Another writer, Caroline Norton, was a key player in initiating legal changes for women in the nineteenth century, and she too had included many of her own personal experiences in her fictional and non-fictional work. (In fact, it was she who was largely responsible for children under the age of seven being able to remain with their mothers *at all* – there will be much more about her actual campaigns in Chapter Five.) By reading such works it is possible to imagine *how* women may have actually discovered their lack of rights during a domestic incident, or heated discussion, between man and wife. In Caroline's *Stuart of Dunleath* a fairly recently married woman, now Lady Penrhyn, wished to continue to deploy some of the money she brought to the marriage on charitable ventures. She double-checked with her husband but did not anticipate the following reply:

> *'D—m it, how stupid women are in all matters of business. Your fortune's mine: do you understand that?'*

> *'The fortune my father left me?'*
>
> *'The fortune your father left you. No married woman has a fortune of her own, as you call it, that isn't specifically settled on her. There's no such settlement in your case… I'm your husband and [your fortune's] mine.'*
>
> *'I do not understand it.'*
>
> *'Oh confound it. I am not going to spend the whole morning talking business with you. Everything that's yours is mine. The clothes you have on, the chain round your neck, the rings on your fingers, are mine.'*

In real life a woman may have turned to a close male relative for advice, perhaps to a male friend if she was lucky enough to have one, maybe even to a professional. But the answer she received would have still been the same. It was true – as a married woman she had few, if any, rights. How did women react to their discovery of this? Predictably their reaction was one of total shock and disbelief. There is an abundance of evidence for this in both real life and reflected in the fiction of the day. A few examples are all that is necessary to prove the point.

> *She was going now… to ascertain if such could in reality be the law of England – if any set of men, however mannish, could have ever legalized so monstrous a system of oppression against our sex.* [29]

> *She sat perfectly aghast. In her ignorance she had never contemplated such a state of things.* [30]

> *No legal claim to my own child that I brought into the world. No claim! I – his mother. No right to provide him with the necessaries of life… Oh it cannot, cannot be true!* [31]

It was not just the women who were to comment on the state of legal affairs. Just as Thackeray was to comment on men's selfishness, so other contemporary male authors were to make many valuable contributions to the debates about women. Wilkie Collins, Charles

---

[29] Emma Robinson, *Mauleverer's Divorce: A Story of Woman's Wrongs*

[30] Dinah Mulock Craik, *A Brave Lady*

[31] Florence Marryat, *Her World Against a Lie*, 1878

Dickens, and Anthony Trollope are to name but three. In his preface to *Man and Wife*, Collins wrote:

> *This time the fiction is founded on facts, and aspires to afford what help it may towards hastening the reform of certain abuses, which have been too long suffered to exist among us unchecked.*[32]

In this novel one of his key female characters, Hester Dethridge, was to ask:

> *Please to answer me this, sir, I says. I have been told by wiser heads than mine that we all pay our taxes to keep the Queen and the Parliament going, and that the Queen and the Parliament make laws to protect us, in return. I have paid my taxes. Why, if you please, is there no law to protect me in return?*

To find yourself in such a position must have been very distressing, and it could also be a very lonely one. Eliza Lynn Linton described the situation in detail:

> *The most desolate creature in the world is a married woman whose husband has ceased to be her support. Women cannot help her and men must not... As lonely as a widow, and without a widow's liberty – as unprotected as an orphan, without an orphan's future – she is like one turned adrift with bound hands into danger, unable to help herself and not suffered to be defended. Anyone may help an unmarried woman, but a wife must bear her own cross without a friend to share it, if her husband fails.*[33]

There was not surprisingly a growing cynicism regarding women's faith in the laws that were supposed to protect them. From the early eighteenth century women had commented on the unfairness of laws regarding them; there was nothing new about women continuing to do it in the nineteenth. Women were beginning to feel isolated from the legal process – they were expected to be governed by it, but were unable to make any contribution to it. Their voices were unwanted and unheard. The situation could be easily summarised:

---

[32] Wilkie Collins, *Man and Wife*, 1870
[33] Eliza Lynn Linton, *Sowing the Wind*, 1867

*English law is simple enough when applied to women. It consists of
stripping them of all rights and denying the vindication of wrongs.* [34]

*And then you are surprised that some women should prefer freedom and
poverty to the bondage of your crooked marriage laws. Why it's enough
to make the whole female race rise up as one woman and swear never to
have anything to do with matrimony again... Bah, a fig for your laws!
They are as useless as the men who made them.* [35]

One of the problems about using quotations from a variety of
different authors is that, although you get a very clear picture of
specific problems at given points in time, you fail to appreciate the
way a particular person developed his or her ideas as they grew older
and they experienced real life problems that could shape their own
choices and opinions. Margaret Oliphant was a very interesting case
in point; at the age of twenty-eight she wrote the article 'The Laws
Concerning Women' and stated clearly her belief at that age:

*There is no man in existence so utterly separated from one half of his
fellow creatures as to be able to legislate against them, in the interest
of his own sex.* [36]

She also believed it was not necessary to go through the whole legal
process to change particular laws for the benefit of a few random
individuals. They would just have to put up with it:

*Nor can we accept individual hardship in a dozen or two cases as
sufficient motive for the alteration of a rule which regulates the fate
of millions, which is no invented tyranny, but which to a plain and
visible arrangement of nature, pronounces its emphatic Amen.* [37]

But with the benefit of experience she was to completely change her
tune; some twenty years later she was to comment:

[34] Emma Robinson, *Mauleverer's Divorce: A Story of Woman's Wrongs*
[35] Florence Marryat, *Her World Against a Lie*
[36] Margaret Oliphant, 'The Laws Concerning Women', *Blackwood's Edinburgh Magazine*, 1856
[37] Ibid.

The sentiment of men towards women is thoroughly ungenerous from beginning to end, from the highest to the lowest... As men seem to think the laws which bear hardly upon women are the bulwarks of their existence, it is very unlikely that they will ever be entirely mended. It is curious that they should be so anxious and confine and limit the privileges of the companion who is avowedly the weaker vessel... And it is a curious thought, when we come to consider it, that the man, who is such a fine fellow and thinks so much of himself, would after all be a complete nonentity without the woman he has hustled about and driven into a corner ever since she began to be.[38]

What women were undoubtedly aware of was the double standard that permeated both the legislation and the traditions of society. It was not just a question of property ownership and income. There were totally different expectations of behaviour for a man and a woman. What was acceptable in a man was despised in a woman. A woman was to be pure, to keep herself wholly only unto her husband – but it was perfectly acceptable for a young man to sow his wild oats and for a husband to have a mistress. Many women discovered their husbands were unfaithful and, regardless of the emotional suffering and distress that it could inevitably cause, were powerless to do anything about it. Conduct books from the eighteenth century onwards had advised women to turn away their eyes.[39]

If a husband caught his wife having an affair, he could easily divorce her, providing he had the money to pay for it, but she was forced to remain with the man who mistreated her, who committed adultery, and deprived her of the necessities of life. As Eliza Lynn Linton said, 'If he simply cares to keep within the letter of the law he may do pretty much as he likes.'[40] A wife labelling herself 'A VICTIM TO BAD TEMPER' summarised the whole situation by asking simply, like others before her, 'May we not make marriage more bearable by recognising legally, and socially, that both sexes have equal rights?'[41]

Just like the young Margaret Oliphant, other women too could

---

[38] Margaret Oliphant, 'The Grievances of Women', *Fraser's Magazine*, 1880
[39] Elizabeth Griffiths, *The Delicate Distress*, 1769
[40] Eliza Lynn Linton, *Ourselves, A Series of Essays on Women*, 1870
[41] Letter to the Editor, *The Daily Telegraph*, Balham, 13th August 1888 quoted in Harry Quilter, (ed.) *Is Marriage a Failure?*, 1888

not believe that it was possible that men had been deliberately legislating against women out of selfish motives or, *if* they had in the past, then those ideas were now outdated. Women only had to get the parliamentarians to realise, and appreciate, the problems that women were currently facing, and then change would swiftly follow. Caroline Norton was one such person when she was looking at the question of child custody:

> *I apprehend, that no right-minded man can read through the examples here given without admitting the necessity of some such alteration in the law.*[42]

Although she was correct on that generalisation, the belief that once men *knew* of the plight of women they would instantly rectify the situation was rather naive. It was not going to be that simple. Of course it was imperative that everyone should have a very clear idea of the problems women were facing, across the board. Publicity through journalism and literature would spread that awareness and hopefully raise public interest in making changes in the law, but media interest could serve another purpose. Over time it became increasingly important to the activists that every woman should be educated about the reality of what getting married actually meant, in legal as well as personal terms, before she took her vows. It would ultimately become every female's responsibility to make sure she knew what she was letting herself in for, and to ensure that she really did make the right choice.

From Rosina Bulwer Lytton again:

> *Alas my young lady friends, it should be at least part of your education to know that notwithstanding the much boasted British constitution, it does not contain a single law for the protection or redress of married women.*[43]

And Anthony Trollope was to refer to the solemn marriage vow a few years later:

---

[42] Caroline Norton, *Observation on the Natural Claim of the Mother to the Custody of Her Infant Children, as affected by the Common Law Right of the Father*, 1837
[43] *Very Successful*

No educated woman, we may suppose, stands at the altar as a bride, without having read and reread those words till they are fixed on her memory. It is a great oath, and a woman should know well what that is, to which she is about to pledge herself.[44]

In the same vein Florence Marryat wrote:

Really, the ignorance of our sex upon matters of general information is astounding. I should have thought it was in the interest of every married woman in Christendom to make herself acquainted with the relief the law contains for her. It's little enough, my dear, I can tell you, and would burden no one's brain to get it by heart.[45]

So, having realised that the laws really did work against them, women were beginning to accept that if they wanted change, they were going to have to take a more active part in the proceedings. Sometimes this would be as individuals, sometimes within a group. The first stage in the process had been to raise the issues, and then see if the men would actually listen to their concerns. As we will see in Chapter Five, before Victoria had come to the throne that was exactly what some women had tried to do – but had categorically failed to gain either their full attention or support. For as Eliza Lynn Linton stated:

If we appeal for protection to the law we appeal to that on which we have no claim, which does not recognise that we have grounds of complaint, and which cannot and will not help us.[46]

It was time to move on. The second part of the process of change was therefore realising that it was going to be necessary to get the law changed themselves – no matter how long it took. It was to be a combination of using emotional appeal and working the system. To have any chance of success they had to change tactics. Whereas the women of the eighteenth century had highlighted problems, the women of the nineteenth century were to get properly organised –

---

[44] Anthony Trollope, *The Bertrams*, 1859
[45] *Her World Against a Lie*
[46] *Ourselves, A Series of Essays on Women*, 1870

they would write propaganda, they would take part in discussions, they would hold meetings, they would set up campaigns and committees, and in various ways they would take on Parliament. At last, and throughout the century, there were women who were prepared to fight for their rights.

In 1854 Caroline Norton had a pamphlet printed for private circulation called *English Laws for Women in the Nineteenth Century*, and as its initial epigraph she chose to quote Charles Dickens. In his novel *Bleak House*, he had had a particularly apposite one liner that could be directly applied to the plight of women, even though it had not necessarily been his intention for it to do so: 'It won't do to have TRUTH and JUSTICE on our side, we must have LAW and LAWYERS.'[47] A political activist and writer, campaigning for justice for women like herself, Caroline was collating examples of legal cases and combining them with a fictional quotation from a well-respected male writer who had an interest in social justice. For those who were listening it added a very definite and popular support to her argument. (Dickens had already made use of some of the incidents of her plight as part of his storyline in *Dombey and Son*, published in 1848 – so this inclusion was highly appropriate.[48])

The following year Caroline lampooned men's attitude towards changing the laws concerning women, even when there was, eventually, an acknowledgement that some complaints were justified no remedial action would take place, for:

> ...*they would be very glad to do <u>something</u> towards amending the laws for women but, really, the subject is <u>so</u> surrounded with difficulty.* [49]

It sounded far more like their excuse for procrastination. While men had asserted the myth that the laws favoured women, and enough women had accepted it, they had also apparently accepted that there was no need to change those laws. Serious questions were now being

---

[47] Charles Dickens, *Bleak House*, 1853
[48] Charles Dickens also used her early court appearances in *Pickwick Papers* (1836); other male authors were to make use of Caroline's life – Anthony Trollope, *He Knew He was Right* (1869); George Meredith, *Diana of the Crossways* (1885).
[49] Caroline Norton, *Letter to the Queen on Lord Chancellor Cranworth's Marriage and Divorce Bill*, 1855

asked; the subjects were at last under public debate; progress was being made, however slowly. Society was having to face a few home truths:

> *We are told year after year … that we may absolutely and always rely on men to prove the deepest and tenderest concern for everything which concerns the welfare of women, shall we not point to these long neglected wrongs and denounce that boast of the equal concern for women as – a falsehood?*[50]

As we shall see in the next four chapters, for *each* separate cause that women wanted to change, men, and more specifically Members of Parliament, would have to be approached and convinced enough to take the issue forwards in the Houses, for they alone could effect the changes that these women so desperately sought. Rather than just follow an overall timeline, I have followed each theme individually, so inevitably there will be some overlap and occasionally it will be necessary to turn the clock back. The process of change did not run smoothly; rather it should be considered as layers of progress – and as each subsequent layer was achieved the position of married women would grow a little stronger.

It is time at last to see what women actually did to change the rules.

---

50 Frances Power Cobbe, 'Wife Torture In England', *Contemporary Review*, April 1878

Chapter Five
Personal Battles

Challenging the institution of marriage, or rather challenging some of its key ground rules, was never going to be a simple or an easy task. As marriage was well established over centuries and reinforced by Church and State, each tiny proposed change would face continuous attacks, counter justifications, and endless legal and emotional debate. One of the fundamental principles that had underpinned the state of matrimony was that husbands took care of the interests of their wives: they were legally responsible for them; they protected them; they nurtured them; they valued them for their moral attributes and gentle femininity. It was the husband alone who was to have dominion over his home and, therefore, over his wife and children. A reality check had shown that the arguments of those men who spoke out so determinedly in favour of the continuance of the status quo were based on their own personal interests – and their absolute determination to leave that sacred domain as near completely intact as possible. Those who benefited from the rules of marriage as they stood had little or no desire to change them. Any proposed change therefore would inevitably take time: time to establish the need for any change, time to gain support from critical parties, and time for legal and social precedents to be introduced. It would also take considerable courage and determination by any woman who was prepared to face the public scrutiny and scandal that such a direct challenge would inevitably provoke.

As we saw in Chapter Four there were certain common areas for married women that had caused them great suffering and distress – problems of physical and mental abuse, questions of money and property and, perhaps most precious of all, the desire for a continued relationship and contact with their children. According to the traditional rules of marriage these were all areas where the husband had virtually complete control, even if the marriage failed, but all of these were to be challenged and altered to some degree during the course of the Victorian period. Perversely, though, the very first changes that took place, that were ultimately to affect the lives of all married women, were not changes that were required *within* the state of marriage, but *without*, and they were not brought in as part of a planned campaign on behalf of all women, but rather because one particular woman needed them, and was prepared to fight for them, no matter what the consequence.

So after years of merely raising voices of discontent, what did it take to make a real difference? What was the trigger for change? Take one determined, and angry, intelligent woman responding emotionally to mistreatment and public humiliation by her husband, who had falsely accused her of having an affair with a public figure, dragged her through the law courts with no chance of defending herself, and then deprived her of the love and comfort of her children... Light the blue touch paper and watch the explosion. Hell hath no fury like a woman scorned and Caroline Norton *was* furious.

To understand the part that Caroline was to play, to see how the rules of marriage began to change, and how married women began to be regarded as something other than the mere chattels of their husbands, we have to start with the children. Innumerable distressed women over the centuries had lost their children because they could no longer find it in themselves to remain with their husbands. Within unhappy marriages those who chose to remain living with their husbands, thus keeping close to their children, continued to face situations of hardship and suffering. The children provided both the necessary comfort and the strength to keep going.

> *How many [women] have been saved from despair or sin by the voice and smile of these unconscious little ones? The woman who is a mother dwells in the immediate presence of guardian angels. She will bear on for her children's sake. She will toil for them – die for them – live for them – which is sometimes harder still. The neglected, miserable, maltreated wife still has one bright spot in her home: in that darkness a watch light burns: she has her children's love.* [1]

---

[1]   *Stuart of Dunleath*

Other writers were to make a similar point:

That little voice roused her from her dumb despair; and as she raised the child and clasped him to her breast, she understood more clearly than she had ever done before, the blessed value of motherhood and the meaning of its duties. Were it not for the brighter future, who could bear the darkened present? Were it not for the love of others who would value his own existence?[2]

According to the law, the children within a marriage were to be regarded as the property of their father; a mother may have been the primary carer for her children, but she had no actual rights over them. It did not seem to matter how bad a husband and father a man may have been, he still had the right to deprive a mother from not only the custody of her children but also *any* access to them. This could be used as a threat to control the wife's behaviour within marriage or as the hidden penalty if she chose to leave the game. It was a cruel way to exert power and domination, and was guaranteed to cause extreme pain to any true mother. From the eighteenth century onwards women writers had repeatedly exposed this as one of the major injustices they had to suffer at the time.

For a woman, issues of custody and access were personal matters. There was no concern with power or control; at this point in history a mother had no such rights. Whenever a child was removed from his mother, virtually the first thing the father had to do was to find a woman capable of looking after him – a sister, mother, governess or servant, or even his mistress. A father may genuinely have loved his child, but that was not the only consideration for him.

To have a son or daughter somehow seems to a man of more importance than a woman. A woman's idea of offspring is like that of a little girl longing for a new doll; it is something to play with and to fondle, to dress and to undress, to scold and to love, to hold in her arms and to teach how to walk. A man's idea of offspring is much more serious. He realizes none of the little thrills of delight, the choosing of little garments is wasted upon him, the little pink legs have no fascination.

---

[2] Eliza Lynn Linton, *Sowing the Wind*

A man's idea of a son is a copy of the creator. His son seems to him his own creation, for in him he thinks he sees himself or what he would have wished to have been. It is like a man who sees his own reflection in a glass without his knowing it, and says, 'What a fine looking man.'[3]

When Caroline Norton was prevented from seeing her children, she desperately wanted to get them back, but she was by no means the first mother to actively seek the custody of her children. At the beginning of the nineteenth century there had been the shocking De Manneville case, where a young mother had run away from her husband, taking her infant child with her. The father pursued them and discovered the wife in the process of nursing her tiny infant. What caught people's attention was not merely the fact that he took the child away, but that he actually tore the child from the mother's breast while she was in the process of feeding him. Mrs de Manneville applied for custody, but the court refused to even read the affidavits and upheld the father's claim without question.

In 1827 Mr Ball was openly living with his mistress, and his wife was granted a type of divorce by the Ecclesiastical Court (*divorce a mensa et thoro*), which was basically a legal separation, but still the court refused to give her any custodial rights over the children. Trying to play the legal system, Mrs Ball approached a different law court, the Court of Chancery, but to no avail. Although the Vice Chancellor (a Mr Shadwell) did at least acknowledge the cruelty of depriving a mother of all access to her children, he still said, 'I do not know that I have ANY AUTHORITY TO INTERFERE'.[4] Mr Ball was thus able to keep his children, and in doing so deprived his innocent wife of all contact with them.

In 1836 Henrietta Greenhill was so desperate to keep her children when her marriage failed that she took the unprecedented step of abducting them and moving to France, thus escaping English jurisdiction and the risk of her own imprisonment for not returning the children to their father. It could have happened. Her husband had already shown extreme cruelty to both her and the children, but

---

[3]   Lucas Cleeve, *The Woman Who Wouldn't*, 1895

[4]   Caroline Norton, *The Separation of Mother and Child by the Law of 'Custody of Infants' considered*, 1838

wanted to compound it by actually *giving* the custody of the children to his mistress. At the time Lord Denham reaffirmed the husband's unlimited right to the custody of the children by saying, 'There is nothing in the case stated, with respect to his conduct, which has ever been held sufficient to deprive a father of the custody of his children.'[5]

It is with this background that we now return to Caroline Norton. Who was she and what made her take such a strong stand against the establishment? Caroline's grandfather was Richard Brinsley Sheridan, a playwright and statesman; her father had been employed in the colonial service, but he died when she was a child, leaving her mother, sisters and herself hard pressed for cash. A real beauty, she was spotted by George Norton, the younger brother of Lord Grantley, while still at school and he was determined to marry her, even prepared to wait a couple of years. As the family had little prospect, Caroline agreed to marry him and by the time she did so he had become an MP. It was not to be a successful marriage. He was violent and demanding; she was impulsive, lively and witty, and definitely unwilling to take on a submissive role. As a result of one of their quarrels he beat her and she miscarried; his beatings were not uncommon. In society she was popular and knew many of the nobility and politicians of the day, but she became rather too close to one in particular – Lord Melbourne, a family friend. Even though her husband, George, had made use of the friendship to acquire his own employment, he still accused her of having an affair with Lord Melbourne (then prime minister) and took the case to court in 1836.

In those days a man could sue if his wife had engaged in 'criminal conversation' (a polite way of describing adultery) and he could demand damages from the accused male, for she was now considered damaged goods. George was hoping to gain financially from the resolution of the case. As a wife Caroline was allowed no opportunity to defend herself in court, for she had no legal identity separate from her husband, and so she became the subject of great slander and scandal. George failed to win his case; Caroline was deemed innocent, but the damage was done. A divorce would seem to have been an ideal solution as the pair were so unsuited, but a woman's adultery was the legal prerequisite for it at the time. George and Caroline would have

---

5   Ibid

to remain married in spite of all their differences and the fact they lived apart. To then compound all the intense distress she had suffered during these events, George denied her access to the children.

Over the subsequent years he was to play a cat and mouse game with Caroline, using the children as pawns in his game, promising her access if she agreed to the financial restraints he wished to impose upon her. And when she agreed terms, he continued to keep the children at a distance, kindly pointing out that in the eyes of the law any agreement made between husband and wife had no validity, because the wife had no separate legal position of her own. It is easy to imagine her distress. When George initially removed the children, and took them to his sister's house, she rushed over there and, though allowed in, was denied access to them. She wrote to her friend Lord Melbourne, 'I could hear their little feet running merrily overhead while I sat sobbing below... If they keep my children from me, I shall go mad.'

Caroline was not one to take things lying down. She loved her children and she desperately wanted to see them and to be with them. George on the other hand was happy to delegate care of the children to his sister, his mistress, even his servants. So how did she react? What could she possibly do to fight against her husband's vindictiveness, and legally re-establish her relationship with her children? Like many intelligent women before her she decided to use her literary skills to make her point. In her case she wrote and distributed pamphlets. The first move had been to thoroughly research her subject, checking previous legal cases where a mother had been denied custody of her young children, through no fault of her own, and then using them as evidence to support her own case. Unlike earlier writers, Caroline made sure that her arguments were read by influential people who not only supported her, but were themselves in a position to help. She had some very powerful friends and acquaintances amongst the aristocracy, including Members of Parliament and even the Prime Minister himself. She made use of the available literary media at the time, as well as her own social network. There is no doubt about it, Caroline was the right person, in the right place, at the right time.

Totally disregarding the criticism and the slander she would receive because she dared to publicise the personal sufferings of her own marriage, and because she chose to make her demands very public, Caroline made use of the public sentiment that earlier child custody disputes had generated, and drew attention to the gathering support for change. She knew that few people had been aware of the details of custody law, as it stood in relation to women, and had herself been shocked by the discovery. Each of her published pamphlets had its own focus, raising key points, examining and countering possible objections and, while clearly promoting her own claim as a mother, never, ever, daring to tread or encroach on the husband's prerogative to be master in his own home. A key issue for her was that a mother's need to be involved with her children, particularly when they were small, had been ignored and her rights as a mother, if she indeed had any, were not considered at all.

One of her early publications was a pamphlet entitled *Observations on the Natural Claim of the Mother to the Custody of Her Infant Children as Affected by the Common Law Right of the Father*. In this she was to argue that, though a mother had an entirely natural claim, it had no acknowledged existence in the law, and she then cited a whole series of cases, including the ones I have already mentioned, where a mother's claims had been denied. She also raised an extremely valid point – while acknowledging the father's right to his child she wanted to know, 'Why should the father, whose utmost care is insufficient for the care of his infant children, have the power to take them from the mother?' She was to back up her argument by reminding people that God himself had fitted her for the task of motherhood and deemed that it was her function to nurture her children. 'It should not be in the power of any human to wrest from her a charge appointed her, not by MAN, but by GOD.'[6]

She referred to this point more emotionally later in one of her novels:

Idiots are they who in family quarrels seek to punish the mother by parting her from her offspring; for in that blasphemy against nature they do violence to God's own decrees.[7]

But the law as it stood in 1837 was quite clear. A husband had the right and responsibility for all decisions regarding his children – a mother did not count – and he could remove the children from her

---

[6]   Caroline Norton, *Observations on the Natural Claim of the Mother to the Custody of Her Infant Children as Affected by the Common Law Right of the Father*, 1837
[7]   *Stuart of Dunleath*

care any time he wanted to. Caroline was to argue that if a father denied the mother access to her children, he should at least have to justify it – and it should be illegal for any child still under the age of seven to be seized from his mother's care. Referring to earlier cases she said the law was both 'absurd and unnatural' ordering a guiltless mother to give up her young children to an unfaithful father, whereas if the case was reversed a guilty wife would have been likely to lose both her children and her home. Fundamentally it was wrong that no justification was required from the man for his actions and no proof was required to show that his decisions were sound. What Caroline wanted was a change in the law that would provide some justice and protection for a mother; regarding the husband, she asked pointedly, 'She belongs to him and his children, do neither belong to her?'

Caroline had been wise to stress that she wanted only to be able to be with her children – for that did not really encroach on the father's rights over his child – and to limit custody to that of the 'tender years' where a mother's input was indisputably appropriate. Backed up also by a religious justification, all these helped to create an admittedly emotional yet logically sound argument in her favour. One of her subsequent pamphlets, *On the Separation of the Mother and the Child by the Law of 'Custody of Infants', considered*, pointed out a serious anomaly within the current law that was to add significant weight to her argument about the need for change. Although a wife had no legal right to the custody of her child, somewhat perversely, a mistress did. Since the 1834 Poor Law Amendment Act an illegitimate child belonged to the mother right up to the age of sixteen; the 'Bastardy clause' had been introduced as a way for men to legally avoid taking any financial responsibility for their own indiscretions, but Caroline carefully avoided referring to that detail.

Once more Caroline stressed the powers given to men had at times been 'grossly and savagely' abused as a means of vindictively punishing an innocent woman, by separating her from her children and refusing her all access. In this pamphlet she again presented evidence of earlier cases and stressed the fact that members of the judiciary involved were showing increasing support for a change in the law. They were well aware of the fact that they were powerless to give any consideration to the mother – no matter how much sympathy they may have felt for her. She noted that some years after the Greenhill case, when the lords were debating the issue, one of the trial judges involved referred back to the case and actually stated, 'I believe there was not one judge who did not actually feel ashamed of the state of the law.'

What Caroline needed, though, was a spokesman, a champion and standard-bearer, who would carry her ideas into Parliament. Through her contacts she met Mr Serjeant Talfourd, an MP who had been involved in the notorious Greenhill case, acting at the time on behalf of the infamous husband (although personally being very concerned at the injustice served to the wife). He agreed to introduce a Private Member's Bill into Parliament on her behalf that sought the legal acknowledgement of a mother's right to have custody of, or at least access to, her young children.

Not surprisingly Talfourd's Bill provoked serious opposition. Entitled *A Bill to provide for the Access of Parents, living apart from each other, to their Children of tender Age*, it raised several immediate issues. Of course patriarchal justifications to keep the law as it then stood soon followed.

> *The father requires no new provision by law to secure to him the right of access to his children be they of years tender or robust. By the law, as it stands at present and so has stood for the last 1000 years or more – ever since there has been a law at all in England – he already possesses this right in its fullest extent and can exert it at any and every moment, so far as his wife is concerned, from the first hour of his children's birth… And this right no one can disturb or force from him, nor in any way deprive him of… Except in the case of permanent insanity, or of some deliberate and criminal act of his own, no father can forfeit or lose his paternal right.* [8]

This was reaffirmed elsewhere:

> *On the conduct, so on the good education of his child, the law has obliged [the father] to stake his purse, his reputation, his parental feelings, his happiness, the peace of his house, the honour of his name and his hope of leaving an honourable paternity after him. Every feeling and interest that can affect the heart of a man, even his own*

---

[8]   Handley, Edwin Hill, 'Custody of Infants' Bill', *British and Foreign Review*, Vol VII, 1838

liberty and life, may be endangered by the bad education and the immoral education of his children. He may in a single moment be ruined utterly. And though the absolute power that confers it on him is a great one, it is not a whit too great to answer the responsibility. The law is just and equal.[9]

Having control over the children was also seen as one of the perks of marriage, and there were great fears that an unhappy wife might abduct her children and run away – as Mrs Greenhill had done.

When a man marries he is sure of only one blessing… if he has children by her, he will have the satisfaction… of bringing them up as sons worthy of himself… else why should the man take the trouble to bind himself by an indissoluble bond unless it were in this hope and with this assurance.[10]

There had also been initial outrage in Parliament because the first draft of Talfourd's Bill would have allowed consideration to *all* wives in custody cases. Adulterous wives would have to be excluded from any considerations for *any* Bill to make progress for, it was argued, children should be free from exposure to any 'contaminated' woman… naturally exposure to 'contaminated' fathers, themselves guilty of adultery, did not raise any concern, nor any possible exposure to their mistresses. As Caroline had been the innocent party, Talfourd could easily agree to amend that part of the Bill and so it was able to continue on its way through Parliament.

There were other criticisms, though, for it was asserted that the Bill was immoral, it was unconstitutional, it was unjust to private individuals (husbands) and it was anti-Christian.

The paternal power is the oldest and most sacred right belonging to a man – the right that ought to be most religiously guarded… Such being the doctrine deducible from the authority of the Christian

---

[9] *A Brief Exposure of the Most Immoral and Dangerous Tendency of a Bill affecting the Rights of Parents now under Consideration of Parliament, or Summary of Reasons why this Bill, entitled 'Custody of Infants Bill', should not be allowed to become Law of the Land,* 1838. This was a pamphlet published by Richard and John E. Taylor, and hereafter will be referred to as *A Brief Exposure.*

[10] Ibid

scriptures... [the Bill] outrages and violates the dearest and most sacred feelings of Englishmen... it is a complete violation of the right of paternity. [11]

These types of responses were somewhat predictable, but a close examination of some of the other issues raised by these publications are indicative of the way in which child custody was openly considered as a means of exerting power and control over the women themselves. I have already briefly mentioned the threat of losing her children could be enough to prevent an unhappy wife from attempting to leave her home. It was one of the ties that bound her to her marriage and for some there was a perhaps natural and extreme reluctance to remove that penalty. There were genuine fears that allowing separated women to have access to their children would lead to a greater number of failed marriages and separations. As paternal power was seen as the foundation of society, it was also thought that if the Bill became enacted it would be disastrous consequences for society.

We are convinced that if that [power] be broken into pieces, or removed from its place, the most terrible and irreparable downfall of the constitution would inevitably ensue; that the most horrible destruction of private virtue and public principle and social happiness would be its inevitable consequence. [12]

The concession of granting child custody to the mother could apparently lead to all sorts of other evils, including the loss of the empire. Take the belief that the only thing that prevented wives from indulging in extramarital affairs was the thought that they would lose their children. Apparently it followed that, if you allowed separated women freedom of access, it would therefore give them licence to lives of lust and debauchery.

What madness then and atrocious wickedness it would be to take away, not merely the least, not merely one out of a number but the greatest, the last, the only bar against the outbreak of ever tempting lusts. [13]

---

[11]   Handley, Edwin Hill, 'Custody of Infants Bill'
[12]   Ibid
[13]   Ibid

It was ever the woman's fault!

What I found even more disturbing in these criticisms of the Bill was the argument that it was only because a wife actually lived with the husband, and continued to fulfil *all* his conjugal requirements and domestic services, that she was entitled to have *any* contact at all with *his* children. If she left him, for any reason, it was only right she lost that privilege. A mother may have borne the children, but any on-going contact thereafter had apparently been merely her reward for services rendered.

> *Never, until the concoction of this immoral Custody of Infants Bill, has been attempted to establish by law that maxim that the mother may desert the sphere of her maternal duties and yet enjoy her maternal rights… Providence has wisely ordained that the enjoyment of maternal rights and privileges, the first of which is the right of access to their children, should be the highest actual reward for the performance of maternal duties, the first of which is living together with them, and consequently their father and natural protector.*[14]

The author of this particular article also stated that any man who chose to marry a woman in favour of these changes in the rules was mad, and he should immediately book himself into a lunatic asylum for his honeymoon. He had also conveniently failed to notice that Caroline and Talfourd were solely concerned with fathers who had not provided that 'natural' protection. Both of them were to be slated for their involvement in the cause: she for her audacity and unwomanliness; he for supporting her against such well-established traditional principles. *A Brief Exposure* showed no sympathy for her at all:

> *Let not Members of Parliament be lectured and sentimentalized into voting for such a law, only to serve the private ends of a woman who probably deserves all she suffers.*

Some women were to be unsympathetic, like Harriet Martineau, herself a reformer, who criticised Caroline for selfishly pursuing her own specific interests in the matter of child custody rather than

---

[14] Ibid

campaigning on behalf of all women. There was some truth in this, for at one point Caroline thought she had won access to the children, with her husband's consent, so there seemed to be no need for Talfourd to continue on her behalf. The Bill was withdrawn. Unfortunately, as soon as her husband, George, realised she was no longer taking action, he then promptly withdrew his consent for access. Somewhat embarrassed, she in turn had to ask Talfourd to renew his efforts in Parliament, which he fortunately agreed to do.

In the process of her campaign Caroline was called a she-devil, and it was implied that Talfourd was merely her puppet, singing and dancing along to her tune, especially when he was directly quoting large chunks of her work during his speeches in the House. Nowadays the allegations would have been considered libellous. She was falsely accused of writing an extremely radical article, *An Outline of the Grievances of Women*, and slated for having so audaciously attacked the position of men in society. Serjeant Talfourd was (correctly) accused of 'disarming opposition' by modifying his original Bill, but he was slated for his rhetoric, his misunderstanding of the law of paternity and being ignorant of the law in general. Setting a pattern for the future campaigns of women, he was publicly mocked for being a male supporter of their claims. At least Talfourd had the opportunity to refute those criticisms, in Parliament and elsewhere, for he could sue over any false allegations, but Caroline had no form of legal redress for the slanderous criticisms of her. She was able to write letters to the newspapers in protest, one even got reprinted in *The Times*, and she at least continued to receive support elsewhere.

Although in favour of child custody for the mother, as she herself had similarly been denied access to her own children, the writer Rosina Bulwer Lytton did not think Talfourd's Bill could possibly succeed, for it was not actually in men's interest to pass it. Openly stating her opinion in another preface to one of her novels, she then added, 'Men are members of nature's inquisition, who's profligacy can only flourish and be protected by keeping the instruments of torture in their own hands'.[15] These were bitter and cynical words, but they did have some validity – while those in power had the means of retaining privileges

---

[15] *Cheveley, Or, The Man of Honour*

and benefits that they valued, it was very likely that they would show resistance to any but the slightest change to them.

As part of the on-going debate, one writer, R. Mence Esq., published a pamphlet in 1838 that acknowledged:

> *The proper treatment of the wife has been hardly touched upon by political writers any more than by legislators, but left from age to age, to a sort of instinct or chance as if it were too insignificant for the exercise of our reasoning powers.*[16]

He too was to become emotive in his response believing that:

> *The gross and revolting tyranny existing under, and supported and sanctioned by the law of the land, is now uncurtained and become notorious. It offends the eyes and stinks in the nose of every man, except those, who in temper and spirit at least, if not in actual commission and daily and hourly exercise, belong to the tribe of monsters that the debates upon the Bill have dragged to light and held up to disgust and indignation.*[17]

He also pointed out that most of the general public had had no awareness of the situation regarding the non-existence of rights of custody/access for mothers prior to the debates on the Bill – a point that had been repeatedly raised by Caroline and that her own publications had tried to rectify.

Although her pamphlets had won her support, articles like *A Brief Exposure* and the *Custody of Infants* (from the *British and Foreign Review*) were undoubtedly damaging to some degree – but Caroline still had one more trick up her sleeve.

A Brief Exposure had originally been sent to the Members of the House of Lords while they were discussing the Bill in an attempt to get them to throw it out. In response to it, Caroline upped her game. She wrote and published *A Plain Letter to the Lord Chancellor on the Infant Custody Bill* (1839); it was to be her *pièce de résistance*. Echoing women writers from the eighteenth century onwards, she used a male voice to

---

[16] R. Mence Esq. *The Mutual Rights of Husband and Wife with the draft of a Bill, to replace that of Serjeant Talfourd, for the Custody of Infants*, 1838

[17] Ibid

add authority to her arguments, deciding to write her next pamphlet under a male pseudonym, Pearce Stevenson. In it she countered all the main points raised in *A Brief Exposure* (and elsewhere). Rather than using her own 'feminine' and emotional style, she adopted a more considered and logical one, arguing the case as a third party, on behalf of Mrs Norton.

'Pearce' reminded the Chancellor that God had allocated the task of motherhood, and even St Paul had told husbands to 'love their wives and be not bitter against them'. In spite of Biblical teachings on adultery no attention was being paid to the misdemeanours of a husband, nor to any other examples of abuse or neglect. Even when the wife was totally innocent, there was the 'strange and appalling fact' that in all cases concerning the children, a husband was awarded custody. Pearce succinctly asked, 'Where are the checks upon men?' Like R. Mence Esq., Pearce stressed women's ignorance of the law and their belief that:

> ...*The strong arm of the law would interfere to protect them... This was believed in error and in ignorance, but it was believed... [Caroline] knew nothing of the supposed check which was to be held in terrorem*[18] *over her... she knew nothing of the operation of the law, which aided the oppressor to tyrannise, punishing the innocent and letting the guilty go free... Simply imagining her own blamelessness and affection for her children... would suffice to establish her claim to protection; she appealed to the English law and appealed in vain.*[19]

Most women falsely assumed that a mother already had rights to her infant child. Pearce said it was therefore nonsense to fear a massive increase in applications for separations and divorce if the law was changed in their favour. In fact, he predicted that having found out they had *no* protection from the law as it currently stood, married women were far more likely to want an immediate divorce. Even if the threat of losing their children had been taken to be a means of preventing wives from leaving their marriages, then it was plainly dependent upon women's knowledge of the law. And that, as we know, was very limited.

One of the other fears expressed in the critical articles had been

---

[18] In fear/terror

[19] Caroline Norton, *A Plain Letter to the Lord Chancellor on the Infant Custody Bill*, 1839

that women would abduct their children, like Mrs Greenhill in the past, if they won custody rights. Pearce countered this by saying that this was a ridiculous idea. In all the cases under consideration the wives were the innocent party, the law-abiding ones, so there would be very little likelihood of them absconding with their children if they were granted legal access. There would be no desire to risk losing that right. Mrs Greenhill had only taken her children to France because she had been denied all contact with her children.

Regarding the personal attacks that *A Brief Exposure* had made, Caroline, under her male pseudonym, gave as good as she got.

It is perhaps on the whole satisfying to find that the only publicity against [the Bill] since its introduction consists of an attack upon the individuals supposed to be interested, rounded on several distinct misrepresentations, and some vague abuse of the female sex.

The author of *A Brief Exposure* was criticised by her for his style, and on a more personal basis:

Indeed it is scarcely possible to believe, on a perusal of the article in question, and on consideration of its utter want of sound and temperate judgment, that such a bombastic schoolboy's exercise on a subject of public interest can be the production of a grown up human being, come to the full maturity of thought and feeling.

His upbringing was also questioned:

Where is the mother of the man? – in her grave or on this earth, when he undertook to speak of the whole female sex, as animals who require caging and chaining?… Did this author never see that usual and customary sight, a modest and affectionate wife?

The *Plain Letter to the Chancellor* concluded by stressing that the only legal change that was being sought was to give some justice to those innocent women (like Caroline herself) who had been left in such a vulnerable and tragic position by the actions of their husbands and had no legal claim of their own. There was no challenge to a husband's position or his authority over his children.

Once completed Caroline sent a copy to every Member of Parliament, while they were in recess, just before they were due to return to London for their final consideration of the Bill. Every plea and justification for their support would therefore be fresh in their minds when they took their vote.

The combination of Caroline's applied pressure to friends and contacts, the media coverage (in newspapers, etc.) and the ensuing debate meant that decisions about child custody were very much in the public domain. Support was there. Very much as a result of her interventions and sheer determination, the Infant Custody Bill became enacted in 1839 and from that point onwards virtuous mothers gained at least the right to petition for the custody of their children up to the age of seven, and have access to older children thereafter. Caroline had been proven virtuous in the eyes of the law, so therefore she could now apply.

One can only imagine how she must have felt when, after all that effort, all that publicity, all that outpouring of her situation and stirring up of the public feeling for support, it came to nothing. When the Act was finally passed, and it was granted that Caroline could obtain legal access to her children, in spite of her husband's activities, George then outwitted them all; he took the children off to Scotland, out of her reach, and out of the jurisdiction of English law. In time she did get her access, but sadly during the interval one of the children, William, was to die after a riding accident, because he had been given insufficient supervision while under the husband's care.

Although Caroline had protested that hers was a personal quest, and had claimed that she was not challenging the husband's authority in a marriage, there were some who had been convinced that such a change, however small in itself, would inevitably have an impact on the institution of marriage, on society and its legal system. Such changes would bring dire consequences. They issued the following warning:

If ever there was a dangerous and revolutionary measure, this Custody of Infants Bill is one… Open your eyes, good easy husbands. Here it seems to lie the gist of the whole matter; no marital tutelage … Marriage henceforth to be a state of perfect liberty for women to do as they please … It is a demonstrable certainty, that if the equality of the sexes be assumed as the fundamental principle, an entirely different system of legislation and society must necessarily spring from it.[20]

---

[20] Handley, Edwin Hill, 'Custody of Infants Bill'

In this particular author's opinion such changes had to be avoided at all cost. At the time it seemed highly unlikely that this prediction would ever prove accurate, but his fears were not without some justification. In spite of Caroline's protestations the Custody of Infants Act 1839 began the painstakingly slow process of setting boundaries to the powers of husbands and fathers. Harriet Martineau commented that the Act of 1839 was 'the first blow struck at the oppression of English legislation in relation to women'.[21] By conceding any access and custodial rights to mothers, this new law acknowledged the fact that there were circumstances where a man could not expect to have unlimited power over his wife and children, and where indeed, if only for a limited time, a virtuous wife may have a greater claim to those children than he had. Although it was accepted that a husband could commit adultery without direct penalty, it was not to be so acceptable for him to hand over his children to his relatives, or even his mistress, or deprive his wife of her children without just cause. It was to be the thin end of the wedge; it marked the shift away from the previous insistence that where problems in a marriage existed they were always the fault of the wife.

It was to be many years before mothers gained the right to seek custody for older children or before there was to be any real acceptance of the equality of the claims of mother and father, or before the considerations of the children themselves were to become paramount. Until then women had only a chance to claim custody for children of 'tender years' – and of course apart from having to find the financial resources necessary to challenge a husband's legal claims, they would be totally dependent upon gaining the sympathy of the male judiciary at the time.

One of the disturbing elements of investigating women's history is to see just how frequently men, in their capacity of legal functionaries, ignored or belittled the sufferings of women and supported each other. Thus, for example, in one child custody case some years later, although a wife had been granted a separation on the grounds of cruelty, Lord Ardmillan still left the child in the custody of the father. His justification for the decision was that 'to leave his little child in his house is, or may well be, to introduce a soothing influence to cheer the darkness and mitigate the bitterness of his lot'. Where was

---

[21] Harriet Martineau, *A History of the Thirty Years' Peace, A.D. 1816-1846*, 1878

the empathy for her? Where was the justice? As one periodical later commented, 'The desirability of cheering the darkness and mitigating the bitterness of the wife's lot does not seem to have crossed the judicial mind at all'.[22]

There was also the problem of what would happen to the children after they reached the age of seven and were no longer legally entitled to their mother's custody. As female writers continued to point out to their readers, after that initial Custody Act the problems and emotional distress of being separated from one's children would still occur once the children reached that specific age. Although Rosina Bulwer Lytton, mentioned above, had supported the legal change, she too was unable to benefit from it. Rosina's children were older, so Caroline's actions provided no relief for her; she could not gain the precious custody of her children, and her husband continued to make access very difficult. Rosina complained bitterly:

> *English women have but one privilege – they may devote their lives to the education, welfare and care of their children, without ever being able to obtain one single, or conventional, or legal right over them, while the father, be his vices what they may, or his neglect ever so unnatural, still possesses, by our wise and moral laws, the whole and sole control over the unfortunate little beings who may be destined to feel all the disadvantages of his power, without reaping any of the benefits of his protection.*[23]

Some thirty years later the same problem was still causing distress:

> *He can take them from her, denying her even access to them and bringing them up exactly as he chooses, within certain limits, which the law, jealous of interference in paternal authority, usually makes broad enough. In fact until they become of age they are as much in his power as the wife is – mere goods and chattels, for whom he is responsible to no one so long as he offends society by no open cruelty or crime.*[24]

---

[22] John Chapman, 'The Law in Relation to Women', *Westminster Review*, 128, 1887

[23] *Cheveley, Or, The Man of Honour*

[24] Dinah Mulock Craik, *A Brave Lady*

Florence Marryat even asked:

> *What is the use of it all if it is to end like this? That after having reared my little one through the dangers of infancy and kept him alive only by my labour and care he is to be torn from my breast as though I were nothing and nobody. Why do we ever bring children into this world? Why do we suffer so much for a reward like this?*[25]

When she had initially started campaigning, what Caroline had sought was personal justice. She had managed to secure the right for a virtuous wife to *apply* for the custody of her children up to the age of seven and access up to the age of sixteen, but no more. Caroline's campaign was once referred to as 'Justice to women. *No* fanciful rights, no unreal advantages'.[26] However, in spite of her success in changing one of the rules that bound women so tightly in marriage, Caroline's problems continued, and it was as a direct result of her continuing personal battles, and her increasing determination to gain further personal justice, that led to the next major change for women. It was still connected with Caroline and her children, but this time the focus was upon money.

Life could be very hard for a woman. As a wife she could have many problems, but if it became necessary for her to live separately from her husband, they could get much worse. Obtaining a divorce, prior to the 1857 Act, was extremely expensive – and involved three separate phases. Firstly, a trial for criminal conversation, where the adultery (of the wife) was legally established, followed by an appearance in the Ecclesiastical Court, which had the power to legally separate the couple (*divorce a mensa et thoro*) and then, lastly, an expensive private Act of Parliament to allow a full legal divorce (*divorce a vinculo*). After this final stage the couple could go their separate ways, start new lives and marry again if they wanted to. Choosing to live separately, rather than going through expensive court proceedings, was often a sensible and practical option – although it denied the two ex-partners the opportunity to marry again.

In Caroline's case her husband, George, had failed to prove her guilty of 'criminal conversation', so they could not get a divorce.

---

[25] *Her World Against a Lie*

[26] Eliza Lynn Linton, 'One of Our Legal Fictions', *Household Words*, April 1854.

Caroline found herself in the same uncomfortable position as many other married women for, unless she was financially independent, and few women were, a wife living separately to her husband would still be dependent upon him making some financial arrangement for her. Some husbands were prepared to do this, not all, and as such arrangements were not enforceable by law it was often necessary to find some form of employment to supplement those funds.

As we have already seen with Caroline's husband earlier, while men were legally able to exert so much power over their wives, there were plenty who were fully prepared to exploit that situation to the full and deliberately make life very difficult. Just as he had manipulated the children, George was to do the same with money. It did not matter that Caroline and George had separated – as far as the law was concerned they were still man and wife, and that meant that he was still entitled to all the legal privileges of a husband. When they were together he was quite happy to live off her earnings; when they were apart he still wanted to make use of them.

We already know that there were various ways of interfering with a wife's earning potential from the work of a number of women writers. In the eighteenth century although Charlotte Smith no longer lived with her husband, he would turn up regularly whenever she was due to receive money from her publisher and he would walk off with it – as he was legally entitled to do; their marriage had not been legally terminated. A century later Rosina Bulwer Lytton used yet another preface to one of her books, this time to bemoan the treatment she had received from the publishers, who had been pressurised by her husband into refusing to publish her works, and thus causing her even more anxiety and further financial distress.[27] George Norton chose to assert his rights in a different way – he used the fact that Caroline was a good writer as a way of getting out of his previous agreement to pay her an allowance, and reduced the sum he was prepared to pay. It therefore put additional pressure on her to earn enough to replace that amount, while at the same time enabling him to have additional funds to spend on his own pleasures.

Caroline's experiences were to highlight additional financial problems, for a wife's inheritances were subject to just as much

---

[27] *School for Husbands,* 1852

interference and control by a husband as her earnings. Caroline was to receive two such bequests. One was from her mother (d. 1848) and one from her family friend Lord Melbourne (d. 1851), whom George had previously taken to court for criminal conversation with her. Caroline decided not to tell her husband about the additional income – and so when he heard about it he was determined to take a stand. Their deed of separation from 1848 had agreed an income for her; on hearing about her inheritance money he stopped paying it. Caroline thus found out another little legal detail to the detriment of separated wives – husbands were not legally bound to pay these agreed allowances – only 'honour bound'. For a man who chose to act 'dishonourably' there was no legal consequence.

For a while Caroline chose to live abroad, but she returned in 1853 and found the situation had not changed. She was in debt, she owed money – and one of the supposed financial benefits of being a wife was that the husband was liable for her debts. So she encouraged her creditors to sue George. He appears to have been totally intent on destroying her in public at this stage – totally obsessed, utterly vindictive, he subpoenaed everyone connected with her financial affairs, including Caroline herself, so that every tiny little detail of her life became exposed to public view again. In court he taunted and bullied her – and he got away with it. He brought up the legacy from Lord Melbourne and, referring back to her alleged relationship, played the sensation card again. Caroline got angry. She defended herself and won the applause and sympathy of the courtroom, but George still got off on a technicality, and thus avoided paying her debts.

It also did not seem to matter that he had again slandered her in court, giving misleading and false evidence about her; because of a wife's non-existence in the law she had no way of suing anyone or claiming damages from them. Any legal action concerning a wife had to take place through the husband, so it was a particularly problematic situation if the person who was causing the trouble was actually the husband himself. At the time she commented, 'I do not ask for my rights. I have no rights; I only have wrongs.'

In her anger Caroline turned naturally to her writing. At first this was through a series of letters to *The Times*, between herself, George, members of the legal profession and friends. She then decided to write one of her pamphlets and again get it privately printed and distributed.

There is no denying that Caroline had the ability to write powerfully and effectively. Regarding child custody, she undoubtedly had helped to change history, but her publication in May 1854, *English Laws for Women in the Nineteenth Century,* was not the document to do it again. It was passionate, it was personal and it was overdone. Although her experiences had been terrible, and the laws obviously did not protect women when they separated from their husbands, she lost the plot; it was unlikely to persuade anyone of her cause, it was much more likely to kill their interest.

Caroline was not the first woman writer to consider how English law treated them; there had been several before her and indeed another woman, Barbara Leigh Smith (whom we will encounter more in Chapter Six) engaged in a similar activity shortly afterwards, but Caroline was capable of doing a much better job of it. As we know, when she was married to George she had discovered that wives did not have a separate legal existence, and that state continued even if a separation had taken place. Caroline may have been powerless according to the law, but she was still a very capable woman. She also had had experience of changing the law. We do not know when Caroline reviewed her work and decided she could do better, but an incident occurred that certainly helped her in the process of doing so. In June, a month after the production of her *English Laws,* Lord Cranworth decided to introduce a new bill in Parliament that aimed to reform current laws concerning marriage and divorce. Six months later Caroline had not only rewritten her arguments but had found a publisher – Longmans – who felt that it would sell.

Caroline Norton's *A Letter to the Queen on Lord Chancellor Cranworth's Marriage and Divorce Bill* was published in 1855, and was both well constructed and well received. Although she made use of her own personal experiences, her anger and her frustration did not interfere with the purposes of her writing. As a writer she used some of the techniques that had brought her success in her quest for child custody, for again she highlighted injustice, gave real life examples and evidence of support for change by members of the government. Once again she was to acknowledge counter arguments, and then effectively knock them down, but this time there was to be a new twist. She addressed her document to the Queen, as head of State, and more importantly as a woman. She drew attention to the fact that no other queen had ever taken on board changes to support their women subjects and, in fact, even queens had not been treated well by the law. She pointed out that regarding divorce law the Queen's subjects could receive different treatment according to where they lived in the realm. Just like today's concern about postcode wars – regarding treatment from the National Health Service, for example – Victorian women could sue for divorce, but only if they lived in Scotland. And Victorian men could sue for divorce, but only if they were rich. 'Is that not a ridiculous state of things to exist in any kingdom?' she asked. She drew the Queen's, and everyone else's, attention to the fact that other countries in Europe looked after their women better than we did, under English law as it then stood, and made it a question of national pride – or shame.

This was such an important document that I think it is necessary to look at it in considerable detail here – and I apologise in advance for the extensive quotations given, but I do think that they help to show just how far women's writings had come and why it would be difficult to ignore them on this particular occasion. The remainder of the quotations in this chapter are from that document.

For clarity Caroline had started by setting out a list of the key problems for separated women, and had shown that far from being protected by the law such women were simply at its mercy. Married women had no legal existence and years of separation or desertion seemed to make no difference, 'for the legal fiction holds her to be at one with her husband, even though she may never see or hear of him'. It is not necessary to repeat all the problems she faced again, but her summation of the situation was simple and effective:

As her husband he has a right to all that is hers, as his wife she has no right to anything that is his. As her husband he may divorce her: the utmost divorce she can obtain is permission to reside alone – married to his name. The marriage ceremony is a civil bond for him – and an indissoluble sacrament for her; and the rights of mutual property which that ceremony is ignorantly supposed to confer, are made absolute for him and null for her... There are bad wanton irreclaimable women, as there are vicious profligate tyrannical men: but the difference is this: that to punish and restrain bad wives, there are laws, and very severe laws (to say nothing of social condemnation);

while to punish or restrain bad husbands there is, in England, no adequate law whatsoever.[28]

Later in the document she reminded her readers of her own position.

I am not divorced and I cannot divorce my husband; yet I can establish no legal claim upon him, nor upon any living human being. My reputation, my property, my happiness are irrevocably in the power of this slanderer on false grounds; this rapacious defender of his right to evade written bonds. I cannot release myself; I exist and I suffer; but the law denies my existence.

She also raised the subject of money – a particularly sensitive issue for her at the time. Mr Norton, as she referred to him in this document, had made an arrangement for an allowance to be paid after their separation but had failed to keep to it, kindly reminding her that she could not do anything about it. He had gained the benefit of her inheritances and her income, even pointing out that 'I am so able with my pen, I might *earn* £500 a year if I worked hard enough!' While she struggled for an existence he, in the meantime, could continue to spend her money. For those married women who had unsupportive husbands and had neither skills, nor resources of their own, the future would be very bleak.

Some five years previously a Royal Commission had reported on marriage and divorce law, but no further debate or action of any significance had taken place. A good starting point for Caroline therefore had been looking at the new proposals that Lord Cranworth had made; she dismissed his efforts very quickly. He had suggested Church Courts should lose their power over divorce decisions – and that power should be transferred to the already struggling Court of Chancery. Although she agreed that a different civil court should become responsible for divorce cases, Caroline felt a new, separate court should be established, and that it should be given powers *from the outset* to ensure that its decisions would be carried out.

Lord Cranworth had proposed that marriages should become

---

[28] Caroline Norton, *A Letter to the Queen on Lord Chancellor Cranworth's Marriage and Divorce Bill*, 1855

dissolvable by statute law – rather than expensive individual acts of Parliament in each case – but clearly believed that only men could apply for them. Caroline could not agree with that; we have already seen how women like her suffered in marriage, and wanted some changes in the basic rules, including the question of divorce.

One of the key issues here was the double standard. Caroline thought that it was immoral, as well as unjust, that a husband could get away with adultery, without consequence, but for a wife it meant the end of her marriage. It was said that such a fault in a man was 'but a little sin'; it was the wife's duty to ignore it. What the argument actually boiled down to was something called 'spurious offspring'. These were the children who were of questionable paternal parentage. If a wife had an affair and returned to her husband's home, any children she then bore may not have been the husband's; they were the spurious offspring. An adulterous wife was therefore a serious risk in terms of a husband's honour and his property, with the possibility of despoiling his home, and affecting the future inheritances of his family. It was said that adultery was therefore much more serious in a woman's case than in a man's. Caroline pointed out the absurdity of the argument:

> *What does it mean, his sin is comparatively harmless? It merely means in his home the sin has no result. Why is he to have liberty to wrong others – by a wrong that in his own case would be so intolerable and unpardonable – when the same reason may be applied to the wrong he does, as to the wrong he suffers? May not he also be the father of a spurious child – one born in a friend's home?*[29]

It was a very good question, and was raised by other women writers, like Rosina Bulwer Lytton.[30]

Caroline was also perfectly aware that, for many men, considering women's issues or the possible need for reforming them was a matter of complete indifference or, worse still, a matter for scorn. She noted that in Parliament, on 10th May 1855, when the Solicitor General had informed the House that the delayed marriage bill would be

---

[29] Ibid
[30] *Very Successful.*

brought forwards as soon as the House had expressed an opinion on the Testamentary Jurisdiction Bill:

> ... *There was a good humoured laugh at the very vague prospect held out – but nobody murmured; for nobody greatly cared when it should come on; or whether it ever came on at all.*[31]

In spite of this Caroline was aware that there *were* Members of Parliament who were more sympathetic towards the plight of married women. Lord Eldon, for example, had stated that he saw no reason why 'a woman was not as much entitled to sue for divorce as a man', and Mr Hallam believed:

> *Nothing can be more absurd than our modern privilegia; our Acts of Parliament to break the marriage bond; neither do I see how we can justify the denial of redress to women in every case of adultery and desertion.*[32]

One of the successful strategies in Caroline's campaign for child custody had been to methodically go through arguments that could be used by her opponents. She expected there would be some predictable opposition regarding her demands for justice now; men would say:

> '*What is all this disturbance about? Woman's rights and woman's wrongs – pooh pooh nonsense; Bloomerism, Americanism. We can't have that sort of thing in England. Women must submit; those who don't are bad women. There are not bad men.*'
> '*But this really is a monstrous case.*'
> '*Well yes, it's all very wrong – very shabby, very unprincipled – certainly; but we can't meddle; all the laws respecting women are in a hopeless state of confusion and it is much better one or two women should suffer unjustly, that the authority of husbands should be doubted.*'[33]

Caroline was armed and was ready to challenge them all, to force them to justify their entrenched position and she asked, 'Why is

[31] *A Letter to the Queen on Lord Chancellor Cranworth's Marriage and Divorce Bill.*
[32] Ibid
[33] Ibid

it better that a couple of women suffer?' Like other women she had been told that her situation was of incredible hardship and deserving of sympathy, but it was impossible to offer help. Caroline was not prepared to accept any of that. She pointed out that it was a question of law and our laws exist to protect individuals. She did not believe that she was too insignificant for justice, and so she asked:

What were laws made for but the redress of private wrongs?... A very shallow reader of history might prove that from time immemorial, changes in the laws of nations have been brought about by individual examples of oppression. Such examples cannot be unimportant for they are and ever will be the little hinges on which the great doors of justice are made to turn.[34]

Caroline was fully aware of her key role in this, as a woman who had suffered under the law, as a woman writer, and again as part of the actual process of reform.

If I had been a man I would have worked out their revision and reform: but I am only a woman – and in the land which my queen governs, women count for nothing in important matters. I am only a woman. Even now friends say to me – why write? Why struggle? It is the law, you will do no good. But if everyone lacked courage with that doubt nothing would ever be achieved in this world. This much I will do – woman though I be. I will put on record in French, English, German and Italian – what the law for women was in England in the year of civilisation and Christianity 1855 and in the 16th year of a female sovereign. This I will do and others who come after me may do more... I believe that I am permitted to be the example on which a particular law may be reformed... In our little corner of the earth – where so much besides is busy and fermenting for change – the time is ripely come for alteration in the laws for women. And they will be changed.[35]

---

[34] Ibid
[35] Ibid

Whenever women had wanted change, men had always come up with excuses, with plenty of reasons for procrastination and delay. Caroline was ready to face that too. In her own words she 'had learned English law piecemeal, by suffering under it'. Because of her efforts other women would study the history of legal development for women, and question the reasons given for delaying the necessary reforms, and they would inevitably reach their own conclusions.

> *And when they have read all which they have time, patience or inclination to read and ability to understand − they may take their crochet-work, or embroidery… and ruminate over their needles… how it is that laws continue to be in force which such men have so repeatedly condemned, as a mass of folly, indecency and contradiction!*
>
> *I hope, during this period of tranquil reflection, the rebellious thought may not occur to the tapestry working sex, that the obstacle to this legal reform must be, that men fear to curb the license of their pleasures. It is impossible seeing how eager, energetic and enthusiastic men are in other reforms, whose necessity is once proved and admitted, not to fancy that the reason why this particular difficulty is 'so surrounded with difficulty' is because it is extremely unpalatable to the reformers.*[36]

Caroline knew her power as a writer and felt that this time she really was fighting on behalf of all women. She knew that many other women suffered as she had suffered. She had learned from some of the mistakes she had made when campaigning for child custody and so stressed her public mission. Of her writing she said:

> *God had made me dream that it was meant for a higher and stronger purpose… It was meant to enable me to rouse the hearts of others to examine into all the gross injustice of these laws, to ask the nation of gallant gentlemen whose countrywoman I am, for once to hear a woman's pleading on the subject… My plea to attention is that in pleading for myself I am able to plead for all these others. Not that my sufferings or my desserts are greater than theirs; but that I combine, with the fact of having suffered wrong, the power to comment on and*

---

[36] Ibid

explain the cause of that wrong, which few women are able to do. For this I believe God gave me the power of writing. To this I devote that power. I abjure all other writing, till I see these laws altered... once more I deny that this is my personal cause; it is the cause of all the women of England.[37]

We do not know if Queen Victoria actually read this document, even though it was directed as a personal letter to her. But we do know that it was read widely, roused public opinion and inspired significant others to work for change regarding women and the law. During subsequent debates on Lord Cranworth's Bill – albeit a much amended bill – Caroline's friend Lord Lyndhurst not only made reference to her *Letter* but actually read out significantly long passages from it during the parliamentary session. Through her experiences and through her powerful writing, Caroline had once again influenced the course of history. Even though she was the subject of much personal criticism and had felt the need to ask her female critics, 'Will none of you heed the case that I advocate, and forget that it was advocated by me?', she could rightly claim, 'Many a woman may live to thank heaven that I had courage and energy left, to attempt the task.'[38]

Looking back to the earlier women writers, the significance of their works had increased considerably over time. From personal records of discontent, to printed novels and treatises and major innovations like Mary Wollstonecraft's *A Vindication of the Rights of Woman,* it could now be rightly claimed that women writers had at last played a direct part in the legal process and that, thanks to Caroline, some of their suggestions were now actually written, virtually word for word, in the statute book.

In 1857 the revised Bill was passed as the Matrimonial Causes Act, though it is more commonly known as the Divorce Act. There is much more to say about the Act itself in Chapter Six, but, for now, it is necessary to note only the specific changes relevant to Caroline's concerns. A new, separate Divorce Court was established, which would have the power to direct maintenance payments. It was confirmed that a husband needed to prove only his wife's adultery in order to sue for a divorce. The double standard was to remain intact, but a woman

---

[37] Ibid
[38] Ibid

could now at least apply for a divorce *if* she could prove the adultery of her husband *and* had at least one other specified complaint. These were bestiality, incest, rape (of another woman), cruelty, bigamy, or desertion for more than two years. In certain circumstances a legal separation could be granted without adultery having to be proven. Caroline had already obtained that. The most significant change in the rules of marriage, as far as she was concerned, was the law now accepted the position of separated women and allowed them to be considered as single women again. Being 'femme sole' meant that any future earnings and inheritances would be their own, and they also regained the right to sue. Once again limitations were being set on the powers and privileges of a husband. Caroline had done well; separated women like herself were now being recognised by the law – they had found a way out of the game. For women who were actually married the task of changing the rules was just beginning.

PART FOUR

PUBLIC CONCERNS

Chapter Six
The Property of a Wife

When women had started to challenge the rules of marriage they discovered the fact that men took the issue of property very seriously. Any children, as we have already seen, were considered to be the husband's property; any property the wife had already owned before her marriage had become his, and anything she should gain thereafter would join his list of possessions too. What is also clear is that she herself was considered to be just as much his possession as her property and the children. By the power and authority invested in him by law, and sanctioned by the Church, a husband had control of a wife's property, her person, her voice and her sex. Eliza Lynn Linton was to refer to him as a 'marital gaoler':

> *An absolute Lord is this marital gaoler. He holds the person, property and reputation of his conjugal prisoner in as fast a gaol as ever was built of granite and iron... the prisoner wife is not recognised by the law.* [1]

To try to unravel just how the laws regarding the ownership of a wife and her property were challenged, and to examine just how much they changed during the rest of Victoria's reign, is actually very complicated. The marriage question consisted of a series of interconnected elements and one should not consider them in isolation. The complex ties that bound a wife to her husband had made it almost impossible for a woman to break away from her marriage, as we saw in Chapter Five, and that put her husband in a very powerful position over her. The fact that both the Church and the State supported traditional marriage meant any challenge to it was likely to be perceived as a threat by both.

---

[1] Eliza Lynn Linton, 'Marriage Gaolers', *Household Words*, July, 1856

We begin by turning the clock back a little and returning to Caroline Norton.

During the eighteenth century some women writers had believed that you only had to expose the injustices that women suffered and then the men who governed would automatically intervene and rectify them. Caroline had shown the absolute fallacy of that belief. Her efforts also publicised the fact that, prior to 1857, English law supported the idea that women should not be able to leave their husbands and so denied them the right to be self-supporting if they did. A wife who dared to leave her husband deserved what she got. Thanks to Caroline, significant gains had been made for separated women, but it would be misleading to leave the impression that the law had been changed due to Caroline's efforts alone. It had not. Her experiences and her use of them had been significant and influential – indeed, I doubt if the law would have been changed at that time without them – but there were others who were trying to change the status of all married women at that time.

We do know that women were not interested only in following Caroline's story; they were moved by her sufferings, and some were directly influenced and even inspired by her actions. One of these was a woman called Barbara Leigh Smith (later Bodichon). Like Caroline, Barbara was well placed; her father was an unconventional MP (he himself never married) and she too had some important friends and acquaintances. These included Thomas Talfourd, who had been so useful for Caroline when she was fighting for child custody rights, and a family friend, Matthew Davenport Hill, a judge, who was Recorder of Birmingham.

Barbara was interested in the law; she wanted to establish how women were being treated by it and, in doing so, she also wanted to see what difference it made when they changed their marital status. At the time she was not married, but had a permanent relationship in mind. She spent time researching her subject and analysing her findings, as a result of which she published a pamphlet entitled, *A Brief Summary, in Plain Language, of the Most Important Laws of England Concerning Women,* in 1854. This was a remarkable document. It was concise, very cheap – costing only a few pence – it sold well, and went to a second edition within two years. Its contents were discussed widely. Using simple language, it listed all the laws for women and showed just what a raw deal they received under English law. It was clearly laid out and the information it contained was detailed and well organised. There were sections on the Legal Condition of Spinsters, the Laws Concerning Married Women, Precautions against the Law Concerning Married Women, Laws Concerning a Widow, Laws Concerning Women in Other Relationships, and Laws Concerning Illegitimate Children and Their Mothers. The total collection led her to believe that 'women more than any other members of the community suffer from over legislation'.[2]

At least there would be no confusion after this for any female regarding a woman's position in the law at the time. A few years after it was published Emma Robinson was to comment she had:

> ...dreamed not the full infernal egotism and oppression for women of man-made English law... The law of England contemplates a species of absorption or suspension of the separate existence of a woman during the whole period of her wifehood.[3]

Such publications as *A Brief Summary* had made it plain enough for all to see. Although single women had property rights and paid taxes, they had no civil rights, and married women were simply nonentities as far as the law was concerned. The pamphlet had concluded with a few pages of Barbara's own remarks on the situation. She asked bluntly, 'Why does marriage make so little difference to men, and such a mighty legal difference to women?' She pointed out the obvious anomaly that, once a woman became twenty-one, she was considered to be an adult, an independent human creature, able to earn money and choose how to spend it, but, if she married, the law would demote her and consider her again as an infant. There is more to say about Barbara and her *A Brief Summary* shortly.

Newspapers and journals were beginning to notice more examples of legal injustice towards married women and highlighted the plights of those concerned. We are already familiar with Caroline's story, but there were plenty of others. There were examples of wives who had worked, scrimped and saved, but the husbands had then squandered

---

[2] Barbara Leigh Smith Bodichon, *A Brief Summary, in Plain Language, of the Most Important Laws of England Concerning Women, 1854*

[3] *Mauleverer's Divorce: A Story of Woman's Wrongs*

all the money, frequently on alcohol, to the detriment of the family concerned. It must have been a totally demoralising and depressing experience for them. As one anonymous working woman poignantly asked, if a husband took it all, 'what's the use of a body striving?' There were other situations too where the husband had died and bequeathed all of 'his' property to his mistress, or another relative, leaving his widow and children completely penniless.

In spite of proclamations that a woman received nothing but generosity at the hands of a father or husband, as early as 1838 a Member of Parliament, Lord Brougham, had asked:

Could anything be more harsh or cruel than that the wife's goods and chattels should be at the mercy of the husband, and that she might work and toil for an unkind father to support his family and children, while the husband repaid her with harshness and brutality; he all the time rioting and revelling in extravagance and dissipation and squandering in the company of guilty paramour the produce of her industry?[4]

When Barbara published her *A Brief Summary*, some sixteen years later, there was still no financial protection for these married women.

Another woman, the journalist and novelist Eliza Lynn Linton, was also influenced by Caroline Norton's experiences and decided to make good use of them, including them in an article, entitled 'One of Our Legal Fictions'. Eliza argued that it was a mere fiction that women received protection from the law, and that reforms were long overdue. Charles Dickens published it in his periodical *Household Words* in April 1854. The article highlighted the sufferings Caroline Norton had faced at the hands of her husband, but without actually naming her. Eliza Lynn Linton has often been criticised by modern women writers for the mixed views she showed in both her novels and her journalism, some of which appear to be highly antifeminist. Yet, although I think she must have felt it was both politically and economically sound to write articles on both sides of the fence, 'One of Our Legal Fictions' does seem to have been written from the heart. At the end of the article she summarised:

---

4   Hansard, *Parliamentary Debates*, (House of Lords) 1838, XLIV, 780

And all this is in the laws, the laws which throw a woman helplessly on the mercy of her husband, make no ways of escape and build no cities of refuge for her, and deliberately justify her being cheated and entrapped. All these are doings protected and allowed by her laws – and men stand by and say, 'It is useless to complain. The laws must be obeyed. It is dangerous to meddle with the laws.'

Surely there is work to be done in the marital code of England. Surely there are wrongs to be redressed and reforms to be made that have gone too long unmade. Surely we have here a righteous quarrel with the laws. Justice to women. No fanciful rights, no unreal advantages... no high flown assertion of equality in kind; but simple justice.[5]

In later articles she also noted that both in Europe, and in countries further afield:

...women have the right to their own property; they can trade, earn and keep, and on the whole they are more of a power, both in the home and in society, than they are here.[6]

A similar observation had been made the previous year:

But the American courts, we are glad to say, go further in the rectification of woman's wrongs, than the simple maintenance of her right to that which is her own... They regard her as something else than as a proprietor. They take note of her as a human being.[7]

As things stood, though, in 1854 when a woman married, unless provided with some independent funds that were legally protected by a settlement, all her financial affairs became the concern of her husband. It also meant that everything she had, her clothes, her possessions, her property, from that point onwards were, in effect, his. It is rare indeed to find a comment on how women regarded the actual *possession* of their settlements, rather than just being happy to make use of them; however, Frances Trollope made a most revealing authorial comment

5   Eliza Lynn Linton, 'One of Our Legal Fictions', *Household Words*, April 1854
6   *Ourselves*, 1870
7   W.H. Dixon, 'The Subjection of Women', *The Athenaeum*, June 1869

in one of her novels: 'Did she glory in the power so carefully invested on her settlement? Most assuredly she did.' [8]

Apart from the use of that settlement money, all household finances, all expenses, had to then be approved by her husband. The element of control and power it gave him over her has already been considered in previous chapters, but it is possible to gain further insight into the reality of the situation from some of the women writers. At its simplest level it was undignified to have to ask for every penny for even the most basic purchases in life, let alone personal ones; it could be humiliating and could make a woman very resentful if she had to justify every expense. This was especially true if she had brought a huge fortune with her that the husband was only too willing to control, and then witnessed him spending freely on his own personal indulgences. Emma Robinson once asked, 'Why can't they let women's property be their property until they expressly choose to part with it like the men's, I wonder?'[9] Even with the husbands having overall control of household finances their wives were often accused of being extravagant with money, or having no money sense, but I have found just as many references to the wives desperately struggling to make ends meet, as I have to their squandering money.

Sometimes men would need to be reminded that it was often inaccurate to say that a husband supported his wife and children without any input from her. In addition to her work on the law, Barbara Leigh Smith Bodichon pointed out that 'women who act as housekeepers, nurses and instructors of their children often do as much for the support of the household as their husbands'.[10] As well as their important, but frequently neglected, domestic and educational role, many women also made a direct contribution to the family income. In 1850 the writer Mrs Gaskell had watched disbelievingly as her husband took her £20 earnings from the publication of her short story *Lizzie Leigh,* and buttoned it up quickly and safely in his own pocket. Eliza Lynn Linton had openly stated that she had always given more in terms of financial support to the family than her husband ever had, and the novelist Florence Marryat cynically once asked, 'Who do you think pays for the butter?' [11]

---

[8] *The Life and Adventures of a Clever Woman*
[9] *Mauleverer's Divorce: A Story of Woman's Wrongs*
[10] Barbara Leigh Smith Bodichon, *Women and Work*, 1857
[11] I am indebted to Dr Catherine Pope for the use of this quotation.

But there was, of course, more to the question of married women having control of property and earnings than issues of personal humiliation or resentment. Married women were in a situation of enforced dependency because of the marriage laws. Without a settlement they were totally dependent upon the financial support of their husbands. Just as the husband's control of child custody bound an unhappy wife to her marriage, so too did his control of the finances. Without employment, or support from friends and family, a woman who left her husband was in a very vulnerable position unless she had money in her pocket. Not only could she be forced to return to her husband if he pursued the matter, but anyone who offered her assistance could also find himself, or herself, in trouble with the law. Financial independence would give her freedom, but it could also lead to a change in the balance of power within marriage itself. Eliza Lynn Linton later commented, 'If women were joint earners and had the power to remove their half of the income and leave, would men be so cagey?' [12]

Having clarified some of the key issues now regarding married women's property, let us return to Barbara and her newly published *A Brief Summary, in Plain Language, of the Most Important Laws of England Concerning Women*. Barbara decided to show her *A Brief Summary* to family friend Matthew Davenport Hill, who was a member of the Law Amendment Society,[13] and he passed it on to them. After studying it, the society decided to conduct their own investigation into women and the law; the following year their report proposed that the law *should* be altered to give married women property rights.

The time was now right for Barbara to move from writing informative pamphlets about the law to doing something more practical. She got together with a small group of friends, drafted a petition for them to use and then, leading the campaign, set about collecting signatures. Using a petition to collect direct evidence of support, to prove women wanted their own grievances to be heard, was not a new venture,[14] but it was one that was to be used frequently during the struggles for emancipation.

---

[12] *Ourselves*

[13] Lord Brougham, mentioned above, had founded this society approximately ten years beforehand, as he sought many reforms within the English Legal System.

[14] One, for example, had been started to show support for maternal child custody in the 1830s, another to support women's suffrage in 1851.

For too long men had said that women were not interested in changing the status quo. The novelist Mrs Gaskell (whose husband had pocketed the £20) was one of 3,000 women who signed it. Regarding married women, the petition clearly announced:

> *It is time that legal protection be thrown over the produce of their labour, and that in entering the state of marriage they no longer pass from the state of freedom into the condition of a slave, all whose earnings belong to the master not himself.*

The petition also pointed out that leaving the mother with control over her own earnings would enable her to ensure that she provided proper moral and physical welfare for her children, rather than being dependent upon the whims of her husband.

Barbara's petition – and the offshoots from it – collected an impressive 26,000 signatures and, supported by John Stuart Mill, these were presented to the Houses of Parliament in 1856. The following year there were *two* different bills being discussed in Parliament related to women's property, but, thanks to Caroline and Barbara, their emphases were different. Caroline as we know was concerned with the plight of married women who were separated from their husbands (or deserted by them); Barbara was concerned with the rights of *all* married women.

Initially Lord Brougham introduced a Bill wanting to give *all* married women the same property rights as unmarried women. A change in government meant that another MP, Erskine Perry, took over with a new Bill. At the same time the law regarding divorce per se was also under consideration, as we saw in Chapter Five. In fact, the second reading of the Matrimonial Causes Bill (the Divorce Bill) took place just nine days after the second reading of Perry's bill.

Unfortunately, Perry was subsequently persuaded to drop his Property Bill with the reassurance that the Divorce Bill would incorporate all his major areas of concern, but he was completely misled. Only Caroline Norton's pleas for separated women were incorporated as amendments to the main Matrimonial Causes Bill, which became law, as we know, in 1857. There was to be no concession for those women who remained married.

Lord Lyndhurst, who had been a real friend and supporter of Caroline in Parliament, had been no friend to Barbara Leigh Smith

Bodichon. He had encouraged the House to agree to the simple amendment that gave property rights to separated/deserted women only, for 'it did not go anything like the length of the Bill which had been in the other House'. And agree to it they did. Barbara, her petitions and all her supporters were left out in the cold. Men, as represented by the Members of Parliament, had certainly shown they did not like the prospect of married women being placed in a 'strong minded and independent position' by being granted property rights of their own.

When Barbara had begun her initial attack she completely underestimated what the general response from men would be; she failed to understand just how deeply embedded the question of controlling women's property was in men's perceptions of marriage. She had stated:

> We do not say that these laws of property are the only unjust laws concerning women to be found in the short summary which we have given, but they form a simple, tangible, and not offensive point of attack.[15]

Clearly she was wrong – for some had undoubtedly been deeply offended. The *Saturday Review* began in a very patronising way:

> So long as the petticoat rebellion was confined to a mistaken petition of literary ladies whose peculiar talents had placed them in a rather anomalous position, we really had not the heart to say anything about it.[16]

However, during the course of the article the tone changed; it went on to talk of defying 'the common sense of mankind' and even of 'revolution', but more revealing was the remark that 'there is besides a smack of selfish independence about it which rather jars with poetical notions of wedlock'. Women who wished to retain their financial independence were thus accused of being 'selfish', and the 'protection' of men was again glamorised with chivalric implications.

Some years later, an article in the more radical *Westminster Review*

---

[15] *A Brief Summary, In Plain Language, of the Most Important Laws of England Concerning Women*

[16] Robert Cecil (?), 'Law for Ladies', *Saturday Review*, May 1856

pointed out for those men who had readily accepted the traditional position there had never been any concern with the 'smack of selfish independence' or jarring of 'poetical notions' regarding their own behaviour. That had apparently been a totally different matter.[17]

Control of property was to be such a key issue in the marriage game. There was obviously a huge difference between putting an end to some basic injustices and actually agreeing to reduce men's previous level of total control by granting all women equality in matters of property and income. Albeit reluctantly, it had been necessary to release a little control over the children and over the property of women who had become legally separated, or those who had experienced long-term desertion as we saw in Chapter Five. The fundamental reason why husbands were reluctant to give up the remaining, significant control of their wives' property was because it gave them power; it reinforced their own authority and position as head of the family (given by both Church and State) and they obviously enjoyed having the benefits of it. Being a husband, having the possession and control of a wife and family, all helped reinforce a man's image and identity. It was one of the visible exhibitions of his masculinity; it was all part of the game. Harriet Taylor put it succinctly: 'We ask why the existence of one half of the species should be mere ancillary to the other … The only reason is, that men like it'[18]

There were other related reasons why men wished to retain the status quo. If married women gained full property rights, it would weaken their overall position in several key ways. While a wife remained alive, a husband would be likely to benefit from any wealth that she possessed; however, when she died, it would be another matter. With equal property rights a wife would be in a position to leave her possessions to whom she pleased – in effect the husband could be disinherited if she chose to leave her property elsewhere. There was another consideration lurking in the background too. At the time not every man had a vote – it was all to do with a property qualification. While it is true that some single women (and that included widows) were wealthy enough to reach that property barrier, there were not sufficient numbers involved to make a significantly strong argument

---

17 John Chapman, 'The Law in Relation to Women'
18 Harriet Taylor, 'The Enfranchisement of Women', *Westminster Review*, July 1851.

about their entitlement to civil rights. If all married women gained property rights, significant numbers would have equivalent wealth to meet the property bar, and so the argument in favour of women's suffrage would become that much stronger. And if women gained suffrage, then the whole structure of law, government and society would undoubtedly be under threat. Those men who enjoyed the benefits of power and control over their wives in particular, and women in general, had no reason to wish for a change in the status quo.

While they continued to enjoy these benefits so thoroughly, men were also very keen to assert their own perceived abilities and denigrate those of the opposite sex. It was regularly stated that women had no business sense and would fritter away and waste family resources if left to their own devices, but rather than going to the trouble of educating women about financial issues, it was considered far better (and safer) to leave things in the hands of the husband. Indeed, as Charlotte Riddell, using her apparently male pseudonym, F.G. Trafford, so eloquently put it, a man would justify such beliefs by proclaiming, 'Good heavens! Women have as much sense of business as cows!'[19] and Mary Taylor explained the situation a little more clearly: 'You see women know little of business, and people are careful not to tell them'.[20]

Another favourite justification of the period, shown frequently in male literature, was that the husband should control all financial matters because of the need for 'unity' in a marriage. Here were 'the poetic notions of wedlock' with the capable and masterful husband lovingly protecting his dear submissive wife. There are frequent references to perceived parallel situations – for example, the much quoted 'if two must ride on a horse, one must ride behind'.[21] I have yet to come across a contemporary recommendation of two riding on separate horses, side by side.

The well-known and respected Blackstone's *Commentaries on the Laws of England,* had clearly stated that, 'When a man and woman married they became one, and the husband was that one.'[22] In the

[19] Charlotte Riddell, *Too Much Alone,* 1860
[20] Mary Taylor, *Miss Miles,* 1890
[21] for example in 'Women's Law: Mrs Norton's Letter to the Queen', *The Law Review 23,* 1855/6. The proverb is from William Shakespeare, *Much Ado About Nothing.*
[22] William Blackstone, *Commentaries on the Laws of England,* 1765-9

middle of the nineteenth century it was still the general belief that the husband should hold the authority position in the family, he should be its voice and of course he should control the money. Any wife who considered otherwise showed that 'smack of selfish independence' so despised by *The Saturday Review*.

In 1839 Rosina Bulwer Lytton stated bitterly, 'Unanimity of opinion, so desirable in wedded life, can never be achieved unless wives are content to live as they must die, intestate'.[23] Similarly, Harriet Taylor, whose ideas were later to be publicly shared by John Stuart Mill, had a similar view: 'A man usually likes to have his own will, but does not like that his domestic companion should have a will different from his'.[24]

It is not difficult to see how easily conditioning had supported this tradition. Boys grew up witnessing the privileges of their fathers and the men around them, and expected to receive the same. Men were taught to be superior and women to be submissive and accepting. For a woman to question or challenge these fundamentals was considered to be decidedly unfeminine behaviour, or so the majority of people seemed to believe at the time that Barbara's petition was circulated.

Florence Marryat summarised the situation very neatly – a husband was speaking: 'It's not love that women want nowadays. It's their liberty, free and uncontrolled. Perhaps they are right, but it's all very different from what I imagined marriage to be'.[25]

Looking back with the benefit of hindsight, the acquiescence of so many women made it easy for men to exercise power and enjoy the privilege of doing so; it is no wonder it took so long for significant changes to occur in law and be accepted in society. In addition to which one can understand how quickly males became protective of the privileges and benefits they received because of their sex. In Chapter Three, I showed clearly how boys were conditioned into their superior role from a very young age. Thomas Hughes had himself attended Rugby School and spoke from experience when he proclaimed in the book:

> *There are no such bigoted holders by established forms and customs, be they never so foolish or meaningless, as English schoolboys... We*

---

[23] *Cheveley: or the Man of Honour*
[24] 'The Enfranchisement of Women'
[25] *Too Good For Him*, 1865

*looked upon every trumpery, little custom and habit that had been
obtained in the school... and regarded the infringement or variation of
it as a sort of sacrilege.*[26]

It was not unknown for Members of Parliament, the judiciary or other
professions to have had a public school education and maintaining
their own privileged status and wealth seems for many to have been a
lifelong occupation.

So married women – as opposed to separated or deserted
women – lost their chance to gain any property rights in 1857.
That situation was not to change for another twelve or thirteen
years. After all Barbara's hard work with *A Brief Summary*, and the
petitions, she must have been very disappointed with the result.
Or rather lack of it. However, she was not defeated; she merely
diverted her energies into other more successful ventures, not just
for married women but for all women. Over the next few years,
amongst other activities, Barbara, along with friends and fellow
campaigners, purchased and ran a woman's journal, supported
higher education for women and helped to found new colleges,
developed working opportunities and improved conditions for
women, as well as developing an increasing interest in women's
suffrage – and Barbara herself got married. This group of women
became known as the Langham Place Group, named after the
premises where they used to meet, and they were to play a key
role in women's history, but sadly there is not space in this book to
pay sufficient tribute to their work as a whole. However, we will
encounter some of their members, including Barbara herself, later
in this and subsequent chapters.

Meanwhile, although Perry's Bill had been abandoned, the need
to improve the general situation for married women had not changed.
There were still plenty of wives whose husbands continued to take
control of the finances, and misuse them, leaving both them and the
children to suffer the consequences. Over the next decade and a half
there were to be repeated attempts to resolve the issue in Parliament;
there were eighteen more Bills concerning it before Acts were finally
passed (in 1870 and 1882) that did much to alleviate the problems.

---

[26] *Tom Brown's Schooldays*

However, after 1857 the situation was becoming far more complex, for interrelated questions regarding the need for women to have a voice (through suffrage), to obtain relief from marital abuse, and the need for a recognition of the separate legal existence of a wife were to be raised again and again both in Parliament and in public. I mentioned earlier that changes in the rules of marriage can be considered as layers of change; as one thin layer was laid upon another the position of women grew a little stronger. The 1860s were to be very important years.

One of the consequences of the passing of the Divorce Act in 1857 had been the establishment of the Divorce Court, and cases heard there were to highlight the sufferings of women in general – even though that had not been the original intention of the Act. With increased negative exposure in the courts and the media, more and more people were beginning to realise that it was no longer justifiable to say that *all* men automatically deserved to be given the right of permanent authority over their wives. Not all men were capable of administering the task with fairness and justice; not all of them were necessarily up to the job. As women began to accomplish more in society through their working achievements, it also could no longer be argued that women as a sex were incapable of greater things than being meek, submissive wives confined to their domestic sphere.

A few years after Barbara Bodichon's efforts failed to win resolution in Parliament, John Stuart Mill wrote *The Subjection of Women*. We have encountered him previously, but it is now time to look at him a little more closely. J.S. Mill was to be one of the greatest and most influential male supporters of women at the time, and he later acknowledged that this book (like other works accredited to him) had been written jointly with his wife Harriet (*née* Taylor) – whom we have also heard from before. Now considered to be a classic feminist text, *The Subjection of Women* was to be a highly significant document, which not only detailed the difficult situations that women faced, but also the role of men in not just creating, but also maintaining them.

J.S. Mill predicted that 'women cannot be expected to devote themselves to the emancipation of women until men in considerable numbers are prepared to join them in the undertaking'. Satisfied with what he had written, he then shelved the publication of the book for approximately *eight years* because he felt that the time was not yet right for its release to the general public. They were not ready to listen. They were certainly not ready to act. He had seen what happened to the work of Barbara and her friends, and he chose to wait.

Four years after he had written *The Subjection of Women*, in 1865 J.S. Mill became a Member of Parliament, and once again women found a strong supporter there. When Barbara asked him what could be done to help further the progress of women's suffrage, he not only advised her to use her petitioning skills, but also said if she got enough signatures he himself would present them in Parliament. Within two weeks Barbara and her friends had just under 1,500 signatures, including those of some of the most famous women of the time – Florence Nightingale (who had been to the Crimea and was busy reforming nursing), Harriet Martineau and Frances Power Cobbe (both well-known journalists), Mary Somerville (a respected scientist), and Emily Davies (who led the campaign for women's higher education and was to found the first women's university college at Girton a few years later).

It was not just a question of collecting as many signatures as possible; it was necessary to have the solid support of well-known, respectable women. Harriet Martineau had been critical of both Mary Wollstonecraft and Caroline Norton in the past because their notorious lifestyles were detrimental to the cause of women. Harriet acknowledged that although their ideas and beliefs had been sound, these two women had made the mistake of allowing their personal feelings and experiences to interfere with their actions. She said:

> *The best friends of the cause are the happy wives and the busy, cheerful, satisfied single women, who have no injuries of their own to avenge, and no painful vacuity or mortification to relieve.*[27]

Barbara's petition in support of women's suffrage had found plenty of such women, but Caroline Norton was not invited to sign.

It was not the first women's petition for the vote – for one had been presented to the House of Lords in 1851 – but Barbara's petition, like her previous one, was again very popular; it was

---

[27] Harriet Martineau, *Autobiography*, written 1855, published 1877

presented to Parliament on 7th June 1866. Suffrage for women became a national issue; organisations and other petitions were subsequently springing up all over the country. Public meetings were frequently held and women spoke openly at them. In 1867 J.S. Mill tried to get an amendment to the Reform Bill, under debate at the time, to remove the sex bar to women's voting, but he was unsuccessful.

Once again women novelists were joining in with their supportive voices. Matilda Hays wrote:

> *I am quite sure that until women have a voice in framing the laws which particularly affect themselves, they will continue to bear, as they do now, unjustly upon them. The law of master and slave is always oppressive to the latter and that with some modification is still the relative position of man and woman.*
>
> *Until quite lately a married woman was only a chattel – a piece of goods – as absolutely belonging to her husband as the table he dined from or the coat on his back. No amount of brutality could free her from bondage, for an appeal to parliament was costly, a solemn mockery of justice for all but the wealthy and the influential. The new Divorce Court has mended this state of things, and the protection it affords to the earnings of married women is a step in the right direction, but women were chiefly instrumental in obtaining this. You remember the petition signed by thousands and thousands of women all over the country for the introduction of this clause.*
>
> *Depend upon it… until women have a voice, direct or indirect, in the framing of the laws which concern themselves, they will bear unfairly upon them.[28]*

Many women were beginning to feel that to get justice in the matter of married women's property it would be necessary to have a say in parliamentary affairs; getting the vote was crucial. I for one had not realised that there were woman suffragists from as early as the 1860s. Many years ago I saw the film *Mary Poppins* for the first time. It was set in 1910. In the film there is a shot of Mrs Banks, the children's

---

[28] *Adrienne Hope, The Story of a Life*

mother, wearing her suffragette sash, preparing to leave for a march. As the front door opened you could see a whole group of suffragettes in the background. And even then I remember asking the question, 'Where did they all come from?' They had obviously been amassing for a very long time.

Whether they wanted equity or equality, or whether indeed they would be able to achieve either, was a matter of public debate. It should also be noted that as things stood, votes for women would not necessarily include *all* women. It was highly likely that property would not be the only bar. If women were to gain any suffrage rights, married women could well be excluded on the old familiar grounds of 'unity' in marriage; it was argued that the husband already spoke for the interests of his wife and children, and also that in giving women suffrage the dominion of every husband would be diminished. They were classic arguments that would be used every time a new claim for women's rights was aired. The editor of *The Athenaeum* stated clearly, 'A man would be ashamed to refuse his wife justice, who would feel no scruple in refusing to give her power.' When later reviewing J.S. Mill's *The Subjection of Women*, he declared:

> *In claiming a full share of public power for women, Mr Mill is preparing for us the greatest revolution ever yet affected on this planet... Mr Mill is working towards no less radical a change than the transfer of the whole of government to women!... The difference in [population] numbers is about a million; and an Act of Parliament which would call the female population to political power would give them, not just a share in government, but the whole. No fact is clearer.[29]*

Men were afraid of giving women the vote. They were afraid of being outvoted, and they were also afraid of losing their home comforts. During a parliamentary debate in 1870 one MP, Mr Beresford Hope, asked:

> *What would become not merely of woman's influence, but of her duties at home, her care of the household, her supervision of all those*

---

[29] W.H. Dixon, 'The Subjection of Women'

duties and surroundings which make a happy home; all these matters must be neglected if we see women coming forward and taking part in the government of the country?[30]

Matthew Browne, a reporter on the House of Commons, admitted:

I can well understand the dismay with which the majority of men flinch from the bare idea of giving [women] votes... We are not entitled, in my opinion, to restrict liberty of action... but we are entitled to look with jealousy upon whatever seems ever so remotely to threaten those ideals which are dearest and lie closest to all that we hold most lofty and most precious in our lives.[31]

This all sounds very familiar, rather like the comment made earlier regarding public schoolboys wanting to keep their privileges. Maintaining authority and control over women and their property, and enjoying the domestic comforts they provided were still very much amongst those 'precious ideals'. But at least Matthew Browne was to acknowledge:

If women in mass were to demand the franchise, I do not see how we could with justice refuse to give it to them; but I devoutly hope they will <u>not</u> demand it.[32]

At the same time that the suffrage movement was beginning to build up steam, a small group of women, namely Elizabeth Wolstenholme, Josephine Butler and Jessie Boucherett, looked for wider support for married women's property rights to be established. It was over ten years since Barbara Leigh Smith Bodichon and her friends had started work in this area, and later Elizabeth reported that she and her friends had known nothing about that previous campaign. To this day women keep rediscovering their own history.

Just as the Law Amendment Society had helped the campaigning women in 1856/7, this time the Social Science Association (itself an offshoot of the Law Amendment Society) was to give their blessing,

[30] Hansard, (House of Commons) 1870, CCI, 227
[31] Matthew Browne, 'The Subjection of Women', *Contemporary Review*, 1870
[32] Ibid

by reinvestigating the matter, still finding the laws regarding married women's property unjust, and again recommending legal reform. In 1868 these women then formed a well-organised Married Women's Property Committee, an organisation that was open to both sexes, had its executive committee based in Manchester, had growing support in London and branches in Birmingham, Dublin and Belfast. Through their tireless efforts, property reform became a national issue. Many important names are associated with it – Lydia Becker (treasurer), Ursula Bright and her husband (also an MP), and Richard Pankhurst, to name but a few. Richard was a member of the Social Science Association and he drafted the Married Women's Property Bill for them[33].

This property committee was built on a much larger scale than the small group of friends that Barbara had originally worked with. Reform was no longer just the concern of 'a few literary women' (like Barbara) or a scorned woman acting alone (like Caroline Norton). The Married Women's Property Committee organised meetings, printed and distributed leaflets, including copies of key parliamentary speeches in favour of their aims, drew up petitions, collected signatures and collated them. To give an idea of the scale of their operation – Barbara's original petition had fewer than 2,000 signatures on it – during the course of 1868/9 the Married Women's Property Committee presented nearly 150 petitions to Parliament with 75,000 signatures from around the country. During the course of this campaign Elizabeth Wolstenholme was to collate a total of 100,000 signatures and issue 135,000 leaflets. Theirs was a phenomenal achievement. The pressure was on.

Once again there were some predictable arguments against the proposed changes in a wife's position. Some had been heard before. In the House of Lords, Lord Penzance expressed concern that even if a wife was financially independent, a husband should still maintain authority over her. Similarly, a barrister and journalist called James Fitzjames Stephen genuinely believed that 'if a wife failed to obey, it showed a base, unworthy, mutinous disposition'. He also made the revealing comment that:

---

[33] He was also actively involved in the moves for women's suffrage and married Emmeline Goulden a few years later.

> *If marriage is to be permanent, the government of the family must be*
> *put by law and by morals in the hands of the husband, for no one*
> *proposes to give it to the wife.*[34]

Since the passing of the Divorce Act, in 1857, there was now the
concern that a wife with financial independence could easily leave her
husband, even divorce him. This seems to have been a great fear for
the opponents of reform, for one of the key chains that bound a wife
to an unhappy marriage was that without financial independence she
had little alternative but to stay. There were a few obvious conclusions
– which the writer Eliza Lynn Linton was only too keen to point out:

> *Many say that womanly independence would weaken the marriage*
> *tie, if so this only shows what the extreme party says is true and that*
> *women are held by self interest and the necessity of food, not love. Is*
> *marriage really nothing but this?*[35]

If the situation did change, and a wife did gain control of her own
money, what were some of the possible outcomes? There were fears
that a wife would herself be able to be a tyrant, over her husband,
because the wealth gave her power.[36] A wealthy woman might even
throw her husband out of her house, leaving him homeless. She could
abandon him for another man. And since the earlier child custody laws
had been established, she could even manage under some circumstances
to take the children with her. It was quite possible that a judge may
decide that *if* the wife had sufficient funds to maintain herself and the
children independently, and knew that a husband without resources
would not be capable of providing adequate care for the children, then
child custody should be awarded to her. These thoughts were truly
shocking and far too alarming for the more traditional males to accept.

More fuel was added to the fire. In the December 1868 issue of
Fraser's Magazine an article appeared by the journalist Frances Power
Cobbe, which has subsequently been referred to by many feminists

---

[34] James Fitzjames Stephen, *Liberty, Equality, Fraternity*, 1874
[35] *Ourselves*
[36] In 1866 Ben Elmy (as a factory manager) had given the wages of married women
    workers directly to them, causing the male workers at the factory (and the husbands)
    to react with extreme anger. Elizabeth Wolstenholme married him in 1874.

as a critical publication. It was also issued as a separate pamphlet. Its simple title says it all. 'Criminals, Idiots, Women and Minors'.

Women were being officially classified amongst groups who were legitimately denied political rights. How could that possibly be right? Frances focused particularly on the property law that so badly affected married women. Using clear logic, she attacked the given arguments for maintaining that law – on the grounds of justice, expediency and sentimentality. Man supported woman, he held authority over her, and there was also the sentimental view of his protection. Frances posed a very simple question. 'The argument is the wife gets an ample quid pro quo. *Does* she get it under the existing law?'[37]

She accepted that some men may be unable to actually support a wife, but, putting them to one side, she raised a vital issue that needed public and legal recognition. It was very clear what was expected of a woman in marriage, the law made it so – but where were the laws that clarified what was expected of a man, and where in particular were the laws that enforced him doing so? If a husband failed to feed or clothe his wife and children, if he failed to provide for her – indeed, if he should squander all the joint resources – where was the law to see that justice was served to her? Like other women writers she also pointed out how men avoided the laws that did exist and then received no penalty for their behaviour. In fact, there was no check at all on a man's actual ability to use the total powers he had over his wife.

Frances used real life examples and showed how a man could avoid penalties for deserting a wife (that would have allowed her a legal separation – introduced after Caroline Norton's campaign), by making sure he kept returning before the stipulated two-year desertion period was up. Each time he returned he could walk off with whatever money and property the wife had managed to earn and build up in the meantime. In such cases a legal separation could not take place and so, because she was still considered legally married, the wife could not even sue her husband for theft. (When Frances wrote this article she had not envisaged just how relevant this example was to be for later events that followed shortly afterwards, as we will soon see.)

---

[37] Frances Power Cobbe, 'Criminals, Idiots, Women and Minors', *Fraser's Magazine*, December 1868

She, too, was to refer to international examples where married women were treated more favourably by the law – this time in Russia and many of the American States. She pointed out that, rather than the 'unity' so desirable in marriage being obtained by granting all the power and control automatically to the husband, 'real unanimity is not produced between two parties by forbidding one of them to have any voice at all'. She was to pose the fundamental question to all men – how would you like it?

We wish we could persuade men more often to try and realise for themselves what is actually the life of a woman... Were they ever to ask themselves how such an existence would suit them, they might perhaps be startled at the reflection which would suggest themselves.[38]

At the end of her article she referred back to the moves towards suffrage and made some very interesting observations. It was only recently that suffrage had been extended to virtually all propertied men, but there had never been any attempt to deny them the right to the vote on purely physical, intellectual or inferior moral grounds. These had all been applied to women claiming the vote. As a moral and intelligent being she claimed her civil rights. 'Can you deny them to me on that ground?' I think it also worth noting that according to her article *The Times,* in 1867, had noted disapprovingly that during the campaign for working men's civil rights, violence had actually taken place. Park palings had been thrown down, but, said *The Times,* at least *the women* were not behaving like that in their campaign. They did not realise that time was yet to come.

By April 1869 John Stuart Mill had decided the time was now right for the publication of his book, *The Subjection of Women.* It is not necessary to give a full resumé of it – it is widely available still – suffice to say that he was only too aware of how women had been deprived of the opportunities to achieve their full potential and how society would gain from their improved education, increased opportunities in employment, and their ensuing achievements. He believed that married women should be treated as individuals and that meant that not only should they be able to control their own property and

---

[38] Ibid

income but that they should also be entitled to vote. Predictably it caused quite a stir, and the same year saw the publication of the third edition of Barbara Leigh Smith Bodichon's *A Brief Summary, in Plain Language, of the Most Important Laws of England Concerning Women.*

Meanwhile, discussions were continuing to take place in Parliament regarding both women's suffrage and their property rights, and then a highly significant legal case hit the headlines, which was to greatly boost the cause of the Married Women's Property Committee. It was very much in accord with the article written by Frances Power Cobbe and concerned a wife who was never completely deserted by her husband. Just before Christmas 1868 Susannah Palmer had had enough of her abusive husband, who had abandoned her and the children, yet kept turning up to walk off with whatever possessions and earnings she had managed to acquire since his last visit. Although the actual details vary, the basic story is the same. He was drunk, violent yet again and finally, reaching breaking point, Susannah grabbed a kitchen knife and stabbed him.

She was convicted of 'wounding with intent to cause grievous bodily harm' and was sent to Newgate prison. So far there were no major surprises – but the following events were to be significant. Public interest had been aroused by previous events, so donations of money and furniture were sent in for her – but it underlined the whole problem for married women when it was realised that it would be *pointless* to actually give them to her on her release. As we have seen previously, any possessions of the wife automatically became the possessions of the husband; the donations of money and furniture for her would, of course, revert to Mr Palmer. It was actually necessary for the sheriffs of London to be named as the legal owners of the donations, in order to prevent James Palmer walking off with the lot. And, like Caroline Norton, Susannah was not going to leave it there. On her release she sent a petition, herself, to the House of Commons pleading for women's property rights to be granted. Russell Gurney, Conservative MP for Southampton, presented her petition and himself already in favour of the Married Women's Property Bill of 1869, (led by Mr Shaw-Lefevre – another MP who was already interested in reform of property issues), now joined forces with John Stuart Mill, Richard Pankhurst, and other supportive MPs, Gurney citing Susannah's case and many similar ones in the process.

With all the background events I have described, it seemed almost inevitable that something was to come out of it in terms of legal change. However, no matter how much hard work and dedication the women outside Westminster devoted to their cause, they had absolutely no control of events once the solid doors of the Houses of Parliament were closed against them. When the Married Women's Property Bill was introduced into the House of Lords in June 1870 it was greeted with a chorus of ridicule and disapproval. During the passage of the Bill between the two Houses of Parliament, somehow the focus slipped away from all married women and concentrated only on the immediate needs of the poorer wives who were considered to be so financially vulnerable.

While it was acknowledged that some men in the lower classes had been abusing their wives, and unjustly taking their money and possessions, those in the wealthier classes had at least the benefit of being able to take out legal settlements to protect the women from such misappropriation. So rather than allowing all married women the same rights and privileges of property as a single woman, poorer married women, like Susannah Palmer, would now receive some limited protection too.

When the Bill was enacted in 1870 it allowed working women to keep their earnings, and they could inherit personal property up to a value of £200. There were not enough men who felt women should receive equal property rights; they preferred to believe that most women did not need them as their husbands did take care of their needs. By treating the property issue as a working-class problem, those in Parliament at the time could be accused of being rather self-interested. The control of major issues of family property and inheritance remained firmly in their hands. There was to be no major change in the financial authority of a husband in any marriage. A working wife could still not sue her husband if he did walk off with her property or earnings. For many women the situation had hardly changed.

In 1873 a new Bill was reintroduced in support of the married women's claims; it passed its second reading, but a variety of parliamentary tactics were then used to block its progress. Lack of quorum, or lack of time because the evening session was going on too late, meant that further discussion was postponed at least *twenty-five times* before it got dropped altogether for over five years. In spite of there being increasing public support for women's issues, those in Parliament still had the ability to squash, or at least minimise, the actual levels of change granted to those who demanded them. It was not in their interest to give up all the vestiges of male authority that they had so keenly purloined.

Any chance of women gaining a say in political affairs was also to be lost – the Suffrage Bill too was defeated in 1870. Many women turned their efforts to more achievable targets. The Married Women's Property Committee continued to work for change, trying to keep the issue before Parliament by lobbying, pamphleting, and working on supportive members of the legal profession, even though they admitted to finding it arduous and depressing work.

Caroline Norton, Barbara Leigh Smith Bodichon, and others like them had drawn attention to the financial concerns of married women, by collecting and using data, and they had won popular support, but some things were out of their control. Just as they could not control the actions of those in Parliament, they were also unable to control external events that affected its composition. Women had learned that in general the more traditional, often Conservative, members of Parliament were less likely to support their moves for financial independence, but some Liberal politicians would, at least, listen to them. Any general election and change of government could have a significant effect upon the progress of their campaigns. When Disraeli became prime minister in 1874, progress in the matter of married women's property came to a temporary halt, until a new Liberal government (under Gladstone) was elected in 1880, and his lord chancellor (Lord Selbourne) became a supporter of women. As a result the Married Women's Property Act 1882 passed through Parliament with far more ease than its predecessor.

This Act gave a married woman the same financial rights as a single woman; she was able to keep all of her own property, earnings and inheritances whether she was married or not. She became responsible for her own debts and she also obtained the right to sue anyone, including her husband, if he encroached on any of her newly gained rights. Even so, it was clear that there were still men who felt that marriage was worthwhile only if it gave them power, authority and financial control over their wives. Only the previous year Lord Fraser had commented:

> *The protection which has been thrown round a married woman is already sufficient, and why she should be allowed to have money in her pocket, to deal with as she thinks fit, I cannot understand.*[39]

Just before the new bill was due to become law, Mr Osbourne Warton, the Judge Advocate General, had made the surprising proposal that the enactment should be postponed for a further *two years* in order to 'give people who were contemplating matrimony time to change their minds when they found the law altered'[40]. In other words he wanted to give young affianced men time to get out of their planned marriages – simply because they were going to lose out on any financial benefits they might have been expecting. Such deeply embedded attitudes as these senior members of the establishment had shown were going to be very hard to change.

When women writers in the eighteenth century were drawing attention to the problems that men were causing them, they often used humour to carry the criticism. Jane Austen was a past master (or should I say mistress?) of the craft. Victorian writers were at times to use similar methods. I must admit I was highly amused to find Margaret Oliphant had turned round to all those who had laughed at women's demands, and shown them, admittedly with the benefit of hindsight, that men's pointed comments had not necessarily been based on honest concerns.

> *'I wish,' said the old gentleman with a little spitefulness, 'that this Married Woman's Property Bill would push on and get itself made law. It would save us a great deal of trouble, and perhaps convince the world at last how little they are to be trusted with property. A nice mess they will make of it, and plenty of employment for young solicitors,' he said rubbing his hands. For this was before that important Bill was passed, which had not, like so many other Bills, the disastrous consequences which Mr Lynch foresaw.*[41]

The following year Florence Marryat made her own snipe at men's

---

[39] quoted in Elizabeth Elmy, 'The Law of Scotland with regard to The Property of Married Women', *The Englishwoman's Review*, Vol 12, September 1881
[40] Hansard, (House of Commons) 1882, CCLXXIII, 1610
[41] Margaret Oliphant, *The Marriage of Elinor*, 1891

earlier behaviour. In one of her novels a wife had been granted a legal separation, but as her husband had been financially dependent upon her he decided to ask the judge to order a compulsory settlement in his favour. The judge refused the request, and stated clearly, 'You ought to be ashamed of yourself for asking such a question.' [42]

---

[42] *The Nobler Sex*

Chapter Seven
The Possession of a Wife

By the late nineteenth century the joint efforts of both female and male reformists had led to the extension of property rights to married women. Equality in marriage had not been achieved – but the situation had undoubtedly improved. Where a woman was separated from her husband legal recognition of her existence had re-established her independence from his control, and it also meant that the penalties for leaving a marriage had been significantly reduced. For a woman who was married, however, even though she was gradually to gain some rights for herself, her husband still remained very much in control of the game; losing control of the property and income of his wife was really only part of what was at stake.

From the onset of Queen Victoria's reign, and indeed for centuries before it, a husband had had certain legal rights over the physical person of his wife. She was considered by many to *be* his property – just as much as the children had been, and just as much as her own possessions were. At the age of twenty-nine Eliza Lynn Linton was to cut through the hypocrisy of Church and State with her radical novel *Realities*, published in 1851. Although she was to include many scathing criticisms of the laws concerning women, and general attitudes towards them, her comment concerning a husband's relationship with his wife was very simple: 'The woman was his property and her excellences were his advantages.' A bride was thus to be no different from any other form of his material possessions, hence:

> *Who is the better for it? I am only a good and a chattel – something to be fed and provided for... just as his horse must be... but a nonentity all the same... a child dependent... not an individual with personal feelings.* [1]

---

[1] Florence Marryat, *Too Good for Him*

Similarly, the following year:

> *He had secured for himself the best thing in wives, as he had the best*
> *thing in horses and modern pictures and dogs. If he held her a little*
> *lower than his short legged hunter, a little less dear than his fawn*
> *coloured pug, he at least gave her as much as she had any right to*
> *expect from him.*[2]

In their struggle for legal recognition as individuals married women
had to fight to regain rights over their own persons and it was not
going to be an easy job to attain them. Years later when *The Daily*
Telegraph undertook its open question *'Is Marriage a Failure?'* one
correspondent proclaimed:

> *The Anglican service lowers the wife and sets the husband on a pedestal,*
> *not at all suitable to him, filling him with notions of marital supremacy*
> *which are the cause of half the unhappiness of married life... what*
> *wonder then that when a man hears himself as a wife's god (The man*
> *is head of the woman, even as Christ is Head of the Church) he should*
> *consider her in the light of his dog, or horse, or anything that is his.*[3]

It all began at the wedding ceremony. Inside religious buildings or,
after 1836, inside civic offices women took a vow to obey their
husbands. The vast majority of ceremonies took place in church,
where before God and the chosen witnesses a woman vowed to accept
her husband and submit herself unto him. According to *The Book of*
Common Prayer (1662), the marriage service, which was not updated
until the twentieth century, had clearly stated, 'The Church is subject
unto Christ, so let wives be to their own husbands in everything.'
Numerous women were to make use of their writings to comment
on how they felt about such blanket obedience. Describing perhaps
her own experience, *The Daily Telegraph*'s correspondent 'Caroline'
summarised exactly how it could affect a bride: 'It publically humiliates
a woman, it makes her feel uncomfortable on her wedding day, and
arouses a spirit of resistance.'

---

[2]   Mary Elizabeth Braddon, *The Lady's Mile, 1866*
[3]   'Caroline', *The Daily Telegraph*, 20th August, 1888

Magazines for both girls and women had continued the process of conditioning that had started in early childhood, frequently emphasising the necessity of accepting the word 'obey' in a marriage. In 1865 a short story appeared in *Townsend's Monthly Selection of Parisian Costumes*, simply entitled 'Margaret; or The Word Obey'. [4] Margaret's friend Grace stated the startling, but naked, fundamental truth regarding the word 'obey' itself – *'I suppose I could not get married if I did not use it.'* It was blindingly obvious. I had never seen it so clearly before. Submission was undoubtedly to be part of the marriage experience. Fortunately, in this particular story Grace's husband did not require much in the way of obedience from her, and only Margaret, the perfectly conditioned 'heroine' of the tale, 'knew how *necessary* a thing it is for a wife's happiness to sweetly, conscientiously, and gracefully, obey'. [My emphasis] Fortunate Grace; unfortunate Margaret.

Novelists too were to find many ways to refer to the rule of obedience and their own questioning of it. In Frances Trollope's *One Fault*, the character Isabella Wentworth was considering her husband:

…who, both by principle and inclination, was of the opinion not only that it was his wife's duty to obey, but that she should do nothing else, and think of nothing else, from morning to night.

For any intelligent woman, who had thoughts and strong opinions of her own, and who then had to suppress these in the apparent submission to those of her husband, it must have been a very frustrating experience. One can easily appreciate why some women wanted to gain the vote from such an early period. Having been told that men, both at home and in government, thought for them, and spoke for them, and that there was therefore no need to gain their own political voice, it was yet another form of control that women had not chosen for themselves. Towards the end of the novel *Realities* there had been an authorial warning:

And oh ye independent women… remember that the majority of men make submission and virtue their feminine synonymes, and endorse that

---

[4] Printed in full in *Victorian Women's Magazines*, edited by Margaret Beetham and Kay Boardman, Manchester University Press, 2001

170

woman alone as loveable who takes such truth as they bestow and speak such words as they endite. Nay, an independent life they may forgive … but an independent thought unsexes her; and love shuddering weeps, and spreads his wings if opinions be retained, intellectual admiration continued, an author read or faith upheld, contrary to masculine authority … She must be rejected, reviled, because she cannot intellectually obey.[5]

In a time of increasing challenges to the authority of the Church and the Bible (for example, through scientific discovery or Darwin and his *Origin of Species*), there were to be many objections to the specific rules and commands regarding women, upheld by Church dogma, particularly in the works of St Paul. He is credited with the Biblical injunction that wives should submit to their husbands in all things. Members of the clergy, husbands and even lawyers regularly referred to him as the absolute human authority in the matter. However, we may have been doing St Paul a severe injustice over the centuries. Modern religious scholarship indicates that rather than being a misogynist he did actually support women, and genuinely encouraged their serious participation in the early Church. It seems an unknown other added St Paul's name to his own writings, in order to give them authenticity and dogmatic weight. Such a discovery came too late for the many women in Victorian times who had bitterly condemned him. A few examples will be sufficient to make the point.

How on earth should dear St. Paul know what it would be right and proper to do 1800 years after he was dead and buried? Such notions really are contemptible.[6]

'St Paul spoke through the inspiration of the scriptures, every word of which we are bound to receive.'
'I dare not receive it when it's against truth and justice… I do not believe blindly in scripture. I believe in my God not yours.[7]

They say it is wrong for a woman to attack the Bible. I say she should. She has so much to gain.[8]

---

5   Eliza Lynn Linton
6   Frances Trollope, *One Fault*
7   Dinah Mulock Craik, *A Brave Lady*
8   Helen Gardener, *Men, Women and Gods*, 1885

Don't try to foist that stale argument – you men are always quoting the Bible for the benefit of your wives. Why don't you study it sometimes on your own account?[9]

For a boy, the habit of arrogance, the habit of looking down on girls, fostered by a hundred other influences in his early life, will derive its main sustenance from the reiterated injunctions of St Paul.[10]

It is rather disturbing to discover that some of the most shocking cases of abuse taken to court actually involved extremely religious men, themselves clerics and vicars. These were not necessarily cases of extreme violent abuse but give a clear illustration of just how far the level of obedience could be taken. Take the case of *Kelly v Kelly*. In 1841 the marriage took place between Frances and the Reverend James Kelly. Because of his extreme religious views, he exacted a disturbing level of submission from his wife based on his claim of divine authorisation. He would demand her total repentance for each and every sin she committed in his eyes, and she would have to abase herself before him, submitting to all his punishments and corrections as a child. He took over the total control of the household. For over twenty years she put up with it all, at times being virtually incarcerated and, banished from seeing friends and family, she even resorted on several occasions to escaping out of windows. Finally, she took her case to court, seeking a separation from him on the grounds of cruelty. Even there, Reverend Kelly continued to justify his actions, and when the court found against him he still actually appealed against their decision, believing he had God on his side.

The promise to obey was just another link in the chain that bound a wife to her husband, and another page in the fiction of unity, deemed so necessary in marriage. A wife having to obey a husband's every command meant that there would always be unity in a household. It was an easy way to control the game. However, it also made a wife appear to be no more than a servant and, in many ways, she could be. Unfortunately, though, unhappy wives did not have the same advantages as servants. In her *Letter to the Queen,* much cited already

---

[9]   Florence Marryat, *At Heart a Rake,* 1895
[10]   Elizabeth Rachel Chapman, *St Paul and the Woman Movement,* in *Marriage Questions in Modern Fiction,* 1897

in Chapter Five, Caroline Norton begged to be considered in the position of servant, as her husband's inferior, for she would then have received far better treatment 'as his housekeeper, whom he could not libel with impunity… as his apprentice, whom he could not maltreat lawlessly… as a scullion, whose wages he could not refuse'.

Frances Trollope had noted too 'no servant is obliged to endure the humours of a master… the wife however beloved [is] the principle victim, for it is only she who can never escape'.[11] Years later, a French writer, Leon Paul Blouet, who taught for years at the famous St Paul's School in London, published his comments on English lifestyles. He reported that an English wife had informed him:

> *I belong to my lord and master, body and soul; the duties of a housekeeper, upper nurse and governess are required of me. I am expected to always be at home, at my husband's beck and call… I often think of what you might say on the servant question and wonder how many of us [i.e. wives] would like to be able to have the cook's privilege of being able to give warning to leave.* [12]

The acceptance of the word 'obey' gave a husband the right to expect his wife's obedience and the justification, as we saw in the case of the Reverend Kelly, if not the 'right', to actually correct her when she failed to fulfil her duties in his eyes. As Frances Trollope put it, 'The law enforces the obedience of a wife to her husband, and the execution of that law I shall now take into my own hands'.[13] It was a dangerous privilege to grant freely to all men for there were many who literally would do just that. Losing a pregnancy because of a beating, being thrown down stairs, losing a limb or even an eye were not unknown experiences for married women at the time.

For centuries one of the accepted rules of common law had been the Rule of Thumb; a man had the physical right to correct or chastise his wife for her behaviour, and so he could beat her with a stick, provided the stick was no thicker than a man's thumb. Modern historians have looked for the original documentation that permitted it, but as far as I am aware they have looked in vain, although there are

---

[11] *One Fault*

[12] Leon Paul Blouet (Max O'Rell), *Les Filles de John Bull*, 1884

[13] *The Life and Adventures of a Clever Woman*

ample references to its declaration by even the judiciary themselves. Whether it did actually exist and subsequently got destroyed, or remains buried in the annals of history, or whether indeed it ever existed at all is uncertain, but countless ordinary people believed in it, and used that belief to justify their actions when confronted by magistrates and legal others in court. It was certainly easy for a husband to justify his aggression towards his wife by saying such things as, 'It wasn't my fault, your Honour, she deserved it' or 'She provoked me, it was her own fault', or as Florence Marryat put it, 'Hasn't a man the right to hit his own wife – the woman he keeps and pays for?'[14]

In 1790 the judge Sir William Scott, later known as Lord Stowell, had helped to set the boundary regarding what was legally punishable behaviour in marriage:

> *Mere austerity of temper, petulance of manners, rudeness of language, a want of civil attention and accommodation, even occasional sallies of passion, if they do not threaten bodily harm, do not amount to legal cruelty; they are high moral offences, in the marriage-state undoubtedly, not innocent surely in any state of life, but still they are not that cruelty against which the law can relieve.*

So, apart from life-threatening violence, a wife would just have to put up with physical and mental abuse. It was, therefore, not surprising to read the following type of comment in women's novels:

> *When I think of his power over me I am horribly frightened. Why do girls marry I wonder?... It is a sad thing when a woman fears her husband. I wish he could kill me outright instead of putting me to slow torture.*[15]

We know women writers had long been using their works to raise awareness of the problems they faced in life. Women in the eighteenth century had been very familiar with marital violence – Mary Wollstonecraft had witnessed her mother being frequently beaten, lying across the bedroom doorway trying to prevent her father's entry

---

[14] *Her World Against a Lie*
[15] Rosa Nouchette Carey, *Only the Governess*, 1840

into her mother's room. Frances Burney too was kept up to date with
her sister's sufferings in her unhappy marriage. Classic nineteenth-
century authors, both female *and* male, were to add their voices too,
condemning mental and physical cruelty to wives; George Eliot (*Janet's
Repentance*, 1857), Anne Bronte (*The Tenant of Wildfell Hall*, 1848),
Charles Dickens (*Oliver Twist*, 1837; *Bleak House*, 1852), Anthony
Trollope (*He Knew He Was Right*, 1869), to name but a few. Until at
least the late nineteenth century authors also pointed out that if a wife
dared to challenge her violent husband, she would, in the long run,
be the one most likely to suffer, as this fictitious conversation with a
magistrate illustrates:

> 'How can you punish him, sir?' says I.
> 'I can fine him,' says he. 'Or I can send him to prison.'
> 'As to the fine,' says I, 'he can pay that out of the money he gets
> by selling my furniture. As to the prison – while he's in it, what's
> to become of me, with my money spent by him, and my possessions
> gone – and when he's out of it, what's to become of me again, with a
> husband whom I have been the means of punishing, and who comes
> home to his wife, knowing it? It's bad enough as it is, sir,' says I.
> 'There's more bruised in me than what shows in my face.'[16]

Writers such as Collins had clearly believed that if there were greater
consequences for the husbands concerned, and if such violent
husbands were actually shunned in society, rather than condoned by
it, the situation would be somewhat different. However, those changes
would be difficult to achieve unless something could be done to raise
the level of awareness and concern of those in a position to make a
difference, and they, in turn, would have to be sufficiently motivated
to do something about it.

Time and again the brutality of husbands – from all levels of
society – would be described by the writers in sickening, gut-
wrenching detail, designed absolutely to shock the reader from his/
her indifference to the plight of others. There would always be far

---

16 Willkie Collins, *Man and Wife*, 1870. This novel was written while the issue of
married women's property was being discussed in Parliament and it is a reflection
of the level of general interest in the subject, as well as the author's own support
for it, that all the key issues were included in the book.

greater emotional impact from a vivid description of unprovoked violence, towards woman, child or animal, whether reported in a newspaper or described in a novel, compared to the cold information provided by a mathematical statistic. Women writers were very good at giving detailed examples, based on their own knowledge or experience.

One such incident occurred in the early popular novel *The History of Betsey Thoughtless*[17] where a much-loved squirrel (a fashionable eighteenth-century pet) was on the receiving end of a nasty, deliberately calculated act of mental cruelty. The squirrel, which had been an earlier present from the loving husband-to-be to his fiancée, had later become the chosen instrument of the husband's power and brutality. From out of nowhere the husband's mood changed, he grabbed the poor squirrel, suddenly, by the neck, and threw it violently and fatally against the marble chimney-piece, just in front of his wife, to cause deliberate and immeasurable distress to her (not to mention the squirrel). The reader would have reeled in shock. It was too awful to imagine.

There were many more examples right through the eighteenth and nineteenth centuries. I have come across irate husbands tearing down doors, or ripping the locks off them, trying to gain access to a cowering wife hoping to protect herself against an intended assault. Whippings; beatings; being hit with thrown pieces of furniture or objects from a nearby table; these were common occurrences for an abused wife, but, occasionally, and even more disturbingly, there would be attacks on the children. These ranged from using a whip on an infant in its cot to attempting to smother one with a pillow, in front of the wife, in order to not only cause obvious pain to the children themselves, but frequently to cause further distress to their mother.

When such incidences took place in women's literature there was more to it, though, than just a physical description, however short. The reader was made to experience the whole thing: its horror; its brutality. They could share the victim's personal reactions to it, as well as consider their implications. The following example of physical abuse makes pertinent reading. It was written in 1865, but I am sure it reflects abuse in past and present marriages equally well.

---

[17] Eliza Haywood, *The History of Betsey Thoughtless*, 1751

A second blow. She felt it keenly. The first had staggered her, but after the first shock she had come to persuade herself it must have been a mistake – a passionate mistake into which he had been surprised and it could not happen again. But now it had happened again; and he had said she was a child and should be treated as such. Was she to be beaten all her life for everything she did wrong? Was she never to have a different opinion from her husband: never to be allowed to act for herself?[18]

Before Victoria had come to the throne there had been a few concessions to wives regarding the violent behaviour of their husbands towards them. The 1828 Offences Against the Person Act allowed a wife to bring charges of common assault and battery against her husband using the local magistrates court, but, as indicated above, it could bring further problems for her if she did so. In ecclesiastical courts a legal separation had occasionally been granted on the grounds of *extreme* cruelty, but the wife had to prove she was terrified and that her life was actually under threat. Anything else just did not count and just because a woman lived separately to her husband did not prevent him from turning up and attacking her if he wanted to.

Some writers were to make comparisons between the laws regarding animals and the lack of laws regarding cruelty to married women. The first Cruelty to Animals Act was passed in 1835, following an earlier act in 1822 for the protection of cattle. Animals had obvious market value. It is particularly telling that in one of her novels (1839), Rosina Bulwer Lytton, who had suffered brutally at the hands of her husband, Edward, had commented, 'There should be some Cruelty to Animals Act that would extend its protection to [a wife].'[19] She made a similar snipe in her semi-autobiographical novel, *Miriam Sedley* (1851): 'A woman was the only beast of burden not included in the Cruelty to Animals Act.'[20]

---

[18] Florence Marryat, *Love's Conflict*

[19] *Cheveley: or The Man of Honour*

[20] Even as late as 1884 a wife was still in an unfavourable position compared to that of an animal. A Member of Parliament, Mr Macfarlane, had raised the cruelty issue with the Home Secretary after hearing about some particularly dreadful cases that had received very lenient treatment by the magistrates concerned. He was told that sentencing was up to the magistrate's discretion. Mr Macfarlane responded by saying that women *would* have been better off if they *had* been included in the Cruelty to Animals Act. Rosina was not so very far off the mark, then, with her initial remark forty years previously.

Unfortunately, too many people, both male and female, had accepted that it was legally acceptable for a man to hit his wife. When the subject was raised in Parliament it often provoked laughter, but by the 1850s there is some evidence that attitudes were at least beginning to change.

Between 1846 and 1852 a series of essays written by Harriet Taylor and John Stuart Mill appeared as newspaper articles in the *Morning Chronicle* and elsewhere. One of these was entitled 'William Burn' and concerned a man who had actually been convicted for severely beating a horse.[21] Although the judge had intended to award the maximum sentence because of the brutality of the attack, the man got off with a simple fine because the judge became concerned about how Burn's large family would suffer, if he had to pay the set forty shillings or was sent to prison for fourteen days. The actual fine that Burn ended up paying was only ten shillings – a quarter of the full fine. The article raised the concern that a man who lost his temper so violently and uncontrollably with a dumb animal that had merely irritated him momentarily was very likely to show similar behaviour towards his own wife and children at home. Any time the husband spent in prison would probably have been a period of respite for the family, instead of which the man was given licence to continue his behaviour, with the knowledge that he had virtually got away with it.

Other articles in the series by Harriet and J.S. Mill exposed the problems of domestic violence and some of its related causes. They noted the link between abuse and the lack of women's political status, and also, like others before them, that there was another strong link between violence and poverty. They were also worried about the fact that justice and its execution in this country was an entirely male affair. Their 'Assault Law' on 31st May 1850 simply proposed that:

> *There should be a declaratory Act, distinctly setting forth that it is not lawful for a man to strike his wife, any more than to strike his brother or his father... It seems almost inconceivable that the smallest blow from a man to a man should be by law a criminal offence, and yet that it should not be – or should not be known to be – unlawful for a man to strike a woman.*

---

[21] 'William Burn', *Morning Chronicle*, 17th November 1846

A later article entitled 'Wife Murder' continued the argument, criticising a legal system that considered it a far more serious legal offence to murder a stranger than to murder a wife. Within a few days, four wife murder cases had come to their attention and, like Caroline Norton before them, they thought it was 'a deep disgrace to our Government that in the fifteenth year of the reign of a woman nothing has yet been done for their relief'.[22]

Harriet and J.S. Mill knew that more was required from the law than merely awarding severer penalties for wife beating; unhappy wives often wanted to be able to escape, permanently, from such situations, and they did not want to wait until they were virtually dead before anyone would take any notice.

> *All that would be requisite is a short Act of Parliament, providing that judicial conviction of gross maltreatment should free the victim from the obligation of living with the oppressor, and from all compulsory subjection to his power – leaving him under the same legal obligation as before of affording the sufferer the means of support.[23]*

In other words, an abused wife should be entitled to a legal separation from her husband, and he would still be required to support her financially. If he was convicted for abuse he should not, under any circumstances, be allowed to return to her and repeat the offence. Women who had suffered repeated abuse would be only too relieved to find a permanent way out of the situation and, before violence alone became grounds for separation or divorce, running away must, at times, have seemed the only way of escape. At the end of the century one female author included an unusual but revealing incident in one of her novels: an abusive husband died and rather than mourning in suitable fashion the widow was actually celebrating, shocking both family and friends.

> *You think me brutal, unnatural; you think that I should show grief – a horror, or some good feeling, whereas I only show relief, and more than that... joy! Do not mistake me in any way. I am glad, glad I*

---

22 'Wife Murder', *Morning Chronicle*, 28th August 1851
23 'Assault Law', *Morning Chronicle*, 31st May 1850

tell you! God forgive me but I have longed for this sweet moment for many a day... You condemn me, I can see. You think me unwomanly. You would have me a hypocrite.[24]

During the early 1850s the MP for Lewes, Mr Fitzroy, too had become increasingly concerned about domestic violence. He had believed the number of abuse cases were rapidly growing and were to be considered 'a blot upon our national character'. He too had noted that animal cruelty was treated more severely than cruelty towards wives. In parliamentary discussion he stated that it was 'the startling principle of English law that women are of less value than Poodle dogs and Skye terriers'. [25] He had also pointed out that any delays in trying violent husbands in court meant that it was difficult for an abused wife to obtain justice anyway – for during that time the husband in question could have ample time to pressurise his wife into dropping the case, and injuries or bruises – so necessary for proof of the assault – would have time to fade. As a direct result of his arguments, and the media attention that Harriet and J.S. Mill had contributed to, the Act for the Better Prevention of Aggravated Assaults on Women and Children was passed in 1853. Thereafter a convicted man could be given a sentence of up to six months or a fine of £20.

Considering the fact that women, and indeed children, involved in such cases were frequently nearly at death's door (and some did actually die from their injuries), it may seem to us that such penalties were totally inadequate. Colloquially it was described by some magistrates as the 'Women's Protection Act', but it did not seem to be very effective. In fact, it was actually noted by many that rather than resulting in a decrease in the number of such cases to have been brought forward, after the Act, it seemed to have resulted in a notably large *increase* in them.

Newspapers and magazines continued to draw attention to the problem. In 1855 the *Ladies' Newspaper* noted the case of a man who had beaten and kicked his wife before pushing her backwards out of a first-floor window, stating it was his intention to kill her; he then received only a twelve-month sentence. After the establishment of the

[24] Margaret Hungerford, *Lady Verner's Flight*, 1893
[25] reported in *The Times*, 12th March, 1853. Once again there were echoes of Rosina Bulwer Lytton's earlier comments about cruelty to wives and animals.

Divorce Court, in 1857, women who cited cruelty alongside adultery in their applications drew further attention to the problem. Ensuing publicity from each case continued to expose the myth that such violence rarely happened and the false assumption that all husbands were indeed good men.

Of course such instances of violence had happened before, but, in the past, women had been encouraged – perhaps even forced – to keep quiet about it. They had made their promise to obey and had felt an obligation to do so. It was all part of the control mechanism, but there were other factors too. To admit to family and friends that you were suffering at home, that your choice of a husband for life had been a bitter, bitter mistake, could cause terrible distress to people who you cared for, knowing they could do little to help alleviate the situation. In addition to which the religious teaching of the time encouraged women to put up with their situations, to accept their duty, to willingly sacrifice themselves in the hope of rewards in the afterlife. They should continue to turn the other cheek, to suffer and be still in this. Adding weight to that rule of silence, magistrates and lawyers together continued to make reference to the dictates of St Paul, so that women, who had hoped to gain some justice from the law, had often been sent back home, unaided, to the continued tempers of their violent husbands. To add insult to injury there are many records of the judge also giving the wife a lecture on how she should stop provoking her husband. By breaking silence in increasing numbers, women themselves were beginning to demand change.

The ineffectiveness of the Aggravated Assault Act led to several proposals for its amendment, most of which seem to have been based on the rather odd idea that one way to discourage wife beating was to introduce corporal punishment as a consequence. Part of the logic here was that it would at least inflict some pain and suffering on the husband for a change; however, such a view was short-sighted to put it mildly. Violence is not, as a rule, cured by violence. An abusive husband punished in such a way and angry after public humiliation would be only too likely to revenge himself on his wife when he returned home. Nonetheless, the suggestion was put before Parliament repeatedly throughout the rest of the century, but the real penalties were never increased enough.

With the additional public focus on other women's issues during the 1860s, namely married women's property and the early moves for suffrage, the publicity drawn by the Susannah Palmer case, mentioned in Chapter Six, where the abused wife finally flipped and attacked her husband, conveniently highlighted all the problems, including that of marital abuse, in one go. In spite of the fact that she had suffered from violent attacks on many occasions Susannah had been imprisoned because she had once lost her temper. Yet, within the confines of prison space, hemmed in by four stone walls, Susannah was actually happy. She said openly that at least, in there, 'her husband could not get at her'. Most men had failed to grasp that the constant threat of violence was an unpleasant, frightening experience – let alone the physical hurt itself. Philanthropic organisations, like the Society for the Protection of Women and Children, were set up over time, to assist those who suffered from all sorts of abuse – providing a variety of services to them (legal advice; a safe place to stay; food; clothing) – but the law provided no real disincentive for the abusers themselves.

The laws of this country had ensured that any injury a man received or any slight on his character, or theft of his possessions could be taken to the courts of justice. A wife had to suffer much before they would even consider her claim. Somehow the idea of protection had slipped out of view. In 1871 a police constable intervened when he saw a man beating his wife, but it was the constable who ended up before the magistrate, being fined for common assault. The legal penalties for assaulting a man were greater than those awarded for assaulting a wife and, somewhat disturbingly, the penalties for stealing another man's property (like his sheep) were far greater than those received by a husband convicted of his wife's manslaughter. The combined facts that the laws had allowed husbands to abuse their wives to such a degree, that the penalties for severe cruelty and violence towards them were so small, and that the magistrates who enforced the laws so frequently chose to administer nothing but the lowest penalties all mean that no further explanation is really necessary as to why the problems of violence towards married women continued for so long. Even though they were being more open about their injuries, women remained under men's control and they continued to suffer.

In spite of the attention drawn to scandalous cases like Caroline Norton's and Rosina Bulwer Lytton's, some people felt more comfortable thinking that such violence only ever occurred in the lower echelons of society, however false that belief may have been. Only the rough working classes behaved in such an ungentlemanly way towards the female sex, in particular towards their wives. This belief was certainly held by some Members of Parliament, but I have also come across references to it in at least one late-nineteenth-century novel. Rhoda, a battered wife, revealed herself to her cousin Tom:

> 'I tell you, you know nothing… I hid all I could. I hid what few women would have concealed. Twice. Twice he struck me.'
>
> 'Rhoda, this is horrible.'
>
> 'Beat me… Oh I know what you think! People in good society never do such things. So I thought or I believed. But he – beats me, nevertheless. It sounds… as though I were a common sort of person, doesn't it? One of those whom we read in the papers daily… I assure you I have felt like them – those poor women to whom retribution is unknown.[26]

The way Rhoda had managed to hide her bruises from everyone was very simple. She always wore long-sleeved dresses.

Until sufficient men involved in government, and in the legal profession, were prepared to empathise with the physical situation or the emotional experiences of women, until they could really appreciate the question 'How would you like it?' little seemed likely to change. Wives would continue to be legally bound to violent husbands. Something else needed to happen and it is generally agreed that the actions of one particular woman played a significant part in the next important change in the rules of marriage.

Frances Power Cobbe had been lead writer for the *Echo* when the Susannah Palmer case hit the headlines in 1869 and had already been moved by stories like hers; she even visited Susannah in prison. Using her position as a journalist, she decided it would be her job to educate the public about the realities of wife abuse. She and other women writers continued to draw attention to the problem in a variety of publications, including the *Women's Suffrage Journal* and, like Harriet Taylor and J.S. Mill before them, continued to link the terrible plight

---

[26] Margaret Hungerford, *Lady Verner's Flight*

that faced many women with their lack of political status. In a letter to the *Spectator* Frances Power Cobbe wrote:

> *If we, the women of England, possessed constitutional rights, the very first exercise of our power of political pressure would undoubtedly be to compel the attention of our representatives in the Legislature of these crimes of wife beating and wife murder. Can you, men of England, wholly acquit your consciences, while you tie our hands, and never lift your own?*[27]

The following year she was so horrified by what she was reading in another newspaper that in her own words 'I got out of my armchair, half dazed, and said to myself: "I will never rest till I have tried what I can do to stop this."'[28] Just as Caroline Norton and Barbara Leigh Smith Bodichon had undertaken specific research in their areas of concern, Frances too researched the problem of abuse, receiving some help in collating material along the way. The article 'Wife Torture in England', appearing in the *Contemporary Review* in April 1878, was to be her *pièce de résistance*.

It had been reported that years before, in Parliament, John Stuart Mill had called for the use of statistical evidence to reveal the numbers of married women beaten and kicked to death, and to compare the punitive sentences given to their husbands with those given for offences against property for, as he said, 'We should then have an arithmetical estimate of the value set by a male legislature and male tribunals on the murder of a woman.'[29] The article that Frances produced was full of such statistics and numerous dreadful examples, the following being just a tiny sample:

> *James Mills [no relation to J. S. Mill] had cut his wife's throat as she lay in bed. He was quite sober at the time. On a previous occasion he had nearly torn away her left breast.*
>
> *Frederick Knight jumped on the face of his wife (who had only been confined a month)[30] with a pair of boots studded with hobnails.*

---

[27] Frances Power Cobbe, *Spectator*, 50, 1877
[28] quoted in William M. Thayer, *Women who Win: Or, Making Things Happen*, 1897
[29] Emily Faithfull, 'Admission of Women to the Electoral Franchise', *Victoria Magazine*, 1867, Vol 9 p243
[30] After childbirth.

John Harris, a shoemaker, at Sheffield, found his wife and children in bed; dragged her out, and, after vainly attempting to force her into the oven, tore off her night-dress and turned her round before the fire 'like a piece of beef', while the children stood on the stairs listening to their mother's agonized screams.

Robert Kelly, engine driver, bit a piece out of his wife's cheek.

William White, stonemason, threw a burning paraffin lamp at his wife, and stood quietly watching her enveloped in flames, from the effects of which she died.

George Ralphy Smith, oilman, cut his wife, as the doctor expressed it, 'to pieces', with a hatchet, in their back parlour. She died afterwards, but he was found Not Guilty, as it was not certain that her death resulted from the wounds.[31]

There are many, many more tales of horror contained in the article.

Although she acknowledged that abuse of wives did occur in the upper classes (Caroline Norton was but one example), Frances stated that it was more common and more life-threatening in the lower social ranks. She initially acknowledged the progress that had been made for women, but pointed out that certain fundamentals had to be addressed or the overall situation would not change.

At the present time, though things are improving year by year, thanks to the generous and far seeing statesmen who are contending for justice to women inside and outside of the House of Commons, the position of a woman before the law as wife, mother and citizen, remains so much below that of a man as husband, father and citizen, that it is a matter of course that she must be regarded by him as inferior, and fail to obtain from him such a modicum of respect as her mental and moral qualities might win did he see her placed by the State on an equal footing.[32]

She too referred to the conditioning process and questioned the consequences that arose from it:

---

[31] Frances Power Cobbe, 'Wife Torture in England', *Contemporary Review*, April 1878

[32] Ibid

How is a lad to learn to reverence a woman whom he sees daily scoffed at, beaten and abused, and when he knows the laws of his country forbid her, ever and under any circumstances to exercise the right of citizenship?[33]

She painted a grim picture clear enough for all to see:

Wife beating in process of time, and in numberless cases advances to wife torture, and the wife torture usually ends in wife maiming, wife blinding or wife murder.[34]

Like other women before her she examined the legal situation and pointed out that it was twenty-five years since the Assault Act and, in spite of growing media attention, nothing more had been done for injured wives since then. The Divorce Act of 1857 had allowed separations on the basis of *extreme* cruelty – but did nothing to appease the situation before it got to that. Even when cases were heard, long delays took place and women changed their minds over whether to continue (often under pressure from their husbands), and sometimes, in traditional fashion, even taking on the blame for their injuries themselves. Frances referred to one case, cited in Parliament, where a woman had 'appeared without her nose, and told the magistrate that she had bitten it off herself!' Like Caroline Norton, Frances pointed out that women were still not allowed to give direct evidence against their husbands in court. Others had to do it on their behalf.

She recommended a new Bill should be passed in Parliament to give poor women at least the same assistance that rich women could obtain in the divorce courts, for they could at least support themselves after a separation. This time, though, it would not just be a question of punishing the abuser; there would be relief for the victims too. The proposed solution would give an abused wife a legal separation, a Protection Order, child custody, and maintenance for her and the children. Women who suffered abuse should be able to have the same relief, through legal separation, as those who had been deserted by their husbands.

---

[33] Ibid
[34] Ibid

Frances did not stop there. Like Caroline and Barbara, she got assistance from one of her legally qualified male friends, Mr Arthur Hill, who drew up a suitable Bill for her that would serve as a starting point for discussion. The Bill was '*Intituled an Act for the Protection of Wives whose Husbands have been Convicted of Assaults upon them*'. The key clauses were included as a separate section towards the end of her article.

It entreated the gentlemen and the ladies of England:

To take to heart the wrongs and agonies of our miserable sisters, and lift upon their behalf a cry which must make Parliament either hasten to deal with the matter, or renounce for very shame the vain pretence that it takes care of the interests of women.[35]

People took notice of her article, and they read the Bill. At the same time Lord Penzance was trying to make some amendments in Parliament to the earlier Divorce Act, and the proposals Frances made were actually incorporated into one of its clauses. From 27th May 1878 legal separations could be granted to women if their husbands were convicted of assault, and the wives could be given mandatory maintenance payments and custody of children up to the age of ten.

It was a huge step forwards and it has been widely acknowledged that the article 'Wife Torture' by Frances Power Cobbe had played a significant part in the process. Another of the ties that bound an unhappy wife to her husband had been broken, and his control over a married woman had been limited again – or at least in theory. Unfortunately, magistrates still had too much discretion, and many at least tolerated the idea of a husband chastising his wife, and often chose not to enforce the payments – in addition to which they could take a surprising attitude towards the whole issue. In one particular case, discussed in the *Westminster Review* in 1887, an abused wife was granted her separation, 'not as a protection to her, but rather because to leave her with her husband were to subject him to an influence, exciting him to violence'.[36] It was still her fault.

We only have to look at current affairs to see that domestic violence

---

[35] Ibid
[36] John Chapman, 'The Law in Relation to Women'

has not gone away. Even modern laws have failed to prevent its presence in considerable numbers. It has more to do with attitudes and values in society itself, as well as the psychological state of those who inflict violence in the first place. At least the Victorian women did help to make some changes here, though, in the marriage game – in a pattern that should be all too familiar now. They had helped to raise emotional awareness, in their novels, in their journalism and other works of non-fiction; they had gained the support of significant men who helped to get matters raised in Parliament; and they had helped to get the laws changed. Unfortunately, the underlying problem remained. The year following Frances and Mr Hill's Amendment, Florence Marryat felt it necessary to reaffirm:

> *I don't consider it my duty to submit to being treated more like a dog than a woman... women and children are not animals that you can kick, or ill use, and you are not the first man who has had to learn that lesson.*[37]

Knowing that he could still get away with violence, providing he did not go too far, obviously gave a great deal of licence to any husband who chose to resort to such methods. There were other ways, though, of ensuring a wife's obedience or punishing her for the lack of it. These may not have been as common as wife beating, but they could be equally disturbing.

While a wife was considered to be the legal property of her husband, he was allowed to control her movements. I have already mentioned that if she wanted to go anywhere she had to have his permission and he could have her brought back if she refused. If she continued to refuse, she could end up going to prison and so could anyone who helped her. However, if he wished to *prevent* her from leaving in the first place, or from getting up to any mischief (in his eyes), he could also lock her up – at home or elsewhere. Just like having controls on her financial resources or using her dependency on her relationship with her children, being able to control a wife's physical freedom to move about was another way for a husband to limit his wife's ability to get away from him permanently – by forcing

---

[37] *Her World Against a Lie*

her to remain exactly where he wanted her to be. He could force her into submission.

Early in Victoria's reign there was the case of Cecilia Cochrane. Cecilia had left her husband the year before Queen Victoria came to the throne and went to live abroad. Her husband decided to sue for the restoration of his conjugal rights and won his case, but after a couple of years' absence Cecilia had still not returned. So, setting up a rather elaborate fraud, he engineered her return to England. Apparently a man who purported to have been in debt to her father, sometime in the past, wished to give the outstanding sum back to her. The meeting was conveniently arranged to take place at her husband's home. Cecilia, unfortunately, did not smell a rat. She returned to this country, arrived at the house and found no stranger waiting for her. Instead her husband took the opportunity to lock her inside, proceeded to nail down the windows securely and refused to let her out. When the case was eventually heard in court, it was clear Cecilia had no intention of remaining with her husband. The judge awarded against her, kindly advising her that there would be no need to lock her up if she would happily accept what was clearly her duty.

Twelve years later there were signs that attitudes were beginning to change; although a husband retained most of his previous rights of 'ownership', he no longer had a carte blanche. When a Mr Sandilands was upset that his wife had left home and gone to live with their son instead, a judge informed him that he had no right to force his wife to go back to live with him. Once through the door, though, he could force her to stay. You may remember the case, mentioned earlier, of the Reverend Kelly who kept locking his wife in the house, forcing her to escape through the window on various occasions.

Frances Trollope had one of her characters clearly warn her readers:

> *There was no law which could prevent [her husband] locking her up and keeping her on bread and water until she obeyed his commands.*[38]

What is more frightening is that, apart from keeping a wife strictly under lock and key in her own home, there were other places where a Victorian husband could keep an unwanted wife out of his way. He

---

[38] *The Life and Adventures of a Clever Woman*

could have her declared insane and confined to a madhouse. There were many reasons for this: it could get rid of a troublesome wife; it could be used to cover bigamy; it could enable an unscrupulous husband to get his hands on his wife's personal money; and so on. There were obvious advantages to having her detained away from home – it was away from the prying, inquisitive eyes of those who knew her and expected to see her going about her normal duties, and could easily be covered, if necessary, by saying she had gone to a relative's house or she had taken ill elsewhere and sadly died. If the woman in question had few friends or relations, who would know?

During the long eighteenth century there had been many instances of wives being locked up in madhouses, for the convenience of their husbands. The writer Mary Brunton had one male character humorously point out, 'Mr Smith, if you shut up all the women who change their humour every minute, who will make our shirts and puddings?'[39] Genuine lunatics, or people suffering from any mental disorder, were often badly and cruelly treated in 'institutions' of different forms at the time, and the system was open to abuse by unscrupulous men. Not everyone, male or female, who was confined was actually mad. Legislative reform in 1774 had started to put some of the worst abuses of the system under control. After that date licences for the institutions had been introduced, with the requirement of adequate record keeping and the necessary certification provided by members of the medical profession. However, as many continued to find out, there were still plenty of ways and means to get around the new law.

In the 1830s a medical man called John Conolly introduced some very progressive changes at the Hanwell Asylum, just on the edge of London. No longer were patients to be routinely treated with such inhumane methods as physical restraint, in any of his institutions. Many were to follow his radical recommendations; he won the reputation of being 'a good man'. However, in 1849 he still openly recommended restraint and seclusion in an asylum for any young women:

---

[39] Mary Brunton, *Self Control*, 1810

...of ungovernable, sullen, wayward, malicious temper who persist in defying all domestic control, or who want that restraint over the passions without which the female character is lost. [40]

This description could easily cover any women who no longer accepted the traditional rules of marriage and their role within it.

By the 1850s Conolly was short of cash and found an easy method of making money. When he had issued the certificate for the incarceration of a 'patient' in a mental institution, he would then pocket 15% of the resulting fees. Easy money. It was never going to be difficult to bribe medical men in need of cash to put their signatures onto the relevant paperwork or to persuade them to take a percentage of the profit; some of them even ran dodgy institutions of their own. In his essay *On Liberty* (1859), John Stuart Mill had alleged that the definition of insanity had been expanded and was now used to cover any generally unacceptable behaviour.[41] It was to be an ongoing problem.

John Conolly was definitely involved in the case of Rosina Bulwer Lytton in 1858. We have met Rosina before – she and her abusive husband, Edward, had battles over child custody, over property, over maintenance – and as we have already seen she used her fictional works, and the prefaces to them, to repeatedly draw attention to her plight. I cannot argue that she was an entirely innocent woman, for she undoubtedly provoked him, but their affairs reached a new level after Edward decided to stand in the Hertford elections in that year. Rosina was in debt (again) and he had become rich; he was due to take his stand on the open hustings there and she decided it was the ideal opportunity to expose his hypocrisy, particularly when he was purporting to stand up for family values.

She had lots of posters printed that named him 'Sir Liar' and, early in the morning of his scheduled appearance, put them all around the town. For some reason Rosina was not there when he started to

---

[40] *John Conolly, A Remonstrance with the Lord Chief Baron touching the Case of Nottidge versus Ripley, 1849.* It should be noted that the same document called for similar treatment for young men who disgraced their families.

[41] John Stuart Mill, *On Liberty*, 1859. Until well into the twentieth century unmarried mothers without sufficient means of support faced the risk of being locked up in mental institutions. There was a major exposé of this in the 1970s when many of these institutions were finally closed.

address the crowd – maybe she had gone back to the hotel for a rest and overslept – so when she did arrive he had already made his speech. However, the crowd was delighted to see her and made way for her – and in front of them all she exposed his cruelty to her, publicly calling him 'Sir Liar'. It is said that he ran away... meanwhile, she kept her audience, ever keen for a bit of juicy scandal, totally enrapt.

Understandably, Sir Bulwer Lytton was not a happy man. He certainly considered his wife of 'ungovernable... wayward, malicious temper' and she had defied all his 'domestic control'. Four days later he had engaged two medical men to assess her mental condition, but after seven hours of tests she was pronounced perfectly sane. A couple of weeks later Bulwer Lytton had successfully bribed two other medical men to put their signatures on the relevant paperwork, and Rosina was carted off to Dr Rowland Hill's Home in Brentford (incidentally not far from the Hanwell Asylum); Dr Connolly certainly visited her there and gave his own approval.

What is interesting is the interplay of elements here – Edward desperately wanting to stop the actions of his wife interfering with his political and financial success; Rosina still wanting some justice over financial settlements and getting desperate; weakness in the laws regarding incarceration being still open to abuse by those who knew how to play the system; and then the public reaction to the case. There was a major public outcry. The people of her home town, Taunton, threatened to march on London, a public enquiry was demanded by *The Daily Telegraph*, and it is even said that Queen Victoria gave instructions that Edward should release his wife. In a sense Rosina won that round, and after a couple of weeks she was released and Edward, however reluctantly, did increase her financial settlement.

The plot of a madwoman in the attic or an innocent individual incarcerated in a madhouse was popular in Victorian fiction. *Jane Eyre* (Charlotte Bronte, 1847), *The Woman in White* (Wilkie Collins, 1859), *Lady Audley's Secret* (Mary Elizabeth Braddon, 1862) and *Hard Cash* (Charles Reade, 1863) were all concerned with the subject. Famous male authors like Charles Dickens, Edward Bulwer Lytton and William Makepeace Thackeray all made use of their knowledge of insanity (for example, through each other as friends or their personal knowledge of Lunacy Commissioners, or by having relatives who ran such institutions) and each of them was to find ways and means to discard their wives, and carry on with mistresses without the impediment of a wife in tow.[42]

Sometime after her own incarceration Rosina read *The Woman in White* and liked it. This story by Wilkie Collins had similarities to her own situation, as it involved the unjust incarceration of a baronet's wife (Bulwer Lytton was a baronet). Rosina even wrote to Collins telling him that she thought his villain was weak, and she could help him create a much nastier character by telling him all about her husband. In 1864 she also wrote to the novelist Charles Reade, who had written a fictional exposé of false incarceration, *Hard Cash,* the previous year, and who had appealed in its foreword for real stories to assist his work investigating the problem, as he was actually one of the Commissioners in Lunacy.[43] In his reply to her, dated 28th February 1864, he acknowledged, 'What facility the Lunacy Law affords for disposing of inconvenient wives' and he also commented that her history rather 'takes the shine' out of the parallel scene in *Hard Cash.*

Although it was not her intention to actually publish the record of her experiences that was sent to Charles Reade, it was published much later, without her permission, under the title *A Blighted Life.* In it she had commented:

> *The most saddening thought that arises after the perusal of this volume is that no change has yet been made in the infamous lunacy laws, for which in the main we have to thank our Whig rulers. Never was a more criminal or despotic law passed than that which now enables a husband to lock up his wife in a madhouse on the certificate*

---

[42] Catherine Dickens suffered from having too many children (ten) and a husband who was too busy to be with them. She lost interest in the domestic scene and he got bored with her, seeking comfort elsewhere. He engineered the failure of their marriage, hinting publicly at some 'long standing' trouble at home, which left him free to his own affairs. Isabella Thackeray suffered from severe postnatal depression after her third child, and her husband was genuinely concerned for her. At the time it was more commonly called puerperal insanity and many women, like Isabella, who suffered badly from it, were permanently sent away to institutions. Similarly, the publisher John Maxwell lived with the novelist Mary Elizabeth Braddon under the appearance of being Mr and Mrs Maxwell, but his own wife was safely tucked away in Ireland, apparently with mental problems of her own. It was only when his real wife died that they could safely marry and live under the genuine married title.

[43] The Commissioners were responsible for overseeing the general condition of asylums and the welfare of those who suffered from mental illness.

*of two medical men, who often in haste, frequently for a bribe, certify
to madness where none exists.*[44]

Rosina's was not an isolated case. Without looking very hard I have
come across two other important instances both concerning women
who had become involved in the fashionable pursuit of spiritualism;
neither of their husbands approved of the interest and both wished
to put them safely out of the way. These two became notorious cases
showing the false incarceration of sane women. There are likely to be
many more. In 1870 Louisa Lowe was forced to enter a mental asylum
after her husband had managed to obtain the two necessary medical
certificates. He had not approved of her spiritualistic activities, and
when she moved away from him he demanded her return, which
she refused to do. Two doctors authorised her removal to Brislington
House, near Bristol, and Louisa was forced to comply.

Apparently there was something wrong with the certification,
which could have led to her husband's prosecution if proven, but it took
months to sort it out and in the meantime Louisa remained incarcerated
in the asylum. Being forced to experience the horrors of a madhouse,
to hear the sounds of lunatics in distress, and being totally unable to
find a way out, cannot have been anything but a most dreadful and
terrifying ordeal for her. During her incarceration she repeatedly tried
to get herself reassessed, without success, and she also discovered that
her husband was busy trying to get control of all her properties that had
been protected by previous settlements. He was wasting no time.

When she was eventually released, she brought a charge of false
imprisonment against her husband, but he got away with it. The
Lord Chief Justice apparently commented that it was not a criminal
offence to incarcerate a sane individual – provided the intent was not
malicious. In Louisa's case it was, according to her husband, for her
own good – so therefore he had but acted *within* the bounds of the law.
Louisa decided to try to use her own experiences to support changes
in the law; she formed the Lunacy Law Reform Association and in
1877 actually gave evidence to a government Select Committee. She
was also able to offer much needed support to another woman who
found herself in a similar position.

---

[44] Rosina Bulwer Lytton, *A Blighted Life*, 1880

Let me introduce Mrs Georgina Weldon, an interesting character to put it mildly. Somewhat unorthodox, certainly an exhibitionist and an eccentric, she, like Louisa, was another spiritualist. She had married her husband, Henry, against her family's express wishes, and was also determined to keep up her theatrical and musical interests after the wedding. She would have loved to have made it onto the professional stage. Georgina was not a follower of fashion and wore her hair short. She was not a conventional wife; there was a *ménage à trois* for a while, and she took a group of orphans into their home, Tavistock House (coincidentally Charles Dickens' old house), determined to form them into a choir. Her methods were certainly unconventional – the children were allowed to yell and scream, and go barefoot; they were undisciplined, and were carted about (literally) in an advertising van used to draw attention to their musical performances. The neighbours must have been horrified. Her husband had by this time separated from her and moved out, leaving her the house and an allowance, but he must have been very embarrassed by her activities. There was talk of her affairs and even the possibility of a lesbian connection. In addition to which she had got into spiritualism and the habit of séances, and was well known in those particular circles.

At some point in 1878 she decided to take her 'choir' to France, and seems to have been guilty of some neglect of them there, but she did leave the children under the care of nuns in a local convent when she had a premonition that she should return to London. She found that a servant had been stealing from her, and started court proceedings, but this was the least of her worries. Tired of all her attention-seeking activities, tired of the constant embarrassment, and tired of having her still making a mess of the house, Henry had had enough. He decided to go for the madness route – that way he could get Georgina out of the way, take over his much-neglected house and solve all his problems in one go. Over a couple of days she received several unusual and disturbing visits by men pretending to be interested in her spiritualism, but these turned out to be doctors in disguise, arranged by her husband to assess her. One of these visitors, Dr L. Forbes Winslow, was the owner of a madhouse in Hammersmith.

Spiritualists had already felt they were vulnerable as a group for being unorthodox, and warned each other about the dangers of being confined in an asylum. Louisa Lowe had already warned that 'women in general' and 'wives in particular' were especially at risk. That evening Georgina wrote to the editor of *The Spiritualist* to tell him of her current concerns.

The following day, coincidentally while Louisa was visiting Georgina for the first time, an attempt was made to remove Georgina out of the house to an awaiting carriage – but fortunately Louisa was quick thinking enough to get the assistance of 'two stalwart policemen' to step in. A third policeman turned up and, assessing the situation, demanded to see the Lunacy Order that required Georgina's confinement. He saw that it had been signed by both her husband, and by one of the visitors from the previous day. Georgina did not want to believe that her husband had been responsible for arranging her confinement, nor that he had so easily obtained false evidence against her. That third policeman helped her escape down the road; he even got her a cab and refused to look at its number – so he could not be made to give that evidence against her. She thus escaped to Louisa's house, alongside her new friend.

Georgina went to Bow Street Magistrates Court, but, as she had not actually been confined, there was no case to answer, no legal redress and of course, at that time, she could not sue her own husband for his actions against her. Georgina went public instead, as Charles Reade himself (the Lunacy Commissioner) had advised her to do – giving interviews, speaking on public platforms and, like Louisa, campaigning for the reform of lunacy laws.

Her lecture was entitled 'How I escaped the Mad Doctors'.[45] In the same way we hear talk of conspiracy theory nowadays, Georgina believed that physicians then were involved in a male conspiracy against women, agreeing to label any female resistance as madness – just as John Conolly himself had recommended. She aimed to use her lecture 'to arouse public indignation and righteous wrath... to force Parliament to amend the state of things'. In 1880 Rosina Bulwer Lytton's own experiences were published in *A Blighted Life* and three years later Louisa Lowe published *The Bastilles of England, or the Lunacy Laws at Work*. All of these works were to draw public attention to the vulnerability of married women, as well as the

---

[45] She also published *The History of My Orphanage, or the Outpourings of an Alleged Lunatic and How I Escaped the Mad Doctors,* in 1882.

need for legal reform regarding the definition and treatment of madness.

We are not yet finished with Georgina; she still has a significant part to play, but for now I want to leave her there – raising public awareness over a situation where she suffered at the hands of her husband and, like others before her, wanting to not only do something more to help other women, but also (rather like Caroline, and Rosina) wanting to get her revenge. We shall return to the rest of her story later.

During the course of this chapter I have shown how a Victorian wife herself was seen as her husband's possession, and how women began to resent that view and fought against it. Having looked in turn at a husband's expectation of her obedience, and at how the rules of marriage allowed him to exercise control over her through chastisement and even incarceration, I then showed how these particular rules were challenged and how they started to change. There is one specific area, though, where a man had significant legal and physical power over his wife – as his possession – that I have not yet considered, and that was believed to be a fundamental part of any marriage. I have deemed it necessary to devote the whole of Chapter Eight to it. I refer, of course, to the matter of sex.

Chapter Eight
Delicate Matters

Although in the past sex was considered to be an indelicate topic, certainly inappropriate for literary discussion, this chapter will not be subject to any such consideration. If we are to investigate the rules of marriage and see how they were to be challenged by Victorian women, we cannot escape from the subject of sex. We need to know what women knew about sex, how they felt about it and how it affected their lives. We also need to know if they were in a position to do anything about it. There may be facts within this chapter that you did not know and could find absolutely shocking. I know I did when I encountered them for the first time. I make no apology for raising them here.

It has already been clearly established that a Victorian wife was the possession of her husband. It took years to establish that a married woman had any legal rights to property of her own and, as we have seen, women had to fight long and hard to achieve that. What the law also allowed was that, once the vows had been taken, a husband had the physical possession of his wife, not just in terms of her freedom to leave home and travel about, but more specifically over her body and her sex. These were his conjugal rights, and were deemed to be an unchallengeable rule – but what do we know about it from the wife's perspective?

Unfortunately, when a girl accepted the proposal of her suitor, no matter how much she loved him, it was very rare indeed that she knew what fulfilling those rights would actually entail for her. What she had clearly understood from her preparation for the event was that she would be fulfilling her duty as a wife if she obeyed her husband in all things. What she had failed to understand was that her husband could demand fulfilment of his conjugal rights whenever he was in the mood – whether she wanted to or not. And until very late in the Victorian period sex education was not likely to be part of a young girl's curriculum; she was unlikely to learn about the act of sex itself from either parent or teacher. How, then, was it that sex was considered to be such a vital part of the rights of a married man, but yet it was carefully concealed from the unmarried and unknowing young maidens? According to contemporary sources, a fashionable physician of the period apparently advised the mother of a nubile young lady, 'Tell her nothing, my dear madam. For if they knew they would not marry.' [1]

Although during the nineteenth century the importance of education for girls was increasingly being recognised, human biology was still not generally considered to be an appropriate subject for girls. There were some things you just did not talk about. As Helen Gardener wrote:

> Our English practice of excluding from literature all subjects and references that are unfit for boys and girls, has something to recommend it, but it undeniably leads to a certain narrowness and thinness and to some most nauseous hypocrisy. All subjects are not to be discussed by all and one result, in our case, is that some of the most important subjects in the world receive no discussion whatever. [2]

When a young Victorian girl did meet a suitable young man and a relationship evolved, it would not necessarily become very physical. Where the girl lived in close proximity to others, where, for example, housing conditions were badly overcrowded and several people shared a bed at a time, knowledge of physical love would have been greater, and so her relationship may have developed at a more natural pace. My focus has primarily been on the literature written by women, and about women, and as that has necessarily been more focused on the middle or upper echelons of society, I cannot claim to write with authority on the general pattern of girls' physical behaviour in the lower social classes. However, there were many members of the working classes who also wished to be considered 'respectable' and when respectable girls of any class were being conditioned and educated for their future roles in life,

---

[1]   Quoted in Dr C. Willett Cunnington, *Feminine Attitudes in the Nineteenth Century*, 1973.

[2]   Helen Gardener, *Is This Your Son, My Lord?* 1890

their physical behaviour was much more likely to be closely supervised. Innocent young girls should not be present when any unsavoury subjects were under discussion, and that ignorance could leave many very unprepared for what would happen in the marriage bed.

Although written in 1937, I think the following quotation is particularly apt here – looking back to the late nineteenth century when she herself had been growing up, Rachel Ferguson wrote:

> *There had been nothing to observe, no hint even of that side of matrimony. Why – with a backlash of fury Gertrude remembered it – she and Clarence had very seldom been permitted to be alone together in the drawing room during the engagement. And then – THAT!*[3]

Any girl who had had a fairly sheltered upbringing would have looked forward to her wedding day with an entirely different focus. To leave the family home by choice or necessity, to hope for more freedom and personal satisfaction, future dreams combined with practical considerations; a wedding was certainly an opportunity for a girl to be centre stage for once.

A wedding has always been an attraction for a woman, particularly if it be a handsome one. The carriages with their grey horses, and favours and bouquets, the dresses of the ladies; above all the interest that clings about a bride and bridegroom; all combine to make our English slave-sales very pretty shows.[4]

Marriage was often referred to as a contract between two people, but its terms were very different to contracts usually transacted as a matter of business. As Harriet Taylor wrote in 1831, marriage was:

> *...the only contract she ever heard of, of which a necessary condition in the contracting parties was that one should be entirely ignorant of the nature and terms of the contract... the fact that a woman knew what she undertook would be considered a just reason for preventing her undertaking it.*[5]

Much later Sarah Grand was to ask:

---

[3] Rachel Ferguson, *Alas Poor Lady*, 1937, (reprinted Persephone Books 2006)
[4] Florence Marryat, *The Root of All Evil*, 1879
[5] *The Nature of the Marriage Contract*, 1831 in *The Complete Works of Harriet Taylor Mill,* (Ed. Jo Ellen Jacobs), Indiana University Press, Bloomington, 1998

If I signed a contract... and found out afterwards that those who induced me to become a party to it had kept me in ignorance of the most important clause in it, could you call it a moral contract?[6]

It raised again the whole question of what a woman's role and purpose really was in life from a somewhat different perspective, and seems to highlight yet again how little choice she had in the matter at the time.

We should also consider how a girl might become aware of such things for the first time, before she even started her honeymoon. One of the surprising issues that is raised in late Victorian literature is that the marriage service, taken from *The Book of Common Prayer*, received open criticism for its inclusion of sexual references within minutes of the beginning of the ceremony. Although the words may have been heard previously, for example, when a girl attended other weddings, such references may have become rather disturbing for a young girl when applied to herself.

The wedding service had been in use from 1662 and remained virtually unchanged until the late twentieth century. The ceremony began with the traditional and familiar opening words, 'Dearly beloved, we are gathered here together in the sight of God' and talked of marriage as 'an honourable estate'. All well and good, but the address then went on to say marriage should not be 'taken in hand, unadvisedly, lightly, or wantonly, to satisfy men's carnal lusts and appetites, like brute beasts that have no understanding'. Marriage, people were then told, was ordained for the procreation of children. Secondly, it was ordained as a remedy against sin and to avoid fornication – so that those persons 'as have not the gift of continency might marry, and keep themselves undefiled'. The third and final given reason was for the mutual society, help and comfort of the two people concerned. When the vows had been taken, the minister finished his task by talking of the duties of the husband and wife. For him, 'to love her and honour her, as the weaker vessel', and for her, 'to submit herself unto him... to be subject to him in every thing'.

Companionship was by no means the greatest consideration, then, when the marriage took place. Indeed, it could even be argued that, according to this service, marriage was all about sex, not companionship.

---

6   Sarah Grand, *Ideala, A Study from Life*, 1889

It acknowledged both man's lust and the need to contain it, as well as the need for procreation. Mutual help and comfort were definitely last on the list.

For any who think that I am reading too much into the actual wording of the service, think again. The correspondence that was sent into *The Daily Telegraph* debate in the 1880s showed there were at least some who felt that, however valid the original intentions of the Church, the wording of the traditional service was, at best, indelicate and those such passages that might embarrass innocent or ignorant girls should be rewritten. And even one cleric, choosing to sign himself off as 'Novus Curatus' wrote, 'If the authorities will not revise this aspect of the prayer book for us we can do it ourselves.' He added that he, along with others of similar mind, could choose to leave out the relevant passages without making the service invalid. I wonder how many did.

A French writer, Leon Paul Blouet, working in England under the pen name of Max O'Rell, published his observations of English life in 1884. He had witnessed the marriage service and was shocked at its use of language, but rather than focus on how an innocent bride might react to the words she had heard, he wondered how the bridegroom might feel after the minister had spoken of lust and fornication:

> *That is how the ball opens. It is promising, is it not? You would give the world to sink through the floor, or be able to seize your dear little wife and fill her ears with cotton wool. You blush as you think of the sweet creatures in blue, pink and white [i.e. the bridesmaids] who are just behind you biting their lips and wondering what those brute beasts, that have no understanding, have to do with the ceremony. And you feel ready to fall on your knees and implore the forgiveness of the innocent young girl at your side for having brought her there to hear such things.*[7]

Suddenly, after the passing of approximately twenty minutes in church, things that were unmentionable, unholy, even sordid were being openly mentioned in front of a congregation, and were to become an accepted part of one's everyday life. Mona Caird tried to capture the emotion of how the girls must have felt:

---

[7] *Les Filles de John Bull*

Poor girls… They awake to find they have been living in a fool's paradise – a little upholstered corner with stained glass windows and rose coloured light. They find that suddenly they are expected to place in the centre of their life everything that up to that moment they have scarcely been allowed to even know about. Every instinct, every prejudice must be thrown over. All the effects of their training must be instantly overcome. And all this with perfect subjection and cheerfulness… Think what it means for a girl to have been taught to connect the idea of something low and evil with that which nevertheless is to lie at the foundation of all her after life.[8]

There may have been a wedding breakfast to follow the ceremony, a celebration with family and friends, but, at some point later, the couple would finally be able to have time to themselves. What could the initial experience of sex be like for a woman who was completely unprepared and unknowing? I have found many short references to 'THAT', and even an occasional 'The morning after the night before…', but few have gone into the explicit, emotional reactions to the initial experience of sex that I found in a translation of a work by the French male author Guy de Maupassant. Perhaps English Victorian women writers were still a little too reserved to go as far as he did. The work was fictional, but I do not think it an unrealistic interpretation of what some girls undoubtedly faced, and consequently the quotation is unusually long. Here the girl, Jeanne, had been given some preparation for the event, surprisingly by her father.

I don't know how much you know of the facts of life. There are mysteries which are carefully hidden from children, from girls especially. Girls must remain pure minded, irreproachably innocent, till the moment we deliver them to the man who will be responsible for their happiness. It is for him to lift the veil from the wonderful secret of life. But girls if they are quite unsuspecting are often repelled. You see the reality is a little brutal compared to their dreams. And sometimes because they are hurt mentally and even physically they refuse their husband his rights. A right which is his absolute due by every human and natural law.

---

[8]   Mona Caird, *Daughters of Danaus*, 1894

But just remember this… and only this… you belong completely and entirely to your husband. [9]

Thus prepared, she awaits the ordeal. On the first night of her honeymoon she got into bed before her husband.

When at last she felt that he was coming she turned over on her side and shut her eyes. She started and was about to jump out of bed at the touch of a cold hairy leg against her own. With her face buried in her hands, almost on the point of screaming with terror, she huddled herself frantically at the edge of the bed…

He clutched her wildly to him as if he were famished for her, covering her face and neck with swift, savage kisses till she was half fainting. She had let her arms drop and lay inert under his onslaught, no longer conscious of what either of them did. Her mind was in such confusion that she no longer understood anything at all. Suddenly a sharp pain tore through her body. Writhing in his arms, she moaned as he violently possessed her…

After that he must have spoken to her and she must have answered. Then he made other attempts which she repelled with horror. As she struggled she felt thick hair against her breast as she had felt it against her leg, and recoiled convulsively…

Then she began to think. She said to herself, in utter despair and disillusion, feeling her hopes and dreams cruelly betrayed and her happiness shattered: 'So that is what he calls being his wife. That! That!' [10]

Fulfilment of her conjugal duties could be a nightly event. For Joanne it was certainly frequent:

Her body and soul still revolted at her husband's incessant desire. Resigned but humiliated she only yielded with disgust. It seemed to her bestial and degrading; an obscenity. [11]

It must be stressed that this extract was not from a pornographic book. It was from a genuinely serious novel, a classic, but it touches on a

---

[9]   Guy de Maupassant, *A Woman's Life*, 1883
[10]   Ibid
[11]   Ibid

highly important point. How a young bride felt about sex, especially if it was a completely unknown or unimagined experience for her, was likely to depend upon how thoughtfully and how gently it was introduced to her, and how seriously a husband took the issue of his conjugal rights. In similar vein the novelist Florence Marryat was to comment:

> *Marriage is such a complete awakening for most women and more especially for an innocent maiden handed over to the tender mercies of a man of the world... It is the means by which many men disgust their wives in the first months of marriage... [Men] overlook the fact that the things which are every day occurrences to them, have been sealed books hitherto for the girl whom they have perhaps selected from her companions for her purity and modesty.*[12]

Much has been said elsewhere of Queen Victoria's comments about her husband, Prince Albert – he was apparently a very considerate lover and she thought he was beautiful. She was irritated that pregnancies followed on so close together and deprived her of his attentions. Not everyone had the same experience. The Victorian philanthropist and social commentator John Ruskin made a conscious decision not to consummate his own wedding night, purportedly because he was so shocked by seeing his wife's pubic hair, rather than the smooth classic forms of statues that he was used to seeing.

However disturbing a first-time experience was, though, for either man or woman, things could undoubtedly get better. One could learn to relax, participate and even to enjoy the activities. Practice too would undoubtedly help, as one female character realised:

> *'Touches and caresses and things of that sort bring thrills and shakes and trembles and flushes, every female novelist assures me of the fact. Well I must practice touches and such, and hope for results. Also I must not let myself shiver and feel sick when I in my turn get them bestowed on me. I wish to goodness I had thought of all this before; it would have been far easier to have begun right from the first.'*

---

[12] *On Circumstantial Evidence*, 1889

She suddenly hid her face in her muff.
'How awful that was, how awful. Oh!' [13]

When the subject of sex was raised in contemporary literature, for example, in the non-fictional works of Dr William Acton (*The Functions and Disorders of the Reproductive Organs*, 1875) and Dr Isaac Baker Brown (*On Some Diseases of Women Admitting Surgical Treatment*, 1866), little consideration had been given to female feelings, desire or need. In fact, not only were women taught to know (or think) little about it before marriage, but they were also taught to say nothing afterwards. These were private affairs. Sexual matters, then, were generally considered only from a male perspective and that could lead to some rather biased opinions and beliefs, notwithstanding the fact that at the time some of the medical thought was based on rather scanty scientific knowledge. Unfortunately, those pieces of information were passed on with the voice of authority and disseminated in turn by doctors and husbands. Dr Acton made some particularly noteworthy remarks, including:

> *I have taken pains to obtain and compare abundant evidence on this subject, and the result of my enquiries I may briefly epitomise as follows: I should say that the majority of women (happily for society) are not very much troubled with sexual feeling of any kind. [14]*

Any rare woman who showed a real or 'unhealthy' interest in sex could be regarded as a nymphomaniac, as someone suffering from a known 'form of insanity' that could again lead to incarceration in a lunatic asylum. Dr Acton also referred to those prostitutes whose apparent interest in sex could be daunting to any young unmarried men who had made use of them, fearing that 'the marital duties they will have to undertake are beyond their exhausted strength, and from this reason dread and avoid marriage'.

In Dr Acton's opinion the vast majority of wives were modest women who would merely submit to their husbands' embraces. He admired such women who were both 'self-sacrificing and sensible', accepting all their marital duties, and he was highly critical of any

---

[13] Iota, *A Yellow Aster*, 1894
[14] Dr William Acton, *The Functions and Disorders of the Reproductive Organs*, 1875

wives who had shockingly declared their aversion to sex. Women who made it too obvious that their husbands' attentions were undesirable, and put their husbands off, were not only to be made to feel guilty, but they also had to take personal responsibility for their husbands' frequent absence from home, and for his finding alternative outlets for his affections. Once again it was their fault if there were problems in a marriage.

The need for women to submit to their husbands sexually was also justified on medical grounds. It was frequently asserted that men would become seriously ill if their own sexual needs were not gratified. Moreover, it was said that if a wife did not oblige her husband, then it could lead to problems for her own reproductive system – so she would be doubly foolish to resist. A wife should therefore merely fulfil her marital duties by submitting to the attentions of her husband, accepting each pregnancy as it arose. We have again returned to the unceasing repetition of having to be a submissive woman; this was her conjugal duty. There were to be no considerations of her personal feelings or the long-term effects of multiple pregnancies on her body. It should be noted that it was also believed that a woman could not get pregnant if she failed to have an orgasm – so perhaps another reason to leave her unsatisfied.

In earlier Victorian times the literary media had made few direct references to sexual matters beyond medical or scientific discourse and the topic was generally dealt with by mere hints and suggestion in fictional works, if not altogether avoided. However, by the late nineteenth century the situation had radically changed – for reasons that will evolve during the course of this chapter – and the contents of women's literature show this turnaround quite clearly.

Using her pen name George Egerton, Mary Bright wrote a short story in 1893 called 'Virgin Soil'. In this a young woman actually went back to confront her mother after her honeymoon and asked:

> Do you think if I had realised how fearfully close the intimacy with him would have been that my whole soul would not have stood up in revolt?... My dear mother, the ceremony had no meaning for me. I did not know what I was signing my name to or what I was vowing to do.

There were many more things for a woman to learn about sex apart from the nature of the act itself. One of the key issues regarding sex within marriage, right up until the end of the twentieth century, was the question of conjugal rights. Even if you look back at earlier centuries when women had been in a stronger position in terms of social and economic status, wives were still tied to the position of sexual slave of their husbands. A married woman was not in control of her own body. Sex was not just a question of initially consummating a marriage; it was within the husband's rights to continually demand its repetition. That often quoted guru of women's conduct books, Sarah Stickney Ellis, had merely warned, 'The greatest trials connected with this state of experience are such as cannot be told, and therefore set the sufferer apart from all human sympathy and understanding.'[15]

In his work on the *Reproductive Organs*, Dr William Acton had clearly stated that if women did have an aversion to sex, it was actually either due to having a disease (!) and if so, 'the sooner the suffering female is treated, the better', or it was due to apathy, or more astoundingly 'a selfish indifference to please'. (You may well be reminded of the comments, made in an earlier chapter, about women being considered selfish when they showed an interest in wanting to keep control of their own money.)

Women did not have the right to say 'No' and Victorian feminists were slowly beginning to realise that this was too important an issue to leave unaddressed. Once again women were to find that marriage was not necessarily a question of mutual love; it was a question of property.

In the eighteenth century the judge Sir Matthew Hale had referred to 'a clear and well settled ancient law' regarding rape:

> *The husband cannot be guilty of a rape committed by himself upon his lawful wife, for by their matrimonial consent and contract, the wife has given herself up in this kind unto her husband, which she cannot retract.* [16]

Since then the traditional belief had remained virtually unchallenged. It is also worth restating that the poor wife was likely to have been

---

[15] *Wives of England*
[16] Sir Matthew Hale, *History of the Pleas of the Crown*, 1736

equally unaware of this part of the contract, for she was to be given no prior knowledge of it, let alone have any choice in the matter. So according to the 'ancient law' a wife was not able to retract a promise that she did not even know she was making.

Disturbing though these issues are, they were not the only ones concerning sex within marriage. I have already said elsewhere that it was perfectly legal to lock up a wife or force her to return to the marital home if the husband wanted to keep her there, and the implication of that is shocking if one now looks at the matter of sex. Any discontented wife who had run away could be forced to return home if the husband won his legal plea for the restitution of conjugal rights. Perhaps out of revenge, perhaps out of his own personal desire, he could then force himself upon her at will, and regardless of her own distress she was powerless to refuse him. To have won a suit for the restitution of conjugal rights was a carte blanche; her rape was legalised – he was perfectly within his rights at the time. It may have been extremely degrading to her, but it is likely that at least on some occasions a wife decided not to resist because she could have faced more serious physical consequences if she had done so. It is a sobering thought. There was also the problem for her that if she ran away from her husband's unwanted sexual attentions, she was actually deserting him and that meant that should he choose not to pursue her she would forfeit all claim to her children and her own maintenance. It would take a brave woman to run away in such a situation.

Serving her husband sexually was thus part and parcel of the marriage and this could have another serious and unwanted consequence for a Victorian wife. The very fact that a man could testify that he had had sex with his wife, regardless as to whether it was by force or not, could be used further against her in the law. Suppose a discontented wife actually wanted to try to obtain a divorce on the grounds of cruelty and adultery. Her husband could argue that rather than condemning him for his negative behaviour elsewhere within the marriage, his wife had shown she had actually condoned it by still continuing to have sex with him (even though it was against her will) and thus acting as his wife again. This was a significant loophole in the law for him. A man could in effect rape his unhappy wife and thus seal her fate to remain at his mercy, rather than getting the divorce she wanted. The laws on sex had acted as an effective trap – a catch 22.

In addition to all of this the laws regarding property had allowed the husband to make sexual decisions *about* his wife's body. During the mid-Victorian period we know there were some women who had made known their desire to leave their husbands, and were hoping to make use of the provisions of the Divorce Act, but, rather than using the legal loophole described above, their husbands chose to use a different method to control their wives' behaviour.

At that time there were some slightly unorthodox doctors in practice, like Dr Isaac Baker Brown, mentioned earlier in this chapter. He operated in London in the 1860s and had performed 600 clitorodectomies on supposedly unhealthy and hysterical women, and was proud of his rate of 'success'. Nowadays we are more familiar with horrific stories about other cultures that inflict this genital mutilation on their women, and there are huge campaigns and constant publicity demanding an end to the custom. Few people realise that this procedure was carried out on some Victorian women in this country as another means of behavioural control.

Although Dr Brown was later to lose his licence for performing a number of such operations on women who had *not* accepted the need for such grossly interfering surgery, it is known from his own printed works that at least five husbands had *paid* him to use the method to control their discontented wives, who otherwise would have chosen to divorce them. Such was the husband's power over an unhappy wife; it would completely subdue her. Dr Brown did not act in isolation; similar practices were conducted elsewhere. On the general subject of castration an American Doctor, David Gilliam, explained:

> *Why do we alter our colts and calves? Not that we expect to abate strength or endurance, nor yet to render them less intelligent; but that we may make them tractable and trustworthy, that we may convert them into faithful, well disposed servants.*[17]

As both Victorian women and men began to question the general rights of a husband over his wife, the issue of sex was to receive some

---

[17] *The American Journal of Obstetrics and Diseases of Women and Children*, 1896 quoted in Susan Kingsley Kent, *Sex and Suffrage 1860–1914*, Routledge, London, 1990

serious consideration. John Stuart Mill had believed that in England a wife was actually worse off than a slave – for in all Christian countries a slave could at least refuse the sexual attentions of her master.

> *However brutal a tyrant [a wife] may unfortunately be chained to… he can claim from her and enforce the lowest degradation of a human being, that of being made the instrument of an animal function contrary to her inclinations.*[18]

Mill himself referred to the 'barbarous restitution of conjugal rights' that was enforced by law in matters of marital disputes. The brute beasts in the marriage service had not gone away after all. However, his view of conjugal affairs did not necessarily please other members of his own sex; not everyone agreed with his views on the subjugated woman. In his work Dr William Acton had encountered 'numerous husbands' who had complained to him:

> *…of the hardships under which they suffer being married to women who regard themselves as martyrs when called up to fulfil the duties of wives; this spirit of insubordination has become more intolerable since it has been backed by the opinions of John Stuart Mill.*[19]

Outside of marriage, rape was classified as a physical assault upon a woman; indeed, until 1841 rape had actually been a capital offence, but thereafter a man could still be severely punished for it, as it destroyed the purity of either someone else's daughter (which could therefore affect her value in the marriage market) or the value of a wife. Rape within marriage did not exist. In 1880 there were even moves towards enshrining this belief into modern statute law – under the provisions of the Criminal Code Bill then being considered. According to this Bill, rape was to be defined as 'the act of a man, not under the age of fourteen, having carnal knowledge of a woman, *who is not his wife*, without her consent'. If it had been passed, generations of women would have suffered from its now overt implications.

While the Bill was under consideration it triggered a response

---

18 *The Subjection of Women*
19 *The Functions and Disorders of the Reproductive Organs*, 1875

from the small, but increasing number of women who wanted to change the rules regarding sex within marriage. These women wanted sex to be a matter of choice for women for they believed:

> *There must be a full understanding and acknowledgement of the obvious right of the woman to possess herself body and soul, to give or withhold herself body and soul, exactly as she wishes.*[20]

One of the most significant names linked to this demand for self-possession was Elizabeth Wolstenholme Elmy, whom we have met before in her support of women's property issues. Elizabeth had spent some years working as secretary to a new organizsation, 'The Campaign for Amending the Law in Points Wherein it is Injurious to Women', which later changed its cumbersome name to the Vigilance Association for the Defence of Personal Rights. Its aim was to monitor parliamentary activity and policy on all laws that affected women, so that no legal actions would take place in the future without the knowledge and reactions of the women concerned. It had been set up in 1871 and though renamed several times it was disbanded only in 1978.

Elizabeth spent so much time studying and observing the legal and judiciary system of this country that she earned the nickname of 'Parliamentary Watchdog'. She realised the Criminal Code Bill was a prime example of planned legislation that would affect generations of women to come. Being well informed, she reacted to the Bill by writing a paper about it and giving lectures on the subject. Like John Stuart Mill in the past she referred to the 'bodily slavery' of a wife and commented that marital rape was:

> *...a violation of a primary natural right, [which] is and ought to be, wholly independent of any legal or otherwise artificially created relationship between the parties, and it would be a gross immorality to enact, as the section I have just quoted [of the Criminal Code Bill] proposes implicitly to do, that any act by a husband, however base and cruel it may be, is justified by the matrimonial consent of the wife once given and never to be retracted.*[21]

---

[20] Mona Caird, 'Marriage', *Westminster Review*, 1888
[21] Elizabeth Wolstenholme Elmy, from a paper read to the Dialectical Society in 1880, but included in 'Judicial Sex Bias', *Westminster Review*, March 1898

Fortunately, the Criminal Code Bill failed to be enacted, but it made little difference. In 1889 Justice Hawkins had affirmed its earlier intentions when he stated that at the time of a marriage a wife gave her husband 'an irrevocable right to her person', and in the same year Justice Pollock said that a wife had no right or power to refuse her consent for 'the husband's connection with his wife'. Until a law was introduced that specifically reduced a husband's sexual rights over his wife the accepted conjugal rights would remain the same. During her lifetime Elizabeth Wolstenholme Elmy made over fifty attempts to try to persuade MPs to introduce the idea of legislation that would do so, but to her dismay not a single Member of Parliament was interested.

It would be distinctly unfair, though, to leave the impression that men alone could have had a specific agenda when they got married. Ignoring those who married for true love alone, for few could actually afford to do that, it was necessary for most women to marry in order to gain financial security and position, and often, also, to please their parents. Without marriage they could be left in very precarious situations as single 'unprotected' women. When a woman chose to marry for reasons other than love she was in effect selling herself for board and lodging, regardless as to whether she personally chose to look at the situation in this way, and even if she knew nothing about the sexual consequences of her action. Mary Elizabeth Braddon, who was an extremely popular contemporary novelist, may have made people pause for thought when she suggested:

> It was like the story of Cinderella... nor does any one know by any means that Cinderella cared very much about the prince. The old fairy story is hardly a love story, but rather a romance of carriages and horses and other worldly splendours, and swift transition from a kitchen to a palace.[22]

In return for providing this home and security a husband would expect the fulfilment of his rights. Increasingly during the nineteenth century women themselves were to realise the connection and make open comparisons between wives and prostitutes, and the way men treated both. It could be an uncomfortable realisation:

---

[22] Mary Elizabeth Braddon, *Strangers and Pilgrims*, 1873

As long as a man demands from a wife what he must sue from a mistress as a favour... marriage becomes for many a legal prostitution, a nightly degradation, a hateful yoke.[23]

There was nothing new in this view of marriage. From at least the eighteenth century onwards writers like Mary Wollstonecraft have described marriage for mercenary reasons as legalised prostitution and she was not alone in her view even then. In spite of sentimental views and religious diatribes about the sanctity of marriage, a marriage of convenience could hardly be viewed in the same light as one made genuinely out of mutual love and respect. Eliza Lynn Linton wrote:

Anyone with money can buy the best in the market... We sell our energies, our brains, our time, our health and strength, for so much coin of the realm... Why not our bodies as well? In the streets it goes by an ugly name, but the church and society call it marriage.[24]

It was apparently only an accident of birth that stopped respectable women in need of financial security being in the same situation in which many of the prostitutes had found themselves. Many women had resorted to prostitution because it could be an easy way to make money. Women writers had also drawn attention to the plight of those who had 'fallen', and the direct link with poverty. Eliza Lynn Linton had called for direct action by those in positions of power, to ensure that women could earn a decent living wage rather than having to sell their bodies. She knew that many:

...are FORCED, loathing, onto the streets for the food, clothing and lodging which their long hours of work cannot give them. This is a fact positively known to those who care to examine into such foul pools as bad social management has allowed to stagnate underneath our stately temples of posterity.[25]

---

[23] George Egerton, *Virgin Soil*, 1893

[24] Eliza Lynn Linton, *The Philosophy of Marriage*, included in Quilter, *Is Marriage a Failure?* 1888

[25] *Realities*

But Eliza's pleas for social change did not just fall on deaf ears. The novel *Realities* was so widely condemned she did not write another novel for fourteen years.

Even if they were aware of the prostitutes' existence, most women generally preferred to remain aloof, either choosing to appear blissfully ignorant about such people or if they did encounter them in the street showing utter disdain or contempt. But as Olive Schreiner pointed out, 'A woman who has sold herself even for a ring and a new home need hold her skirt aside for no creature in the street. They both earn their bread in one way'.[26]

Nowadays we are not unfamiliar with remarks about women being considered as sexual objects. It has been a regular subject for general debate, but it does seem to have been a fair comment regarding Victorian times. A woman was seen as a man's possession, and that included him having full sexual rights over her. Whether you consider a wife being the husband's private sexual property or a prostitute being shared public sexual property, a man's sexuality, his sexual needs, seems to have been given a primary consideration.

Elizabeth Wolstenholme Elmy believed that at the heart of all the problems that women faced in life was the fact that everyone seemed to accept that men were born with a strong sex drive, and could do nothing about it. Men's sexual needs had to be met whether they were married or not. Men's vices, their sexual adventures outside marriage, had always been excused and the laws, being made solely by men, had endorsed such behaviour. As we have already seen, a wife *had* to submit to her husband's attentions. She was given no choice in the matter. She also had to be faithful to him.

A man may have made promises during the marriage ceremony regarding his future fidelity – but it was not considered essential that he kept them. If he did commit adultery, it did not mean the end of his marriage. There are so many references to this double standard in contemporary women's literature we can take it for granted that women often became aware of the situation, even if they chose not to talk about it. I will cite only two key examples here:

---

[26] *The Story of an African Farm*

In the innocence of their hearts and the ignorance of their heads [women] imagine that marriage vows are a dual responsibility; solemn and dissoluble as God ordained them; and on the woman's side so they are, but with men it is very different, they have concocted a code of conventional morality adapted to their needs.[27]

The second example neatly ties the double standard to the spurious offspring, discussed in Chapter Five, which were frequently used as the justification for its existence.

We [women] cannot, we ought not, according to some reasoners, to expect to confine such variety loving creatures as men in the pales they themselves have made, but so easily vault over – we are fixed as rocks in constancy to them; for it is only we who can do the harm in families. We alone taint the purity of the domestic hearth, we alone introduce spurious offspring into the house.[28]

Unfortunately, in England it was still commonly accepted that it was 'only natural' that a man should find an outlet for his sexual needs and, if he was unwilling or unable to get married, say for financial reasons, or he wished to have more sex than he got at home from his wife, there were other women available elsewhere. For a start there would always be some innocent but rather gullible young women who fell for the tale of a lovesick suitor who was so desperate to test how much the girl 'really' loved him. It was then all too easy for a knowledgeable young man to abandon a pregnant girl whom he had seduced, especially if he had been careful to indulge his desires well away from home. We even had laws that protected such men.

The 1834 Poor Law Amendment Act contained a Bastardy Clause that meant that the social and financial responsibility for illegitimate children up to the age of sixteen fell totally on their unfortunate mothers, the fallen women. It allowed those men who had seduced otherwise innocent girls to deny that they had even met them and get off scot-free. Various women writers were to make critical references to this clause in their work. Rosina Bulwer Lytton, in her novel

---

27   Rosina Bulwer Lytton, *Very Successful*
28   Emma Robinson, *Mauleverer's Divorce: A Story of Woman's Wrongs*

Cheveley: or The Man of Honour, had the seducer scornfully tell his victim, 'I suppose your father will disown you… and as for your brat … thanks to the new Poor Laws you have no claim on me.' Some six years later Frances Trollope wrote that the Bastardy Clause 'was not only then to punish the offending woman but to spare the pocket of the fondly protected man'.[29]

Jessie Phillips told the story of a fallen woman, who suffered greatly because of the Bastardy Clause; it was a complete exposé of the injustice of the Poor Law system. It has been said that the insight gained from reading Frances' book may have helped lead to the revocation of the original Poor Law Act some twelve years after its original enactment. For those twelve years, though, the law had continued to protect the male sex drive, and offered no compensation or support for the fallen women affected by it. In spite of this reform, however, some twenty years later a whole series of acts was to be introduced that once again were to protect the sexual needs of men, at the expense of the women, and it is towards the introduction of these acts that we must now turn.

We begin by looking at the fallen women themselves. The term 'fallen women' did not just apply to those like Jessie Phillips who had been seduced by an errant male, but also was generally applied to those who made their living by selling sexual favours. These were the prostitutes of course, the mistresses and courtesans, readily available in all the towns and cities. Prostitution was rife in Victorian England. London even had its own guidebooks as to who could be found, with what speciality – if you knew where to look. Common prostitutes were the lowest of the low, despicable women selling their bodies for money, for greed alone, or so it was said. Dr William Acton wrote, 'A prostitute is a woman, with half the woman gone.'[30]

These women did not just provide a purchasable sexual pleasure for young and not so young men on a fun night out in town, returning home in the early hours of the morning. For those who worked temporarily far away from home the services of prostitutes and brothels provided a welcome and necessary distraction. Soldiers who served abroad found comfort and female companionship in brothels,

[29] Frances Trollope, *Jessie Phillips*, 1843

[30] Dr William Acton, *Prostitution, Considered in its Moral, Social and Sanitary Aspect, in London and other large cities and Garrison Towns, with Proposals for the Control and Prevention of Attendant Evils* – originally published in 1857, reprinted and updated 1870.

especially if their wives were unable to be with them. Apparently the army allowed very few soldiers' wives to be quartered with their serving husbands, for it was feared their strength would be sapped by the very presence of their wives. Yet somehow it seemed to be a totally different situation with regard to the provision of prostitutes. I learned only recently that in each of the major towns in Imperial India the army actually ran its own brothels, and many of these supplied girls of only *twelve years old* for their troops' entertainment.

Unfortunately, one of the problems that the army faced then was that men who frequented these brothels, and made use of the prostitutes, whether abroad or at home, often ended up with an unexpected consequence of their actions. They contracted venereal diseases. In fact, the soldiers suffered from this problem to such an extent that there were more soldiers being treated in the Crimea for it than for physical injuries gained in conflict. Official figures for 1860 showed that as many as 369 men per 1000 were affected by it.

It was naturally a matter of major political, military and medical concern that the British army had such a serious problem. The soldiers were known to be unhealthy because of their use of prostitutes. It was obviously necessary to improve the health of the soldiers. However, it was not to be by introducing improved recreational facilities for bored off-duty men, although that was suggested repeatedly; it was not to be by improving the general health and hygiene levels in the men's quarters; but it was to be by introducing a law to control the sexual health of the prostitutes – by force. It was so easy to lay the blame on them.

One summer's night in June 1864 a new law was quietly passed, without debate, in Parliament. It took only *five weeks* to pass through the various stages. It had been given a misleading name, the Contagious Diseases Act, and when Queen Victoria had to put her signature to it, it is thought she was under the misapprehension that it was something to do with cattle.

This law and the reactions to it were, in time, to have a major impact on the double standard, on the very acceptance of men's sexual nature, and resulted in some fundamental changes with regard to women's knowledge of sexual matters and their own attitudes towards them. It was to affect both married and unmarried women alike, and it was to highlight all the various links between married women and prostitutes.

What it actually introduced was that in eleven named military towns (including Aldershot, Colchester, Portsmouth, Plymouth and Woolwich) any woman who was thought to be a prostitute could be taken off the streets, by the police, and *forced* to have an internal examination by a designated doctor armed with a speculum, in order to establish if she carried a venereal infection. If she refused, she would be brought before a magistrate and she could face imprisonment. If a woman was diseased, she would be taken to a lock hospital for treatment and kept *locked in* (hence the name) until she was considered cured, for a period of up to six months. *Any* woman walking the streets at night in those towns could find themselves under suspicion – so that included factory night shift workers, for example, or any others who had legitimate reasons for being out at night. Subsequent extensions of the Act meant that within a few years the number of military towns included in the provision would be extended to eighteen and a magistrate would no longer need to be involved. It was to be left entirely in the free hands of the police as to whether a woman was considered a prostitute or not, and therefore whether she was forced to see the designated doctor. This extensive power could easily be, and was, abused by them. It is worth noting that London itself had not been included in the Acts – possibly because of the lack of adequate numbers of police to enforce it.

There were many who supported the initial Contagious Diseases Act, because there was a general agreement that 'something had to be done' to improve the functioning of the army; there was, after all, the empire to consider. Some of the prostitutes themselves apparently approved because they got free treatment and even a medical certificate to show they were healthy – at least at the time of the certificate being issued. Some even called themselves 'The Queen's Women', because they were now under her regulations. Even the first woman doctor, Elizabeth Blackwell, was in favour when the original Act was introduced, thinking it was better to protect the health of the nation rather than protect the individual rights of degraded women.

There was, however, another side to the picture, and anyone who took more than a superficial view of the Act would quickly become aware of its implications. There was one woman who was suspicious from the start. Florence Nightingale. There must be few who are not aware of her work in Scutari, supporting the wounded soldiers during the Crimean War. Since then she had become responsible for advising the government and the army on all matters relating to their medical welfare. The first draft of the Contagious Diseases Bill had been prepared in secret and had been circulated only to 'interested parties'. When Florence got to hear about the government plans regarding the initial Bill she was not in favour of it. She felt it was immoral. The government was clearly accepting and endorsing the need for prostitution and ensuring a supply of women for the task who had an apparently clean bill of health. In addition to this Florence knew that the government claim that the recommended procedures would solve the problem of venereal disease was not supported by statistical evidence – and she was a great believer in statistics. She too feared that it was a system that could be subject to abuse and that any honest girl could be locked up all night by mistake.

When she was asked to be involved in the selection of doctors for the process of examination Florence refused. She wrote to her journalist friend Harriet Martineau who published various articles in the *Daily News* in 1863 echoing her concerns, but to no avail. Later Harriet commented:

> *It is an awkward and difficult state of things when legislation is necessary, or is sought without being necessary, on matters unfit to be brought before the eye of a great part of the public... The Bill is of this nature... The object of the proposer is to get the Bill passed with as little noise and as few words as possible.* [31]

Although Florence had passed on her initial concerns, it must have been difficult to know what else she, as a woman, could actually do. Here was a proposal for a new law to be introduced that was to protect men's sexual use of women. It was not merely legalising prostitution, it was putting it under government control. Women alone would be forced to undergo brutal physical examinations and be locked up for treatment. None of the government measures were to be applied to the infected men themselves. It was a corrupt law,

---

[31] *Daily News*, 2nd July, 1864

and it would put an end to the myth that governments protected the interests of women.

Even from her own authoritative position, with all her expert knowledge, Florence Nightingale was unable to challenge the government's decision, and it was even more difficult for ordinary women to know how to react if, and when, they did find anything out. On 20th March 1856, some eight years earlier, there had been a leading article in *The Times* entitled 'The Traffic in Women', which appealed for women to 'use their powers' to stop the progress of 'the enormous wrong' it had exposed. Subsequently a female correspondent (A.J.) had asked:

> *How are we expected to act, to speak, or even to think on such a subject? We have been told heretofore by men whom we respect that it becomes women to be absolutely silent on such revolting subjects – to ignore or rather to affect to ignore such a 'state of things' as you refer to.*

The same problem was to face those who were concerned about the Contagious Diseases Acts (as they were collectively known, and hereinafter referred to as the CDA), but those who were in favour of them could easily justify their support on various grounds. The state of the army was named as the primary concern. Men needed an outlet for their sexual impulses; it was unhealthy for them to resist. Some, like William Lecky, even argued that prostitutes actually protected the purity of other women – by in effect providing a safety valve for men.

> *But for her the unchallenged purity of countless happy homes would be polluted, and not a few who in the pride of their untempted chastity think of her with an indignant shudder, would have known the agony of remorse and despair.*[32]

According to this argument it was implied that without the availability of prostitutes an unsatisfied male could otherwise be a danger to the public, preying on any unprotected female. There was never any question of it being necessary for a male to exercise self-control. It

---

[32] William Lecky, *History of European Morals*, 1869

prostitutes were indeed so indispensable to men, some women felt that we should change the way we viewed them. Thus, for example, in 1880 Ellice Hopkins remarked that 'since prostitutes were masters of purity, brothels should be next to churches!'[33]

By introducing the CDA the government had not only accepted the need for prostitution, but it had also given its blessing; however, many people were, over time, to have grave concerns. For a start encouraging men to use prostitutes allowed them to think of women in general as disposable items. Although he blamed the prostitutes themselves for this, rather than the men who made use of them, Dr William Acton warned a woman would become:

> ...a toy, a plaything, an animated doll; a thing to wear like a glove and fling away, to use like a horse and send to the knackers yard when worn out.[34]

Women were to be seen as sexual objects, and their feelings and any sense of degradation because of the provisions of the CDA were to be considered irrelevant to the purpose. There was also the injustice that the penalty was being applied only to the women concerned. In a pamphlet that she had published Annie Besant wrote:

> Under [the CDA] women are arrested, condemned and sentenced to a terrible punishment and for what? In order that men may more safely degrade her in the future, and may use her for their own amusement with less danger to themselves.[35]

Prior to the Acts the notion of examining all *soldiers* for venereal diseases had been considered, but it had been abandoned because it was feared that the soldiers would prove extremely hostile to the idea. It was so much easier to enforce examinations on fallen women whom nobody really cared about. Annie protested:

---

[33] quoted in Susan Kingsley Kent, *Sex and Suffrage in Britain 1860-1914, p63*
[34] *Prostitution, Considered in its Moral, Social and Sanitary Aspect*
[35] Annie Besant, *The Legislation of Female Slavery in England*, 1876

Men would not submit to it. Of course they would not if one gleam of manhood remained in them, and neither would women with any sense of womanhood submit to it, if they were not bound hand and foot by the triple cord of ignorance, weakness and starvation.[36]

One of the other key issues around the CDA was the loss of individual freedom for the prostitutes – a fundamental loss of liberty if they were imprisoned within a lock hospital without having previously committed any actual crime. Annie Besant felt it necessary to remind the government:

No more inalienable right exists than the right of the individual to the custody of his own person; in a free country none can be deprived of this right save by a sentence given in open court, after a jury of peers has found him guilty of a crime which, by the laws under which he lives, is punished by a restriction of that liberty.[37]

It was an idealistic hope as far as women were concerned at the time; we have already seen in the previous chapter that married women were particularly vulnerable for they could be locked up by their husbands at will.

Although some may find it distasteful, it is also necessary that the actual physical examination of the prostitutes should be considered at this point. Nowadays we are more used to preventative procedures in medicine, and many women have regular internal examinations, which use a speculum as part of pre-cancer screening. At my own doctor's, a nurse, invariably female, conducts such examinations and a twenty-minute appointment is scheduled for *each* one. While the CDA were in operation, Dr William Acton himself attended some of the examinations of women in a lock hospital and recorded that:

The examinations are conducted with great rapidity. In the course of one hour and three quarters I assisted in the thorough examination of fifty-eight women with the speculum.[38]

---

[36] Ibid
[37] Ibid
[38] *Prostitution Considered in its Moral, Social and Sanitary Aspect*

Less than two minutes were spent on each procedure. It is not surprising that there were complaints of brutality, of being treated like a lump of meat, and it being such an unpleasant experience that it was a good idea to get drunk beforehand. For those waiting for local examinations it could be humiliating in an additional way – word got round, local louts came to jeer and mock the women while they awaited their turn, and little children were spotted playing in the gutter – not the traditional 'doctors and nurses' game that we are familiar with, but the contemporary version of 'doctors and prostitutes'.

To those who raised concerns it was reassuringly said that 'respectable women would have nothing to fear from the Acts', but that was false propaganda, for married women were to be affected by the CDA in numerous ways.

Under the terms of the initial 1864 Act a woman who had refused to be examined would find herself in front of a magistrate, but at least she would get a hearing and she could prove her innocence. After the extensions to the Act were introduced, the police and doctors alone were responsible for enforcing the CDA. Just as Florence Nightingale had predicted any woman could be 'suspected' and examined without just cause. We know innocent women, spinsters and wives, had to face the ordeal, and it led to the suicide of at least one blameless wife.

These were not the only risks that married women faced, though, as a result of the CDA, for without treatment for himself any diseased male could easily go home and infect his wife and future children. Mrs Beeton, the famous author of the *Book of Household Management* (1861), was one amongst many women to suffer in this way. Soldiers were not the only ones to use prostitutes. There is evidence from the doctors themselves that they frequently recognised the diseases in wives and children but helped protect the husband concerned by revealing nothing of their specific knowledge. We also know that one of the medical myths of the time was that you could cure syphilis by having sex with a virgin, as were the majority of unmarried women.

One gains the impression from late-nineteenth-century women's novels that a few women at least may have suspected the truth when they saw their own sickly newborns, or young infants, and compared them to those of their family and friends, especially if the men they married were known to have something of a notorious past.

The secrets of the House of Heriot lay before him. On those frail tiny forms lay heavily the heritage of the fathers... When I saw and understood the face of my first baby, when the little hope born of patient effort turned to that – do you not think I did not have my desperate moment?[39]

Well before this women writers also began to raise some very pointed questions, to which Annie Besant had her own particular answer.

If men have the right to demand the protection of the law, why should women be deprived of the same protection? If so necessary for the safety of men, why not necessary for the safety of women?... Any man should at once be arrested, be compelled to prove he is not married, should be examined and kept in hospital if need be until perfectly cured.[40]

It is no surprise that her suggestions failed to be taken up by the authorities.

Returning now to the CDA, within a few years the number of towns covered by them had been steadily increased and, encouraged by their 'success', a select committee had been formed in 1868 to consider extending them to cover the entire civilian population; suddenly, every woman could be at risk. The word got out. The prospect of all women being subjected to such sexual interference and control, however unlikely, was intolerable. Organisations like the Rescue Society and the Social Science Congress denounced the Acts and any further extension of them; the time was ripe for the women themselves to take action.

But what female would be prepared to get involved publicly with such a delicate subject and take on the establishment? Women had been censured for their involvement in moves for child custody and property ownership, but matters of sex were not considered appropriate subjects for them at the best of times – let alone the shady areas of prostitution and venereal disease. Many unmarried women had taken part in the earlier protests, but they could hardly take the

---

[39] Emma Brooke, *A Superfluous Woman*, 1894
[40] *The Legislation of Female Slavery in England*

lead here – they were not even supposed to know about such things. What was needed was a strong, solidly respectable, married woman who was prepared to stand up and fight, primarily on behalf of the fallen women, but also on behalf of the whole sex. Someone who could not be accused of being self-seeking in her actions, as Caroline Norton had been in the past; someone whose virtuous actions would speak for themselves. Elizabeth Wolstenholme (later Elmy) had been present at the Social Science Congress in 1869 when the CDA had been discussed and condemned, and decided to send a telegram to her friend Josephine Butler whom she thought would fit the bill.

Some years before the first Contagious Diseases Act was introduced Josephine had read the novel *Ruth* by Elizabeth Gaskell, published in 1853. This was the sympathetically treated story of a fallen woman. The book had caused outrage at the time; fathers banned their daughters from reading it – Josephine had been deeply moved by it. Later she discovered not only that her husband's university colleagues still felt the book was unfit for women to read, but that one of them was actually responsible for seducing and abandoning a pregnant girl himself. It was outrageous.

She had become increasingly concerned with abandoned girls and fallen women, even taking such poor creatures into the shelter of her own basement. For Josephine it was not just disgust at the hypocrisy of such men; she also felt at least partly responsible for the fact that men had got away with such behaviour for so long. Women's conditioning, and acceptance of the process of conditioning, had in itself helped to condone such a state of affairs. By failing to get involved, by failing to acknowledge the unmentionable things in life, women had failed to challenge men's sexual attitudes towards them, and had suffered the consequences. Later, in a letter to an MP in 1883, she wrote:

> *At the very base of the Acts lies the false and poisonous idea that women have nothing to do with this question and ought not to hear of it, much less meddle with it. Such propriety and modesty [has been] the cause of outrage and destruction to so many of our poorer women… I cannot forget the misery, injustice and outrage which have fallen upon women, simply because we stood aside when men felt our presence painful.*[41]

---

[41] quoted in Susan Kingsley Kent, *Sex and Suffrage 1860-1914*, p74

Within months of being asked to lead the campaign Josephine had started the Ladies National Association for the repeal of the Contagious Diseases Acts and on New Year's Day 1870 *The Daily News* published 'A Solemn Protest' signed by 120 leading women of the day – including Florence Nightingale and Harriet Martineau. It demanded the end to the laws for 'it is unjust to punish the sex who are the main victims and leave unpunished the sex who are the main cause'.

You can understand how shocked women must have felt when they heard about the CDA for the first time. Sarah Grand captured the emotion well when she wrote:

> *It was all as new to her as it was horrifying, and she required time to study both sides of the question. Her own sense of justice was too acute to let her accept at once that the so called civilised men who boast of their chivalrous protection of the weaker sex had imposed upon women a special public degradation, while the most abandoned and culpable of their sex were not only allowed to go unpunished, but to spread vice and disease where they listed. The iniquitous injustice and cruelty of it made her sick and sorry for men, and reluctant to believe it.*[42]

After hearing about these laws, thousands of women joined the Association. Local branches were set up throughout the country. Over 250,000 women were to sign a petition in support of repeal at this stage. Josephine was invited to talk to the Royal Commission and told them clearly, 'Legislation hitherto... has been directed at one sex only. We insist it should be directed against both sexes.' She also felt it was about time that someone pointed out the class issue involved: 'Whereas it has been directed against the poor only we insist, and the working class men insist – that it should also apply to the rich profligate'.[43]

Josephine's campaign involved touring the country, giving all the nitty gritty details of the Acts and their implications, gaining the support of the working-class men and their families whose daughters, and often wives, were most vulnerable. She highlighted the misguided belief of those who had turned aside from such knowledge, those who preferred to believe 'such treatment of women will never be allowed

---

[42] *The Beth Book*, 1897
[43] quoted in Trevor Fisher, *Prostitution and the Victorians*, Sutton Publishing Limited, Stroud, 1997.p105/6

in England while the Queen lives'. It was time for some very straight talking. Of the prostitute herself she stated, 'She is my sister and you shall not use her so.'

In addition to campaigning for repeal Josephine and her supporters were also involved in conducting campaigns against election candidates who were known supporters of the CDA. When challenging General Sir Henry Storks in the Colchester elections of 1870 she, and indeed they, were to face public criticism, open heckling and terrifying mob violence because she dared to challenge the right of men's sexual needs to dominate women's lives. Josephine was undaunted; she faced similar criticism throughout her campaign, as did any who supported her, including her husband, and supportive journalists and politicians. As the journalist Eliza Lynn Linton commented:

> *No school has yet upheld [women] as sober, rational well-informed beings… with courage to attack dark moral problems, and to learn the truth of social conditions which they do not share, yet with purity survive knowledge.* [44]

Storks, by the way, suffered a humiliating defeat.

Josephine also tried to encourage young men to gain a more moral outlook on life. She lectured male students in the universities, encouraging them to learn to accept the need for sexual self-control and personal responsibility, and to join various purity associations and societies that had been set up by other men wanting to reform male sexual behaviour. The organisations spread throughout Europe, to America and even to South Africa.

Some men were totally bewildered to see the extent of the women's involvement in such a 'delicate matter'. A leading politician told Josephine:

> *We know how to manage any other opposition in the House or in the country, but this is very awkward for us — this revolt of the women. It is quite a new thing. What are we to do with such an opposition as this?* [45]

---

[44] *The Modern Revolt*
[45] Josephine Butler, *Personal Reminiscences of a Great Crusade*, 1898

In theory the answer was simple: put an end to the Acts.

By 1880 Josephine Butler had an army of women at her disposal, patrolling the streets, encouraging the protest amongst all classes of men and women. It may be hard for us to appreciate just how significant this campaign was at the time; we are so used to living in a world of multimedia and served by the internet, where no subject is totally hidden from view – if you know where to look – and huge campaigns and protests take place about something virtually every day of the week. It is important to remember that this prolonged and public exposure of sexual matters that Josephine and her supporters had undertaken was unprecedented at the time.

Josephine had travelled widely; newspapers and magazines carried the shocking information into every home, to all readers, and all classes. She had won support throughout the country, from women, from working men, trades organisations and, after a slow start, from both the Church of England and other religious groups. Over two and a half million signatures were collected; over nine hundred meetings took place. Sex was being opened up to the public in ways that could not have been imagined at the beginning of Victoria's reign. The double standard was very much in the spotlight; the sexual behaviour and the morality of men were being seriously questioned; the CDA were being publicly condemned – and women themselves, who had been supposed to know nothing about such matters, were leading the protest.

Josephine herself was very aware of the significance of this:

> Our open defiance of government and of that false public opinion which made it possible for governments to enact such a law has done what years, even centuries, of more silent and private work had never done, and could never do. It forced men to once more call things by their right names.[46]

However, in spite of all the growing support for repeal developing throughout the country, in spite of support from international organisations, in spite of repeatedly getting the Acts reviewed in Parliament, there was as yet no change in the law. There was still far

---

[46] Josephine Butler, *Social Purity,* 1879

too strong a contingent within Parliament, within both Houses, who had no intention of abandoning the CDA. So what more could be done?

We have already seen how important it was for women to have the support of powerful and influential men. One of Josephine's key supporters James Stansfeld, a great statesman, had been a vice president of the National Association (for the Repeal of the CDA). Although it took time, and ultimately cost him a Cabinet position, he desperately fought for change *within* Parliament. Josephine herself had been a tremendous campaigner, but she was not a politician and she did not know how to deal with Parliament. As a woman she of course lacked that form of political experience.

There is not time to do Stansfeld justice here, but he was a wise and effective politician, as well as being a good orator, capitalising on the now vocal public support for the campaign, and he was able to use military statistics to prove the CDA were not effective for the purpose for which they were introduced. In 1883 his proposition was accepted that the compulsory examination of suspected prostitutes should be stopped. It is true that change was now in the air – even in Parliament – but there was still talk of compulsory detentions for those prostitutes who were found to have venereal disease. Stansfeld had not been able to put an end to that. To actually get a full repeal of the CDA something else was needed, something that would put irreversible pressure on the government itself.

The trigger was to be provided by investigations into white slavery, where young English girls and women were being lured abroad with false promises of employment or marriage, and were then trapped into, and unable to escape from, a life of vice. In 1880 a man called Alfred Dyer followed a lead to Belgium and uncovered a horrific tale of the sexual exploitation of young English girls, some aged between only ten and fourteen. He was shocked to find that neither the English nor the Belgian authorities were prepared to either acknowledge it or show real concern. In fact, he actually believed they were often in collusion with the slavers themselves.

Before we discover what happened next it is necessary to go back a little. Ten years previously when Josephine Butler had attended the Royal Commission in 1870 (regarding the CDA) she had denounced the age of consent being then a mere *twelve* years old. Nowadays it is not uncommon to find girls reaching puberty while still at primary school, but in the Victorian period girls reached puberty much later, often around the age of sixteen or more. Josephine was horrified that the age of consent had been kept to a pre-pubescent level. She had told that Commission 'at present for the purposes of seduction, and seduction only, our laws declare every female child a woman at twelve years of age'. Married women had not been considered able to make financial decisions regarding property or be sufficiently responsible to vote – yet females were expected to take on sexual responsibility for themselves from the age of twelve, when as young girls they were far too young to even be able to understand the consequences of saying 'Yes'. Albeit reluctantly, the age of consent had been raised to thirteen in 1875, but it was still too low as far as Josephine and her supporters were concerned.

When Dyer's discoveries about the sexploitation of English girls in Belgium became known, Josephine Butler decided to make a stand. She obtained a thousand signatures in protest about the sexual traffic in children and again called for legal changes. When she handed her petition in she discovered that a new Select Committee was due to investigate the same matter. Its subsequent report led to a new Criminal Law Amendment Bill, which proposed the raising of the age of consent to sixteen, and would also empower the police to intervene in underage prostitution.

However, the Bill was not popular in Parliament. A compromise had been suggested of raising the age of consent to fourteen years, but some of the lords were still not satisfied. It was reported in Hansard that Lord Cranmore and Browne said:

> *He believed that there were very few of their Lordships who had not, when young, been guilty of immorality. He hoped they would pause before passing a clause within the range of which their sons might come.*[47]

That last sentence said it all. Others in the Commons were equally concerned that 'it would make criminals out of the passions of mankind', and fully supported the use of young girls in brothels. There was also an overriding fear that if the law changed, underage girls

---

[47] Hansard, (House of Lords) 1884, CCLXXXIX, 1219

would continue to be willing to have sex but then blackmail the men afterwards. It was similar to the fears that influenced the passing of the Bastardy Clause in 1834. Protecting their personal property and rights, rather than having concern for less fortunate people, as well as the need to meet their own sexual requirements were still primary considerations for a significant number of Members of Parliament.

Such views were not just confined to English politics. In both Europe and America, where Josephine Butler had organisational connections, women fought against legalised prostitution and against low ages of consent. Shocking though it now sounds, in the late nineteenth century *nine* American States had the age of consent as low as *ten*; the record seems to have been set by Delaware, whose governors believed that girls of *seven* were old enough to take on sexual knowledge and responsibility. There were even plans in some States to actually reduce the age of consent – plans that resulted in fierce opposition from American women, as well as encouraging their own political aspirations. In one of her novels, which was written in support of the American women's campaign, Helen Gardener included this conversation between a daughter and her mother:

> '*Don't you believe that if all laws or bills had to be openly discussed before, and with, women it would be better, Mamma, I do.*'
> '*Such Bills as that would never be dreamed of by men if they knew they must pass the discussion of a pure girl or mother – never!*'[48]

In this country too more people were beginning to realise that giving women suffrage would, in time, affect many of our laws, and was therefore another key reason for the delay in granting it. Regarding the parliamentary reluctance to raise the age of consent to sixteen, the editor of the *Pall Mall Gazette,* W.J. Stead, commented:

> *A House of Commons in which women were represented would not display such indifference to a question which really is one of life or death to immense numbers of young girls.*[49]

---

[48] *Pray You, Sir, Whose Daughter?*
[49] *Pall Mall Gazette*, 23rd May, 1885

Two years after the Criminal Law Amendment Bill was introduced it was still being blocked in Parliament, with a variety of delaying tactics being employed in the process – interparty conflicts, calls for quorum, general filibustering and timewasting, all had their part to play.

So, using his own editorial position, W.J. Stead decided to undertake some investigative journalism with a difference. He planned to purchase a young virgin girl, get her set up in a brothel and then send her abroad. Of course he had no intention of letting her be used for sex, but he wanted to make a point. The subsequent articles were to be headed 'The Maiden Tribute of Modern Babylon' (6th July 1885) and, two days beforehand, in an advance warning guaranteed to send sales rocketing, he advised his readers:

> *All those who are squeamish, and all those who are prudish, and all those who prefer to live in a fool's paradise of imaginary innocence and purity, selfishly oblivious of the horrible realities which torment those whose lives are passed in the London inferno, will do well not to read the Pall Mall Gazette on Monday and the following days.*

The sexual exploitation of women, particularly young girls, was suddenly a national scandal discussed over the breakfast table of many households. Stead was to be slated for his insistence on printing such obscene content in a daily newspaper, but he was not to be put off. Other publications were prepared to give passive support. The *Englishman's Review* stated that 'it was naturally silent – but far from indifferent'. Stead kept up the pressure by threatening to expose upper-class and royal frequenters of brothels, he exposed how the police had been involved in the white slave trade and alongside the work of those, like Josephine, who were trying to raise the moral standards of the country, and the nation followed his trail. The only way to get him to stop, as far as Parliament was concerned, was to pass the Criminal Law Amendment Act, which happened in 1885, raising the legal age of consent to sixteen.

With all the activity regarding the age of consent, and the focus on young prostitution, the repeal of the CDA had been pushed a little to one side, but public opinion had been sufficiently roused and the work continued. By 1886 the politician Stansfeld was personally in a strong position in Parliament and had gained sufficient influence there to at last push through a motion for the repeal of the Acts. It had taken a combination of strong personalities, devotion to a cause, and a determination to succeed no matter how long it took. Delicate matters had been taken out of the shadows and exposed in raw sunlight, but the subject of sex did not end there.

Although it has been necessary to digress a little from the main discussion of sex within marriage, the obvious connections between the CDA, married women and prostitution have been clearly cited. It had taken some major political dynamite to expose the darker side of men's use and exploitation of women, but there still had been no direct legal challenge to a husband's sexual rights within marriage. That was still written into the marriage contract and was to remain very much a part of the game. There were, however, to be other consequences for women as a direct result of the public focus on sexual matters in general, and the morality of men in particular. It was somewhat inevitable that there would be a bit of a backlash.

In 1886 Lady Colin Campbell charged her husband with adultery and cruelty, and sued for divorce. During the course of the hearing it transpired that her husband had suffered from syphilis before the wedding and it was necessary to postpone the consummation of the marriage because of the state of his diseased parts. A few months after the wedding she was shown part of a letter, from his doctor, that recommended consummation should then take place because it would help to improve her husband's health. She complied and so caught the venereal disease. Although it took time, and she was not granted a divorce, because neither she nor her husband had adultery charges proven against them, Lady Campbell was able to get a legal separation on the grounds of cruelty, and the specified cruelty being that her husband had knowingly infected her with the contagious disease. Thanks to the scandal of the Contagious Diseases Acts and their ultimate repeal, women had found another way out of an abusive marriage.

Another consequence of the CDA and 'The Maiden Tribute' concerned education. Believing that the conditioned innocence and ignorance in matters of sex had led to problems for women, both as individuals and within society, greater emphasis was to be placed on sex education for girls and women. Rather than leaving this to the practical elucidation of a husband on his honeymoon, Elizabeth

Wolstenholme Elmy and her husband wrote books and articles on the subject including *The Human Flower* (1894) and *Baby Buds* (1895); others began to follow suit.

The purity associations continued their work. Members of the Social Purity Alliance and the Ladies Association believed in bringing up their own sons to respect women and trained them for chastity. The Moral Reform Union was started by a group of women who wanted to study all subjects related to the moral welfare of young people, and they wrote, published, sold and distributed literature on the subject too. In time more girls would learn about the subject of sex and its relationship to marriage, and moral education would be extended to members of the male sex.

In addition to helping protect young girls through education, moves were also made to monitor, and hopefully prevent, the known disrespectful behaviour of officers towards women in other situations. The National Vigilance Association, for example, extended their work so that in time women warders would be employed at police stations and at courts so that women would no longer suffer from the brutality or even vice that male officials had exhibited there.

Women writers themselves continued to expose the events of the past years, covering the Contagious Diseases Acts and the changes in the age of consent, and they drew renewed attention to the horrors of venereal disease and the risks for women and their children. The author Sarah Grand was one of the New Women writers at the end of the century who was most outspoken on the subject, and she had good reason to be. She discovered that her own husband, Surgeon-Major David McFall, was one of the allocated Lock Hospital doctors who were responsible for such brutal examinations of women.

Two of her novels, *The Heavenly Twins* (1893) and *The Beth Book* (1897), were concerned with venereal disease. In *The Heavenly Twins* two sisters were affected by syphilis; the first, Evadne, discovered her husband had contracted it, gaining the knowledge fortunately before she went on her honeymoon, and she refused to consummate the marriage. Later she tried to warn her sister, Edith, who made a similar marriage, and then had to watch as Edith became increasingly affected by the disease – going mad and eventually dying from it. Her infant child was similarly afflicted.

For Sarah Grand herself finding out that her husband was a lock doctor was shocking, and she did not approve of his activities; she knew that he did not hold any particular respect for women, and this is reflected in how she wrote about the doctor in *The Beth Book*. When she first heard about her husband's additional occupation Beth reacted strongly:

> *Disapprove!... The whole thing makes me sick. I ought to have been told before I married him. I would never have spoken to a man in such a position had I known.*

When Beth confronted her husband, in the novel, he tried to justify it and she raised all the questions about women being unprotected from the dangers of venereal disease, and the fact that the men received no treatment, let alone incarceration. She also raised one question with him, as a doctor, that I have not come across elsewhere:

> *And why, if sanitation is your business, do you take no radical measures with regard to this horrible disease? Why do you not have it reported, never mind who gets it, as scarlet fever, and other diseases – all less disastrous to the general health of the community – are reported?*

It had not been in the men's own interests to have their infections publicly recorded, although for women it was a completely different matter, as we have already seen.

The CDA may have been repealed over ten years previously, but it was necessary that they should not be forgotten, nor what they represented as far as women were concerned. Other women writers too wrote in detail about syphilis – in the husband, and transmitted to the wife, with the latter occasionally refusing consummation, or continuance of sexual relations, or in the case of *The Superfluous Woman* (Emma Brooke, 1894) even going to the extent of the wife deliberately inducing a miscarriage, and then committing suicide after the murder of one of her syphilitic children by the other, in order to prevent the diseased lineage of one family from continuance. When such novels were critically reviewed at the time their revelations were considered 'distasteful', but they remained very popular with the readers.

Some years later the subject of venereal disease was also raised in a non-fictional book by Christabel Pankhurst, the suffragette daughter of Emmeline Pankhurst, who again linked it to the need for women's suffrage. It was simply called *The Great Scourge, and How to End it* (1913).

Although it had been feared by some men that the women who had attacked the double standard would reject marriage altogether, and even become as sexually frivolous and promiscuous as their own sex had been, there is little evidence that was so. When Grant Allen brought out his own scandalous book *The Woman Who Did* (1895) there was a swift response in kind, by women – *The Woman Who Didn't* (Victoria Cross, 1895), *The Woman Who Wouldn't* (Lucas Cleeve, 1895)[50] and so on. In fact, *The Woman Who Wouldn't* rejected sex completely – not only keeping herself pure for her future husband, but insisting on keeping herself pure for him afterwards by having nothing to do with sex whatsoever.

At the start of the Victorian period women had been considered pure if they knew or affected to know nothing of delicate subjects, if they were ignorant of vice or immorality. By the end of the period women knew of such matters and rose above it. There had been a direct challenge to traditional notions of male sexuality and large numbers of men themselves had been convinced by it, and there had been a significant change in the expectations of women regarding the men that they married. Rather than being convinced that a virtuous good woman would be capable of reforming even the most disreputable, dissipated man, women were learning to accept that they did have a choice, that they did not have to accept men on those terms, that they did indeed deserve something better:

> *Husbands… forget that the man who comes back to the embraces of his wife is quite as loathsome as she could be, under the same circumstances in his. The rights that women want and which will someday be theirs are the rights to demand purity in their husbands as well as themselves.* [51]

> *Did it never occur to you that a woman has her ideal as well as a man… that she loves purity and truth and loathes degradation and vice more than a man does?*[52]

---

[50] A pen name for Adeline Kingscote.
[51] Florence Marryat, *The Nobler Sex*
[52] Sarah Grand, *The Heavenly Twins*, 1893

In a similar vein Emma Hewitt summarised the situation:

> *The time has come when women should demand that the men they marry, the men their daughters marry, the men whom they receive in their home shall be free of taint.*[53]

Looking back to the beginnings of the CDA, *The 8th Annual Report* of the National Ladies Association held in 1877 had acknowledged that:

> *The Acts were but the expression of the spirit of the time about women; they were no miraculous growth, they had not sprung out of nothing, they could not have been planned or carried or maintained if there had not been amongst us, amongst women as well as men, an acceptance of the doctrine that women are inferior to men, that men's interests are paramount and that, where necessary, women must be entirely sacrificed to those interests; that women are unfit and unentitled to regulate their own lives which must be ordered by men, in the interests of men.*[54]

It is a valid comment. Women had been conditioned to accept such practice. After years of protest and campaigning, attitudes towards man's sexual nature were changing, not only amongst the women themselves but throughout society. Approximately twenty years after their introduction, the CDA were no longer acceptable as laws in this country. There was, sadly, to be no change in the expectation that a husband would have sexual ownership of his wife, and no recognition of the existence of rape in marriage[55] and it would still be easier for a man to get a divorce, citing the single excuse of adultery in his wife.

It is worth noting one final benefit of all the attention focused by the CDA and 'The Maiden Tribute': people finally began to look more

---

[53] Emma Hewitt, *Woman's Duty*, 1899

[54] quoted by Susan Kingsley Kent, *Sex and Suffrage, 1860-1914,* p77

[55] That was not to change in England until 1991. Although many countries have altered their laws in the same way, some still uphold the traditional ways. After the recent publicity regarding widespread rape in India, and the international condemnation of its acceptance (Spring 2015), I was very disturbed to hear the Indian Home Minister still justifying marital rape by saying marriage is a sacred bond. We used to use that argument here.

critically at the morality of the politicians and law–makers themselves. After the successful repeal of the CDA and the raising of the age of consent, the Methodist preacher Hugh Price-Hughes held a public meeting and called for a purity crusade. He said:

> *They must begin by cleansing the House of Commons. They should lay it down as a great political principle, that no man who believes that the daughters of the poor must be sacrificed to the lusts of his own sex is fit to make the laws of England… They should raise the purity of public opinion until it becomes impossible for an immoral man to occupy any public position in this country, from the village police station to the throne of England.*[56]

Times were indeed changing.

---

[56] *The Sentinel*, February 1886, p20-1

Chapter Nine
Reframing the Question

When Queen Victoria came to the throne marriage in England was a well-established institution, supported by the State, the Church and the laws of both. Those who were to become a future part of that institution had well-defined roles to learn and in the process were to develop clear expectations of what they might hope to gain by becoming a member of it. If we continue to look at marriage as a game, the players had to learn the parts they were to play. Girls were conditioned to take on a submissive role within marriage and were led to believe that all their future needs and interests would be taken care of by the husband they 'chose'. They learned to accept their duty as paramount and to take pride and even pleasure in performing it. They learned to accept the limitations such a position could enforce on them – including the loss of status as an independent individual – and they were destined to become an active part of that well-established system themselves, by passing on those values and beliefs when they in turn trained their own children to accept for themselves the roles their parents had performed.

It had been a self-perpetuating system. Yet when I had been studying the long eighteenth century for my first book I became aware that the whole situation was not quite as simple and as straightforward as it had first appeared. There were flaws in the process. Throughout that period women writers had not only drawn attention to the unpleasant situations they faced within marriage but were to set individual challenges to the power holders and the accepted customs of the day. They pointed to the false nature of the assumptions they had been led to believe and accept, and the self-interest of those who had voiced them. But these were like random shouts in a crowd and those who were in control of the game had taken little, if any, notice of them. The individual protests were not part of any mass movement working towards any general or specific change in the lives of women and therefore were all too easily ignored.

Some years ago my son made a significant comment about the work of these women writers. He is very much a scientist in his view of the world and he said, 'It's all to do with critical mass. You have to reach a certain mass before something happens.' The work of the women writers certainly did contribute to that 'mass', but you also needed certain conditions for that 'something' to take place. When Caroline Norton fought back against the mean tricks of her husband regarding the children, she was not the first woman to do so. However, she was the first to be so empowered by her emotions, and so enabled by her own capabilities and the connections and abilities of those around her, to be able to act as the catalyst for change in an environment that was beginning to be receptive to those changes. She may well have received much criticism for being so scandalous, so unwomanly, so *unfeminine* in her actions – but perhaps that *was* what it took to make the difference. A woman who was prepared to stand up for herself in public, and fight for what she believed in, regardless of the personal criticism, slander and scandal she would inevitably face. By challenging the rules of marriage, by showing that the law did not deliver justice in all situations regarding child custody, and later married women's property, Caroline Norton helped to change the rules regarding those who had separated from their marriages, and thereby helped towards changing the definition of what the institution of marriage actually meant, and what it was to become.

For a start some of the fundamental myths regarding marriage had been openly challenged, debated and proven to be wrong. Men had shown that they did not truly protect women, that laws that purported to be for women's protection were actually based on men's own interests, and that women did not always want major decisions of their lives to be made for them, for they were not the submissive, feeble, weak-minded creatures belonging to an inferior sex that they had been considered to be. They no longer wished to be 'protected' or confined, or be told that they preferred it that way. Olive Schreiner asked:

If the bird does like its cage, and does like its sugar and will not leave it, why keep the door so very carefully shut? Why not open it, only a little? Do they know there is many a bird will not break its wings against the bars, but would fly if the doors were open?[1]

Over time women had shown themselves capable of being rational creatures who were capable of acting responsibly; wives who were capable of being good mothers, able to control their own financial affairs, and take a more active role within marriage and life itself. They had also shown that there *were* certain boundaries as to what was acceptable *to women* within marriage, and when those boundaries were breached marriage could not and should not continue. As Emma Brooke wrote:

You think that marriage is an eternal thing that cannot be broken; but that is a mistake. We live in the nineteenth century and not in the middle ages.[2]

Male politicians, husbands and men in general would no longer be the only ones with a voice in marriage.

It is possible to look at these changes and consider that within such a relatively short period of time, from 1837, with the Infant Custody Act, to 1882, with the Married Women's Property Act, a major revolution had taken place. Over two generations a married woman had gained rights that she would never have considered possible at the outset. And it had all happened so quickly, hadn't it? However, I think that it is inappropriate to consider the events of the period in this way. It is so easy to look back at history in retrospect, with the benefit of hindsight, and condense half a century into a paragraph, but we forget that during this period of change real women lived and experienced their whole lives. They struggled with their day-to-day situations, they had to cope with the endless frustrations of their experiences, and to face up to the sheer extent and hardship of their task to make those changes really happen. These changes did *not* happen overnight.

Many women were to devote years to their own particular cause

---

[1] *The Story of an African Farm*
[2] *A Superfluous Woman*

and yet not see any real result from their own personal efforts. Caroline Norton's personal fight for custody may have taken only three years to get the law changed, but it took nearly twenty years of campaigning to repeal the Contagious Diseases Acts, and around twenty-five years for married women to gain full property rights. At one point Margaret Oliphant was feeling very pessimistic.

> *As men seem to think that the laws which bear hardly on women are the bulwarks of their own existence, it is very unlikely that they will ever be entirely amended.*[3]

Women writers had been flagging up the problems since at least 1700, but it was not until nearly two hundred years later that you could say things had really changed for married women.

So why *did* it take so long to achieve? There are many factors to consider here. The most obvious is conditioning – the way children were raised to accept their future role in life according to a very set pattern that would not influence only their own personal choices and behaviour, but would also be likely to affect their attitudes towards any around them who dared to be different. As Eliza Lynn Linton put it:

> *I think they may always count upon a large weight of spotless sisters who can never be stirred up to this hatred of men, but who naturally turn to them and love them and cling about them, like the parasites they are.*[4]

Even if a young girl or woman did feel any unfairness in her life, she had been trained not to complain for fear of being criticised as unwomanly or for failing to do her duty – a criticism that could be levied by members of either sex. It was not just a question of being restricted by 'marital gaolers' as Eliza Lynn Linton had described in her article[5]; women could effectively act as their own wardens. In the words of Mona Caird, 'to make a prisoner his own warder is surely no light stroke of genius'.[6] A more experienced woman could warn a restless young woman:

---

[3] 'Grievances of Women'

[4] *Ourselves*

[5] 'Marriage Gaolers', 1856

[6] Mona Caird, *Daughters of Danaeus*, 1894

*If you don't swim [in the mainstream] you will only tire yourself,
trying to swim against a tide that is too strong for you and nothing
good will come of it. Nothing at all.*[7]

Other writers made similar observations:

*I can understand how women become conventional... it is useless
to act on their own initiative... It annoys everybody frightfully and
accomplishes nothing.*[8]

There was no point, then, in self-assertion. Women were powerless;
they had no civil rights – but it was still very much their concern, as
reflected in this conversation between an aunt and her niece:

*'I am only going to suggest that it is a waste of time – your valuable
time... to make up your mind upon so exceedingly complicated a
subject as this one... for the simple reason that you are unable to assist
its settlement one way or the other. That's all.'*

*'But, Auntie, how can you say I am unable to assist its
settlement? I can't make the State do this or that – I couldn't even
cause my father to support a Bill – but I, in my own person, must
read and think about it, because it is a question that only girls can
settle ultimately.'*[9]

Any potentially rebellious female could easily lose men's respect
and regard (i.e. from those who appreciated a submissive female)
and, more significantly, she could suffer in additional ways if she
happened to be dependent upon those particular men. It was
therefore in her own immediate interest to conform. Max O'Rell
had also noted:

*It is true that since the passing of the Married Women's Property Act
she has a right to possess property; but if she sets the least store by her
peace of mind and the tranquility of the household she quickly gives
up to her husband the rights he already considers his own... You see,*

---

[7]   Helen Gardener, *Pray You, Sir, Whose Daughter*
[8]   Mona Caird, *Daughters of Danaeus*
[9]   Menie Muriel Dowie, *Gallia*, 1895

he takes a wife for better, for worse, and if he is no fool, he manages that it shall be for the better. It is very simple.[10]

As a woman gained a home of her own, with the additional responsibilities of a family it is true that her opportunities for rebellion became severely limited. There was just too much to do – keeping the house in good order; attending to the needs and demands of a husband, a growing family; not to mention keeping an eye on any servants in the house. There could be little time for complaint, let alone active protest. A woman just had to get on with it. Once again the voice of experience could note:

> *...how rigid most people become in a few years, and how the personality grows wooden, in the daily repetition of the same actions and the same ideas... Daily surroundings were not merely pleasant or unpleasant facts, otherwise of no importance; they were the very material and substance of character, the push and the impetus, or the let and hindrance; the guardians or assassins of the soul.*[11]

And even the young could perceive the change: 'I can't understand parents; they must have been young themselves once. Yet they seem to have forgotten all about it.'[12]

Being able to recognise what was happening in the conditioning process and starting to do something about it was part of the process of change. Women also had to ask themselves the question, 'Have these men marred my life or have I done it for myself?'[13] From the early eighteenth century onwards, individual women writers had called on their sex to take more responsibility for themselves, in their novels, their treatises, and in their journalism, to 'rise up', to work together and strive towards a more equitable social system. They could start by looking at their own lives, and they could pay more attention to the rearing and education of their own children. It was their responsibility to help children take on new roles in a developing world; they needed to help promote the girls' abilities

---

[10] *Les Filles de John Bull*

[11] Mona Caird, *Daughters of Danaeus*

[12] Ibid

[13] Florence Marryat, *The Nobler Sex*

and talents as well as the boys'; they also needed to teach boys to respect girls and to value them.

Unfortunately, when women did choose to challenge the rules, they were faced by men who had not only been conditioned themselves into believing they were superior, and therefore had greater rights and predominance in society, but were only too happy, in general, to accept it. It was not difficult for men to convince themselves that they took adequate care of the needs and interests of their women, that married women, for example, had no need of individual property, social or civil rights. Each of the challenges I have considered so far, namely child custody, personal, physical and sexual property within marriage, encroached on the privileges a man expected he would receive by taking a wife. Before he had the benefit of personal experience, Mandell Creighton wrote in a letter, dated 1866, 'Of course at a certain age, when you have a house and so on, you get a wife as a part of its furniture, and find her a very comfortable institution.'[14] In due course he was to become a bishop and, in her turn, his wife was to become an active suffragist!

Women had struck at the very heart of society and the very superiority and dominance of man. They had attacked man's self-image as well as his sexuality. It is hardly surprising that the challenge generated such a heated response. Marie Corelli described the difference between men and women: 'A man in this world does as he likes – a woman does as she must. The two things are totally different'.[15]

In her *Letter to the Queen* Caroline Norton wrote, 'Every man seems to dread that he is surrendering some portion of his rights over women.' Whether you consider this to be purely a matter of male conditioning or take the view that men in general at the time were rather selfish characters, or that some combination of the two was more likely, one has to acknowledge the possibility that an element of selfishness was involved, because giving men alone such privileges had to be at the expense of women.

The novelist Charlotte Bronte wrote to a friend, in May 1854:

Man is indeed an amazing piece of mechanism when you see, so to speak, the full weakness of what he calls his strength. There is not a

---

14 quoted in J.A. Banks and Olive Banks, *Feminism and Family Planning in Victorian England*, Liverpool University Press, 1964, p74

15 Marie Corelli, *Murder of Delicia*, 1896

female child above the age of eight but might rebuke him for spoilt petulance of his wilful nonsense.[16]

Over thirty years later the editor of the *Westminster Review* publicly proclaimed:

> *The most powerful reason for change has not been sufficiently laid before the public – the reason namely, that all our legislation in time past has been directed entirely to the advancement and benefit of man and that in its progress woman has been generally entirely neglected and frequently grievously injured… Little or nothing has been done to protect women and especially wives from the selfishness of that class whose interests most directly conflict with their own.*[17]

Similarly, in 1910 the young Liberal politician and lecturer (later professor in law) at Liverpool University, Walter Lyon Blease, was to state:

> *Not a single disability has ever been removed on the initiative of men. Very few have been removed except in the face of hostility of men. Every step in advance… and in marital relations, has been the result of the exertions of women… Every woman who has worked for her sex during the last fifty years has found among men, here and there, spontaneous help; generally, want of sympathy and indifference; and not seldom blind, unreasoning, and clamant hostility.*[18]

As well as a threat to the stability of society, challenging the male supremacy was seen as gross impertinence: 'For as usual by the aid of man's logic he deemed himself the injured party and she the injuring'.[19] Time and again women writers were to comment on the way men worked together taking a rigid stand against the women's active claims, often condemning them collectively with such derogatory comments as 'the shrieking sisterhood'.[20]

---

16 quoted in Clement King Shorter, *The Brontes and their Circle*, 1914
17 John Chapman, '*The Law in Relation to Women*'
18 Walter Lyon Blease, *The Emancipation of English Women*, 1910
19 Marie Corelli, *Murder of Delicia*
20 This term was used by Eliza Lynn Linton in an article of the same name in 1870, but she had been referring to its use elsewhere. The American novelist Nathaniel Hawthorne referred to 'that d—d mob of scribbling women'.

In her article 'The Grievances of Women' published in 1880 Margaret Oliphant admitted:

> *To be met with an insolent laugh, a storm of ridiculous epithets, and that coarse superiority of sex, which a great many men think it not unbecoming to exhibit to women, is a mode of treatment which affects our temper, and those nerves which the harshest critic is condescendingly willing to allow as a female property.*

However, she acknowledged that progress was being made:

> *The dash in our faces of such an epithet as that of the 'shrieking sisterhood', for example, more effectual than any dead cat or rotten egg, would have driven us back, whatever our wrongs had been, into indignant and ashamed silence. But it is well that there are some bolder spirits who have encountered the storm, and made it apparent not only that rotten eggs are no arguments, but that the throwing of them is not a noble office.*[21]

It is hard to avoid reaching the personal conclusion that some, though not all, of the male members of Victorian society were like spoilt schoolboys, and that their attitudes towards women had not changed since the days when they first discovered their superior position as members of the male sex. I do not think it going too far to say that, for some at least, they were frightened they were going to lose it all. John Stuart Mill had said that the:

> *...disabilities [of wives] are only clung to in order to maintain their subordination in domestic life because the generality of the male sex cannot yet tolerate the idea of living with an equal.*[22]

On matters of property, personal control and financial privilege, on matters of child rearing and custody, and regarding his authority and control over his wife, a man's home was *his* castle and the law was there to make sure it stayed that way.

An equally good, and much used, justification was the ability to

---

[21] Ibid
[22] *The Subjection of Women*

resort, albeit selectively, to such authoritative texts as the Bible; at times Church and law went hand in hand, with judges referring to the Bible, and members of the Church referring to the law. There have been many examples, both in this book and in my first, which showed how women were beginning to question and criticise the religious dogma that they had been conditioned to accept and believe. Whether St Paul was responsible for some very misogynistic comments within the New Testament, or not, he has certainly been given the blame for it. Women who accepted their duty of submission looked to the afterlife for a better world certainly, but there were plenty who thought it would be a very interesting time when it finally arrived. As Marie Corelli said, 'Good heavens what a heavy score we women shall run up against men at the Day of Judgement'.[23]

It is true there were some changes in the Church, as it adapted to reform movements of its own, and occasionally individuals within it would address the issue of women in a way that went against any conditioning they may have received earlier themselves. Samuel Wilberforce, son of William Wilberforce who made such a significant contribution to the abolition of slavery, became the Bishop of Winchester in 1870. Not only did he, as bishop, publicly agree that men had conveniently disregarded the message in the Bible for themselves, but he also talked about their fate on judgement day, somewhat unusually from the women's perspective. He knew that men had been against the advancement of women and warned:

As they [the women] advance they will become juster judges: they will sit in judgment on you, they will weigh you in the balance and you will be found wanting. They will remember that the only true superiority is moral superiority, and when they look for it in you they will not find it. And remember, my friends, that you cannot stop them. This movement is progress and it cannot be stopped.[24]

Naturally not everyone was to agree. As people questioned religious belief more, and the authorities on which it was based, doctrine that held

---

[23] *Murder of Delicia*
[24] Quoted in Harry Quilter, *Is Marriage a Failure?*

women firmly in place did not have quite the same weight. However, there were other developing areas of learning that could be sourced for apparently relevant justifications that kept male dominance firmly in place, in scientific thought and medical advances, for example. New knowledge, especially in areas where women had little strength, could easily fill any gap provided by the dilution of religious justification for maintaining the status quo. I do not intend to go into much detail here, but, for example, discovering that women had smaller brains provided a wonderful opportunity for trying to limit the possible choices a woman might seek to make. She was not thought to be capable of them. Women were also told being involved in intellectual pursuits might interfere with their reproductive functions and so, for example, Victorian mothers should be very wary of allowing their teenage daughters to engage in any physical or serious activity (especially of an intellectual nature) during menstruation.

In 1867 Dr Seymour Heyden described the control the medical profession had over the opportunities and interests of women:

> We are in fact the stronger and they the weaker. They are obliged to believe all we tell them... we therefore may be said to have them at our mercy.[25]

Over time, though, a gradually increasing number of key parliamentary men had become alert to the problems women, and particularly married women, faced and had started to become more critical of the traditional views that they, as men, had previously learned to accept, and wanted to do something in a more practical way to help. Sometimes these men had been convinced by experiences within their own lives. Members of Parliament like Serjeant Talfourd, who was prepared to help Caroline Norton, because he saw for himself how badly treated women had been in an earlier child custody case; John Stuart Mill because he saw the body of a poor little suffocated infant and worried about the woman who led such a tragic and unequal life that led to its death; and James Stansfeld because he had seen how women were banned from speaking at a slavery convention and realised how little their views counted in a male-dominated society that liked to believe it cared for women.

---

[25] *Medical Press and Circular,* April 1867

Before Victoria had even come to the throne William Thompson and Anna Wheeler had referred to man's 'vile cloak of hypocrisy' and warned men to 'cast aside the tattered cloak before it leaves you naked and exposed'.[26] We have seen the effect of the shocking revelations in earlier chapters, but there were plenty of powerful men who chose to turn their backs to the slowly oncoming tide.

Rosina Bulwer Lytton and Caroline Norton had ample opportunity to experience the negative behaviour directly exhibited by their husbands (both Members of Parliament) who strenuously took this reactionary position, and they were also witnesses to the conversation and general attitude of members of the aristocracy, including other Members of Parliament, in a variety of social settings. As a writer Rosina was frequently criticised by editors and literary critics alike for overuse of her personal knowledge and experience, and for making some very obvious criticisms of particular members of the aristocracy – even if she did change their names. In her novel *The World and His Wife* (1858), published just one year after the Matrimonial Causes Act (the Divorce Act) was passed, Rosina portrayed some characters and conversations that she had obviously encountered in real life. One stated:

> *A man's public character being in fact the brass plate and letter box on his front door, as long as they are kept bright and polished for all passers by to see, no one has any business to enquire, much less to meddle with, what may be passing within.*

In this particular work Rosina also gave a significant and highly detailed example of the type of discussions that she herself would have been aware of regarding married women's property issues, prior to the actual passing of the act. A fictional character, Lord Potarjis, began:

> *It's quite alarming the way in which all the women in England are taking Lord Lyncius' Bill au pied de la lettre[27], and fancying that all of us who have voted for it, as a party job, really care one straw for the*

---

[26] *Appeal of One Half of the Human Race*, 1825
[27] literally

cause that the Bill affects to advocate! They cannot see the difference between voting with one's friend or one's party – stopping the gap of a particular cry, and all that sort of thing; and I am really overwhelmed – positively overwhelmed by the avalanche of letters every morning's post brings me from the rebellious Griseldas [i.e. women] who have the folly to take that Bill for a new Gospel, and to suppose that each of their separate Apocalypses is of the utmost importance to its propagation, as if anyone cared how the deuce they were used, and after all, confound it, a man has a right to use his wife as he pleases; as this Bill, if it is ever jobbed through Parliament, will plainly prove to them, by tightening their girths instead of loosening them.[28]

It is probably unnecessary to do more than pick out the salient points here, relevant to the passing of the Matrimonial Causes Act. Caroline Norton was fighting for separated women's rights to keep their own property, and at the time Barbara Leigh Smith had been trying to get those rights extended to cover all married women. Women believed that politicians would be prepared to take up the fundamental issues involved, not just the surface ones (hence the avalanche of letters), but the politicians continued to support what they considered to be the fundamental rights of a husband. The basic principles that a woman was merely the possession of her husband and that the way she was treated was solely his affair were to remain untouched by the changes in the law for many years, and those who remained married would feel more tightly bound to their situations. (You may remember that this Act confirmed that it would be easier for a man to get a divorce from his wife than vice versa.)

Politics could be a highly complex affair. Politicians themselves had to be careful regarding what they voted for – it could be a matter of party politics or keeping in with someone because you hoped to gain political favour, or wished to give it, or it could be connected to a business matter altogether outside parliamentary affairs. Sometimes you had to please party politicians on one particular issue in order to gain their support somewhere else, on a completely unrelated matter. Also debates in favour of women's property or questions of custody were *not* generally taken up as party issues, so there was no force or

---

[28] Rosina Bulwer Lytton, *The World and His Wife*, 1858

power behind them, although Liberal politicians were more likely to look favourably upon them. Women needed real friends in Parliament who would continue to push for the necessary changes in legislation regardless as to which party was in power, and regardless of how it would affect their own political fortunes; even then politicians who supported one aspect of women's reforms did not necessarily support all of them.

Looking back as outsiders, it can be quite difficult to analyse why some politicians seemed to change sides, even in between different Acts that dealt with the same women's issues. Rosina's work is again useful here for its pointers to parliamentary practice – not a subject usually raised in women's literature at the time. Once again an MP is talking:

> *It don't do to mix oneself up in private affairs, and be made the involuntary repository of other men's peccadillos, kickings, bitings, monetary meanness and pecuniary defalcation towards their wives, not only on account of the lex talionis[29] but because when one is making use either of a fellow's brains or capital, or want of principle, or dining, voting and politically coalescing with him, it would never do to commit oneself by animadverting on his private conduct, which after all is nobody's affair.[30]*

It was the old schoolboy loyalty again, and leads me on to another reason why legal changes for women took so long to achieve. As we have seen when Caroline Norton realised that it would be necessary to see about changing the laws for women herself, she discovered she had a lot to learn. As a woman she knew little of parliamentary affairs or procedure and was not even allowed into any of the debates. It is true that women were allowed to view the proceedings – from a special little gallery up in 'the Gods' of the Houses of Parliament, where a fine grille prevented one from seeing properly, and was sufficiently far up to make even hearing difficult. Women were not supposed to be a party to what was going on.

So Caroline, and others in their turn, had to rely totally on male

---

[29] law of retribution
[30] *The World and His Wife*

supporters who would take up the issues as Private Members' Bills. However, when one of these radical bills was brought in for discussion there were many ways to sabotage its progress, within Parliament, and this was something that women were to encounter repeatedly with all their proposed changes, and they could do nothing about it. Parliamentary affairs were beyond their control once the doors were shut firmly upon them.

Using tactics we are all too familiar with nowadays from television and radio coverage in Parliament, those Victorian MPs who wished to prevent the smooth passage of reform bills had a range of tricks to choose from. There were the obvious ones like to attack the speaker in a personal way, to mock or make fun of those who supported the women's cause or to burst out laughing when such matters were even raised. It must have been a great boon that Queen Victoria herself was not a great supporter of women's rights; there would be no additional pressure from her. When Lady Amberley dared to give a lecture in favour of women's suffrage in 1870, the Queen had written:

> *The Queen is most anxious to enlist everyone who can speak or write to join in checking this mad, wicked folly of 'Women's rights' with all its attendant horrors, on which her poor feeble sex is bent, forgetting every womanly sense of feeling and propriety. It is a subject which makes the Queen so furious she cannot contain herself. Lady (Amberley) should get a good whipping.[31]*

Within parliamentary sessions there was also the issue of quorum. If insufficient members turned up to a scheduled debate, the issue would have to be dropped. Valuable time could be taken up by calling for a count, and then checking – time that could be usefully taken up with the debate itself. Of course if the requisite number of members failed to be present anyway, the allocated time would be lost. After the 1870 Property Act had been passed, moves were made by the women again to try to extend its terms, and a new Bill was before Parliament in 1873 to that effect. On six occasions a quorum failed to be reached; there was not enough interest in it at those points in time.

I also discovered a wonderful invention that some Victorian

---

[31] Letter to Sir Theodore Martin, quoted in his book, *Queen Victoria As I Knew Her*, 1901

politician somewhere had invented to block the moves that did not meet with his own approval. It is known as 'the half-past twelve rule'. Any Private Member who had been given a slot to discuss his proposed bill could lose his opportunity, if it was known in advance that there would be opposition to it and the clock reached half-past midnight before he took his turn. On a scheduled day/evening session any MP seriously opposed to the new proposals could just keep talking about whatever issue was on beforehand, and watch the clock go round. In addition to the use of the quorum issue on the 1873 Property Bill, the half-past twelve rule was applied *fifteen* times *on the same Bill*. Similar delaying tactics could be used to 'run out of time', for example, at the end of a parliamentary session. Nowadays we call it filibustering. Josephine Butler had been very frustrated when politicians blocked her attempts to push forwards the raising of the age of consent using similar techniques.

Timing could also work the other way. It was well known that parliamentary attendance during the early summer months, particularly in the evenings, would be light. A quorate group of those approving of a particular bill could rush something through without many people knowing until it was too late to do anything about it. The infamous Contagious Diseases Act was a key case in point. The games some people play.

Relying on Private Members to bring an issue forwards, and hopefully carry it, inevitably put tremendous pressure on one individual – he could not rely on other party members, for example, who could share the work both in and out of Parliament – and of course he would have had other priorities of his own to bring before the parliamentary session. Once the issue had been carried from the women into Parliament they had no further control of its progress there. There has been little mention of other key areas of Victorian politics within this text, but whenever such urgent matters as the Crimean War or Ireland and the question of Home Rule occurred, or key domestic issues like factory reform, public health or education needed attention, any women's issue would automatically be put on the back burner, or dropped altogether. The situations women faced were not 'real' problems like those that faced the MPs; they were insignificant matters and, if absolutely necessary, could be attended to at some vague future date in time.

We also have had to accept that while attitudes were slowly changing towards women, and old laws were re-examined and either modified or replaced, some laws were still being brought in for the benefit of men alone. When child custody rules were changed as a direct result of Caroline Norton's actions, only 'virtuous' women could receive the opportunity to submit a claim for their infant children's care. An adulterous husband was not considered an inappropriate adult to be in charge of them.

Regarding divorce, adultery had been named in the Bible as the only justification for it, but Victorian law had modified the original edict – for men it remained sufficient to prove adultery in the wife; for women the husband now had to have proven both adultery and another 'unnatural' or 'irregular' practice. Similarly, regarding suffrage, one of the key reasons for continuing to deny married women the rights to their own property was because it would take them a huge step nearer to their personal claim for suffrage rights. And as we know the infamous CDA were definitely *not* introduced for the benefit of women.

Walter Lyon Blease commented, 'It is sheer dishonesty to pretend that a man who regulates vice for the convenience of himself or others ... has anybody's interest at heart except that of his own sex'. [32] Florence Marryat agreed: 'You men have made all the laws of society for yourselves and have no authority for them but your own wishes'. [33] Seventy years earlier William Thompson and Anna Wheeler had warned:

> *The moment that power is given ... it is an absolute contradiction in terms to speak of identity of interest; for if the identity existed, there would be no need of power to enforce obedience.* [34]

And they had all been proven right.

Even when progress *was* finally being made, for example, when both Caroline Norton and Barbara Leigh Smith were pursuing property rights for married women, it was always open to the Members of Parliament to go for the easiest route out of the problem, to deal with the surface details and not the real issue. Thus it was perceived to be necessary to address the property grievances of only those 'few'

---

[32]   *The Emancipation of English Women*
[33]   *At Heart A Rake*
[34]   *Appeal of One Half of the Human Race*

women who had exceptionally bad husbands or the 'small' numbers who had suffered 'life threatening' violence from them. It had also been remarkably easy for upper-class MPs to turn a blind eye to the faults of their peers (for example, those listed in Rosina's example) and address those that they preferred to believe existed only in the lower classes (which could be covered by very small financial settlements), or (while ignoring examples such as Caroline and Rosina could have personally verified) likewise asserting that extreme violence towards women occurred only within the rougher levels of society.

In addition to this, for those who sought to retain the status quo it was a relatively simple task to exploit any weakness in the women's position. Just like a military general examining the forces of the enemy it must have been very satisfying to see that Caroline Norton and Barbara Leigh Smith were not even working *together*, let alone working *well* together, and that they were asking for very different changes. It is such a shame that Caroline and Barbara had not been able to join forces; it was such an obvious flaw. For Parliament it was then all too easy to agree to the far smaller changes that Caroline sought and dismiss Barbara's claims for years. Women had so much to learn about solidarity. Long before the Matrimonial Causes Act of 1857 Rosina Bulwer Lytton had written:

> *How different is the conduct of men with regard to their own sex. It is neither their imaginary intellectual nor their real superiority of natural strength, nor even the laws they have made which constitute their omnipotence, half so much as the indissoluble manner in which they support each other.*[35]

There were so many ways that this could work, even to the extent that a popular move supported by the Commons could be sent up to the Lords for a hearing there – and then be completely blocked by them. Once Caroline Norton had realised that you had to use the system to change the system, once she realised it was not enough to claim injustice – even on a grand scale – she understood you had to *prove* your case. You needed solid evidence. Men in their numbers had to be convinced of their own failings. They had to be forced to stop talking on behalf of women and start to really listen to them. It would then no

---

[35] *Cheveley: or The Man of Honour*

longer be acceptable for men to deny the existence of large numbers of women who were not satisfied with the status quo.

Where the eighteenth-century women writers had been successful in raising the problem, on an individual basis, women like Caroline had to learn how to present a case that would stand up in law. They had to learn how to undertake legal and historical research, to make use of scandalous cases, and to work the literary media. They had to extend their written propaganda into an active process. They had to convert those people, both males and females, who had accepted the conditioning process and remained convinced by it, as well as reassure those otherwise supportive, but hesitant women, who feared that men would resort to dominance by force if they lost their right to dominance by law. Women had to learn how to work *together* as women with common aims; how to set up and create organisations that would be able to cope with problems along the way, and continue until at least a goal was reached[36]. They had to form committees, with central and local branches, and coordinate their activities. They had to either provide money for their work themselves[37] or learn how to raise funds to keep them going, and they had to learn how to work alongside other organisations that had similar aims, like the Law Amendment Society, and that could add significant weight to their cause. They had to learn how to write and collate petitions, to make sure significant women signed it (like Florence Nightingale) and make use of important male friends and supporters who could do more than just deliver their petitions to a parliamentary door. Thousands of women were actively involved in the various campaigns mentioned in this work; it would be impossible to mention them all – even if we did know their names.

With all these different factors combining with the long-reaching arms of conditioning it is no wonder that it took time to achieve those new laws for women that I have covered so far. By the early 1880s, though, married women had gained further custody rights

---

[36] The Married Women's Property Committee, the Ladies National Association for the Repeal of the Contagious Diseases Acts, the National Society for Women's Suffrage, and the National Vigilance Association are to name but a few.

[37] This included such things as paying for the publication and distribution of their own books and leaflets, hiring premises, publicity, general organisational costs, covering travel and so on.

(though still by no means equality in that area) and they had earned the right to keep their own property and income both before and after their marriages. Economic independence would mean more personal freedom for married women, rather than the subservience that had gone alongside the financial dependence of the past. The issue of the double standard had been raised, through the CDA and 'The Maiden Tribute', and women were expecting a higher standard of morality from their men, which some at least were prepared to accept. Undoubtedly, during those almost fifty years women had made considerable progress, but within the next ten years there were further developments that would radically change the status of married women in this country for good.

It all started with Georgina Weldon, whom you may remember we left at the end of Chapter Seven feeling somewhat disillusioned, not to mention increasingly angry, with her husband who had unsuccessfully attempted to have her locked up in a madhouse in 1878.

Just a few years after the failure of her husband's plan, the Married Women's Property Act (1882) was passed, which finally allowed married women to keep all their own property and earnings. In itself it was a major step forwards, allowing married women to have the same financial independence as single women, but the implications of the Act were enormous. For a start married women were allowed to make contracts for the first time, and they gained the all-important right to sue. By gaining this right and by (re)gaining their own property rights, married women had not only won the financial independence that Barbara Leigh Smith had sought twenty-five years previously, they had also won legal independence. They had won the right to be considered as independent individuals again, just like single women. After the enactment, Georgina Weldon decided to sue *all* those who had been involved in her attempted abduction – including the owner of the asylum concerned, the doctors who certified her, the men who had tried to abduct her and also, of course, her husband. Women may have been forced to bring charges against their husbands previously, for example, in cases of extreme cruelty, but they had not been allowed to sue them.

Just as Jane Austen had had her books rather than her children, so too did Georgina with her court cases. Georgina became renowned for her legal cases; at one point she had seventeen on the go, and the total reached over a hundred before she died.[38] Rather than rely on the services of the legal profession she generally chose to represent herself in court, and impressed members of the judiciary, the press and the public with her performances. Even though she was a woman, she was not to be intimidated by the process of law.

Her case against the owner of the asylum in question, Dr Forbes Winslow, and her husband, as co-conspirator, was not successful – although it did gain her respect and popularity; she did, however, win the case against Dr Semple, who was one of those who had signed the medical certificate, and she was awarded £1000 in damages. Thanks to Georgina's actions during the course of these notorious trials, many of the infamous practices regarding wrongful incarceration were exposed to the general public for the first time, which added significant weight to the pressure on Lunacy Law reform. (It is worth noting at this point that there was a major change in this law in 1890, when the responsibility for certification of lunacy passed from doctors to a magistrate. It was still possible for urgent cases to be confined for a week on one medical signature, but a second signature would be required and the magistrate's approval gained. In addition there was to be a new safety check – certification was to be on an annual basis.) Revelations by Rosina Bulwer Lytton, Louisa Lowe and, of course, Georgina Weldon had all helped towards this change.

Although Georgina had failed to win that first case against her husband, she worked out an even better way to get revenge on him, again using her newly acquired right to sue. She decided that she would sue Mr Weldon for the restitution of conjugal rights. Applying for the restitution of her conjugal rights implied that Georgina actually *wanted* her husband to move back in with her, but it is more likely that she knew that even *if* she won the case against him, he would still refuse, and she hoped that there would be serious consequences for him if that happened. You may remember that previously if a woman chose to leave her husband, and he decided to sue for her return, she could be sent to prison if she refused. When women gained legal independence the situation could be reversed and Georgina was looking for revenge.

I have read various works that say how much Georgina wanted

---

[38] Not all of her cases were to do with the lunacy issue.

this reconciliation, but I remain unconvinced by them. I think it was necessary for her to *say* she desperately wanted him to return to her, in order to have her case heard, before she could stand any chance of winning it. She *had* to convince members of the legal profession, including a judge, that she loved him and truly wanted him to return to the family home. Yet a woman who was prepared to sue her husband and all his associates for their disgraceful attempt to lock her away, just because she was a bit of an embarrassment, could hardly be said to be exhibiting great love for him.

So Georgina sued Mr Weldon for the restitution of *her* conjugal rights and in 1883 the verdict was announced:

> *The court decided that a husband was required to provide not merely house, servants and an allowance, but live under the roof with the petitioner and the decree can be enforced against him by attachments for contempt.*[39]

According to this testament of events the judge in question, Sir James Hannen, warned that 'if an unwilling husband was compelled to return to his wife, "great difficulties would arise, even murder", slily added his Lordship', and so he was very unhappy about compelling Mr Weldon to follow the court order.

It seemed likely Mr Weldon would appeal against the decision, so there was a delay in issuing any decree against him. This gave Justice Hannen time to rush a Bill through Parliament – it could happen as we have already seen – which meant that if a spouse refused to accept the order for the restitution of conjugal rights, he (*or she*) would no longer be forced to comply with it. It has been generally accepted that the law was deliberately, and specifically, changed so that no man would have to face the same situation of imprisonment that women had been made to accept in the past.

It neatly got Mr Weldon out of a very awkward situation. Georgina had won her case. Without the change in the law her husband would have had to face going to prison; now it was no longer necessary for him to even appeal against the original court decision. Rather than being known as the Matrimonial Causes Act

---

[39] Henry Edwin Fenn, *Thirty Five Years in The Divorce Court*, 1910

of 1884, it is not surprising that it was, and is still, referred to as the Weldon Relief Act.

Apart from the fact that women too would no longer face imprisonment if they refused to cohabit with their husbands, there was an additional benefit for them from this new law. If a husband refused to comply with an order for the restitution of conjugal rights, it could be taken officially as desertion, and could be used as a fast track in separation/divorce cases. No longer would it be necessary to wait for a two-year period before such cases could be considered. Henry Edwin Fenn further commented:

> *It has been taken advantage of to such a large extent it is difficult to estimate. Indeed its benefits cannot be too strongly dealt on with such an important change in divorce law. This very important amendment of the law is known among practitioners as the Weldon Relief Act and numberless ladies owe this redoubtable champion of women's rights a deep debt of gratitude for her action in the matter.*[40]

No prison sentence therefore for Mr Weldon, and for Georgina it meant that she could get out of her marriage, with him being left with a bill for maintenance too. A win–win situation.

Only about five years later another significant event took place that was to have a major impact on the position of wives as individuals. It can be linked to Georgina Weldon fighting against the specific right of a husband to lock up his wife, and to the traditional claim of a husband to be able to treat her purely as a possession. It also illustrates how successful the challenges to the conditioning process had been thus far.

In 1889 Edmund Jackson decided to sue his wife, Emily, for the restitution of his conjugal rights. After their marriage in 1887 she had very quickly decided that she did not want to live with him after all and returned to her family, who were not very impressed with her choice of husband anyway. He had gone off to work in New Zealand as originally planned, but went without her. He returned in due course and expected her to live with him, but, in the meantime, she and her family had developed some financial concerns about his

---

[40] Ibid

ability to support her. I think his love for her may have been genuine, but it does seem to have been based on a rather more traditional view of marriage.

In 1891, somewhat frustrated by the fact that he had won his legal action but it could not be enforced (since the Weldon Relief Act), Mr Jackson arranged that he and two associates would kidnap Emily. As she and her sister left church one Sunday afternoon she was bundled into a carriage and driven away. She was taken to his uncle's house and kept locked up. Her family tried to release her, but, as the police chose not to intervene, they then tried bringing a writ for *habeas corpus*. This was rejected, but it went to appeal. Mr Jackson had to produce his wife in court and subsequently defend his actions. At that time the lord chancellor himself, Lord Halsbury, was presiding over the Court of Appeal and he was firmly against the claimed right to lock up a wife. He said:

> *The authorities cited for the husband were all tainted with this sort of notion of absolute domination over the wife... I confess to regarding with something like indignation the statements of the facts of this case, and the absence of a due sense of delicacy and respect due to a wife, whom the husband has sworn to cherish and respect.*[41]

Mr Jackson was laughed out of court.

Not surprisingly there was a loud outcry from all conservative voices who felt it *was* the husband's right to live with his wife, regardless as to whether she wanted to or not. The *Saturday Review* of 28th March 1891 talked of 'the ruin of domestic happiness', and in one of her more antifeminist articles, Eliza Lynn Linton acknowledged that while:

> *...there has been a loud and well deserved outcry against the injustice and tyranny to which women have been subjected... marriage as hitherto understood in England, was suddenly abolished one fine morning last month... Our law lords have destroyed the old balance as completely as if a tornado has passed over a stately shrine and flung the holy image to the winds.*[42]

---

[41] Court of Appeal, The Queen v Jackson (1891) IQB 671 Note:. Apart from being known as the Jackson case/decision this is also often referred to as the Clitheroe case/decision because of its location.

[42] Eliza Lynn Linton, 'The Judicial Shock to Marriage', *Nineteenth Century,* May, 1891

Likewise *The Times* attacked the judges who had been 'trifling' with marriage law and took a similar line to Eliza's yet it still acknowledged: 'This may be the inevitable outcome of modern ideas and the logical result of modern legislation'.[43] *The Law Times* had agreed and stated that Lord Halsbury's decision provided 'the charter of the personal liberty of the married woman'.[44] A year later, though, the matter was still being debated. Joseph Bridges Matthews complained:

> *A wife upon her marriage undertakes in the most solemn manner to serve, love, honour and obey her husband... It might be supposed that the husband would at least have the right to compel his wife to live with him and render his marital rights.*[45]

After the verdict *The Times* had predicted that the outcome would not be popular in Blackburn, the home region, where it was said 'somewhat primitive ideas prevail as to the rights of man and duties of women'. The prediction was absolutely correct. Emily had decided to return north to her home and as she approached it an angry mob attacked her carriage. Some decided to taunt her by engaging in the community singing of 'For he's a jolly good fellow' outside the house, in loud support of her husband. An appeal fund was set up to enable Mr Jackson to approach the House of Lords, with even the local bishop giving his official support. The judges involved in the original decision were also given a hard time by those who were somewhat concerned that it could lead to even further changes in the matters of marriage law.

Even though there were conflicting opinions throughout the country, because of his position Lord Halbury's decision had weight. He believed that Mr Jackson's actions had been out of keeping with modern feeling. If any such laws had been previously accepted in society, they were very much out of date; such conduct would no longer be acceptable in the late nineteenth century.

The Jackson/Clitheroe decision meant that a wife could now choose to leave her husband, and not only could he not threaten her with prison if she later refused to return, but he did not have the

---

[43] *The Times*, 17th April, 1891
[44] 28th March, 1891
[45] Joseph Bridges Matthews, *A Manual of The Law Relating to Married Women*, 1892

right to prevent her from carrying out her decision in the first place. He certainly did not have the right to kidnap her. A husband still had his conjugal rights while the wife was *willing* to cohabit, but he no longer had the right to force her to stay so he could demand them. A wife was free to leave the house without needing permission to go. She had her personal freedom at last. Elizabeth Wolstenholme Elmy proclaimed:

> *Let us rejoice together – coverture is dead and buried... The legal position of every wife has changed from that of her husband's chattel to that of a responsible human being... It is the grandest victory the women's cause has ever yet gained, greater even than the passing of the Married Women's Property Acts.* [46]

As *The Spectator* poignantly commented, 'Marriage, to be sacred, must be voluntary'.[47]

It is true that there were some further details to sort out. Mr Jackson had still been left with the responsibility for his wife's maintenance, which some, like Eliza Lynn Linton, felt was rather unfair on him. There was also the added point that after this legal decision, if a wife *did* desert her husband, he would not be in a position to get a divorce and find another wife, unless the original wife committed adultery. If she remained chaste, he was forced therefore into the uncomfortable position of either resorting to mistresses or remaining celibate. Nobody seemed very bothered about the fact that women who had been deserted by their husbands had been forced into that similar position – for years.

In retrospect the Jackson decision combined with the Weldon Relief Act and the changes in Lunacy Laws mark a significant period in the development of marriage as an institution. Looking back to the days of Caroline Norton and her early fight for the recognition of the rights of a mother, married women had undoubtedly come a long way by the end of the nineteenth century. Legally a wife had been recognised as an individual, with some rights of her own, and these

---

[46] Elizabeth Wolstenholme Elmy, *The Decision in the Clitheroe Case and its Consequences*, 1891

[47] 21st March 1891

changes would benefit all women, rich or poor. Dinah Mulock Craik, along with many other women writers, recognised that progress was taking place.

> *Fictions, social and otherwise, may have their day, when both the simple and the cunning accept them. But it is not a day that lasts forever. Bye and bye they tumble down, like all other shams.*[48]

The assertion that men would always take care of women had been shown to be a myth. Traditional marriage roles that children had been conditioned to undertake were no longer to be accepted without question, and indeed from as early as 1864 there had been various references to marriage actually being 'on trial' during the period. Justin McCarthy wrote, 'The institution of marriage might almost seem to be... just now upon its trial'[49] and the phrase was still being used some thirty years later.

Since the days of Caroline Norton and the Infant Custody Bill 'the woman question' had become a parliamentary question. No longer was the husband able to exert total authority over his wife without being challenged. The Victorian marriage laws had seen to that. He no longer had the right to just take her financial resources, whether pre- or post-marriage; he could not freely use his wife as his punch bag; he could not keep her under lock and key.[50] He could not prevent her from leaving the marriage, and if she did, she would not have to lose contact with her children.

In a subsequent novel Eliza Lynn Linton asked the question:

> *What can a man do when [his wife] simply says she will or will not, and acts on her decision? He cannot beat her, nor lock her up, nor drag her by the scruff of her neck out of the house and into a carriage. He can but remonstrate, explain, reason, perhaps bully, perhaps coax. But*

---

[48] Dinah Mulock Craik, *Hannah*, 1871

[49] 'Novels with a Purpose', *Westminster Review*, vol 82, 1864

[50] Unfortunately, the penalties for a husband convicted of grievous assault upon his wife were still remarkably low. In 1892 the *Woman's Herald* complained against such leniency. They reported the case of Henry Walker who had actually murdered his wife by throwing her over a bridge, and although he was found guilty he received a sentence of only twelve months.

if she remains inflexible, what is his next move? He has but one –
submission to the irremediable – letting her have her own way because
he cannot prevent her taking it – yielding because he cannot coerce.[51]

It was even asserted that 'the Advocates of Women's Rights have really hardly a grievance left'.[52]

Had the institution of marriage really changed that much? Was it so very different at the end of the nineteenth century? Although there *were* now clear legal restrictions upon what a husband could or could not do, behind the closed doors did a wife actually have any more say within her marriage or about what would happen to her and the children if it failed?

In spite of all the legal changes covered in this work, the husband, the father, still remained the one with the legal voice of the family. It was still taken for granted that he knew best and would be the decision maker for everyone in the household. He still held the reins of power firmly within his hands.

Frances Power Cobbe commented, 'Things are improving, but she, the wife, will still be regarded as inferior until the law recognizes her as an equal'.[53] Women had been actively trying to gain the vote since at least the 1860s, but they had not been successful. Men did not want to share political rights and power, and those in Parliament had ensured that on the domestic front the husband remained very much in authority there too. When the issues had been raised regarding married women's demands for custody rights, for equal property rights, for rights of personal safety, the men did not want to give an inch. It was a struggle every step of the way. Women may not have originally wanted equality across the board, but that was the way it was going.

In 1870 Eliza Lynn Linton reviewed progress so far:

A state of things which put [wives] wholly in the power of a man
when once he was the married master – which allowed him to ruin
them without redress, and to treat them with every kind of cruelty, save
an amount of personal brutality to life, yet held them to their bond,

[51] Eliza Lynn Linton, *The One Too Many*, 1894
[52] Edward Manson, 'Marital Authority', *Law Quarterly Review*, July 1891
[53] 'Criminals, Idiots, Women and Minors', 1868

*and held them close – was sure to produce misery, as it was sure also
to create evil... Now, however, things have got somewhat put to rights
in that quarter, and by and by more will be done, 'till it is all worked
through, and the theory of marriage will be no longer based on the
enslaving of one but on the equality of two.*[54]

In another article, written the same year, she wrote:

*All that we can and ought to do with a large class movement is to
discuss it fairly and endeavour to give it a good and wise direction.
It is cruel tyranny to repress it and for the most part a futile tyranny.
For we might as well attempt to check the growth of a plant or of a
human being by merely wishing, as to check the progress of ideas, by
either refusing to recognize that they exist or by angrily saying they
are bad.*[55]

When I first started investigating the Victorian changes in marriage I
was not expecting to find so much literature in the latter part of the
period where wives were still complaining in much the same way that
they had been at the beginning. A Victorian man who was adjusting
to the changes in society around him (the educated woman, the limits
to his authority and so on) may well have started to respect his wife
and daughters in a way that would have been unheard of in his father's
time, and certainly would not have been understood. As we have seen,
though, it would take time for real changes in attitude and behaviour
to become widespread, however keenly adopted and promoted by
such men as John Stuart Mill. Behind those closed doors, time and
again women were to cry out that they were still being suppressed in
their marriages and were wanting more out of it. The novels of the
New Women, at the end of the century, are full of such examples:

*Am I not an individual like yourself, with the privilege of my own
wishes and feelings? Why are they to be disregarded any more than
yours?... However kind and indulgent our husbands may be, as long
as they treat us like children under control as irresponsible creatures*

---

[54] 'The Modern Revolt'
[55] *Ourselves*

who are not fit to think and judge for ourselves, we are slaves to all intents and purposes.[56]

We demand not protection, but respect.[57]

I have not questioned your authority, but you ask for more than authority. You ask me to surrender my personality. You go too far even for a husband.[58]

Later in the same book there was a wonderful touch of humour: 'If only one could be married without having a husband. He is the drawback.' Other books were to include similar ideas:

She was in reality satisfied with her marriage on the whole. But in this class of union there is generally one item which is intolerable, namely, the husband. He really was the only drawback in this case.[59]

With each new law that we have seen enacted there was to be a slight shift in the balance towards equality. When Caroline Norton won success with the Infant Custody Act in 1839, Harriet Martineau had said that it was 'the first act to strike a blow at the oppression of wives in English law'. George Eliot wrote to her friend Sophie Hennell in January 1856, regarding the proposed changes in women's property law. It would, she said, 'help to raise the position and character of women. It is one round of a long ladder stretching far beyond our lives'. After the 1870 Married Women's Property Act had been passed, Florence Marryat commented, 'Since that blessed Property Act [marriage] is not half the slavery it used to be'.[60]

As each new generation grew up they would absorb more of the challenges and changes that had been taking place in society and in law. Education of the young was to be one of the vital elements of updating the conditioning process; it would take time to inculcate a new generation of women with higher expectations and a stronger,

---

[56] Florence Marryat, *At Heart a Rake*
[57] Sarah Grand, *The Beth Book*
[58] Mona Caird, *The Wing of Azrael*
[59] Mary Cholmondley, *Diana Tempest*, 1893
[60] *Her World Against a Lie*

more confident self-image. From the 1880s onwards girls' magazines like *Atalanta* and the *Girl's Own Paper* would reflect the changing attitudes towards women and be full of advice on how to achieve greater things. There were articles on the Married Women's Property Act, drawing up wills, making investments and living on a budget, in addition to advice on employment, and basic cookery as well as such useful skills as flower arranging and how to identify the china marks on English porcelain.

In 1892 Elizabeth Wolstenholme Elmy published a sex education book for children called *The Human Flower*. It too carried a fundamental lesson for the future:

> *The conviction is every day growing that under no plea or promise can it be permissible to submit the individuality, either mental or physical, of the wife, to the will and coercion of the husband.*

It was all part of the slow process of change but still:

> *...one must have patience; it will take some time to break men of their old savagery. For centuries they treated women as slaves and cattle; it may take other centuries before they learn to treat them as equals.*[61]

In some areas women had been able to make little or no progress regarding equality; a case in point was with regard to child custody, where it all began with Caroline Norton. When Caroline Norton fought so hard to keep her infant children she had accepted that, after the age of seven, the children should return to their father's care and authority, for that was what the law had dictated at the time, regardless as to whether the father was up to the job. Later changes in the law (1873 Custody of Infants Act) had extended a mother's rights to claim *custody* or access from aged seven to aged sixteen, but there was still no equality in the law in this area. The father still had primary rights over his children. Even after this, separated or divorced women could still be denied their children.

In classic style Elizabeth Wolstenholme Elmy, amongst others, fought hard to change this automatic bias in the husband's favour. What she wanted was 'nothing less than the entire re-adjustment of

---

61   Marie Corelli, *Murder of Delicia*

the legal position of the mother in the family'.[62] Using articles and giving lectures, presenting petitions to Parliament with the aid of supportive MPs, together they fought for 'equal' custody rights, but, once again, Parliament was not keen. When the Infant Custody Bill was being discussed in 1884 one Member of Parliament, a Mr Fowler, announced:

> *The Bill started with the idea that the husband and wife were equal, a theory that is against scripture and reason... The man and the woman could not be made equal by any Act of Parliament in the world.*[63]

After it became law any moves for sharing the custody responsibility equally between man and wife were abandoned. There were a few changes, though – if a husband died, the widow *would* now be given custody rights, rather than someone whom he had named in his will. Also if a mother died and her husband was considered 'unsuitable' as guardian, her representative could be appointed too. Gradually wives and mothers were being recognised as equally rational beings. There is a wonderfully humorous example of this. While the Bill was still at the discussion stage, according to a parliamentary correspondent:

> *Mr Warton... solemnly informed the House that it was laid down in Holy Scripture as the Law of God, that the husband should be supreme over the wife. Mr Warton further announced that the best wives always acknowledged the supremacy of their husbands. So for a wife to have a will of her own where her children or her property are concerned is a sign of depravity.*
>
> *There was a time no doubt, when this idea was accepted as a Divine Institution; but civilization has made some progress since then, though Mr Warton is still stranded among the fossils.*[64]

---

[62] Elizabeth Elmy, *The Infants Act 1886, The Record of Three Years' Effort for Legislative Reform, with its results.*

[63] Hansard, (House of Commons) 1884, CCLXXXVI, 823/4

[64] *Sussex Daily News*, 29th March 1884 quoted in Ivy Pinchbeck and Margaret Hewitt, *Children in English Society: From the eighteenth century to the Children Act 1948,* Routledge and Kegan Paul 1973, p381

We should not underestimate just how important a role the literary media played in the process of change. The power of the printed word is taken for granted nowadays, whether it is on screen or in print. We know all about the role of propaganda. Victorian women who sought political and social changes took to speaking in public, but there was no radio or television to broadcast their activities, no internet to spread their ideas. They relied heavily on printed material – their books, their journalism, their pamphlets, and so on – and the media coverage and ensuing debates that resulted as a reaction to their ideas all helped carry them still further. Reports of adultery, cruelty and violence in divorce cases hit the headlines after the creation of the Divorce Court, when private tragedies became public scandals and catalysts for change. One can only imagine the shock to 'respectable' households when 'The Maiden Tribute' article arrived on their breakfast table. *The Daily Telegraph* debate of 1888 has been referred to extensively already; the editor of the newspaper himself felt it had played a significant part in continuing and even opening up new areas in its discussion on the subject. At the end of its featured series its leader stated:

> *Such a correspondence as that to which we have opened our columns…*
> *should provide the social historian of the future with material of no*
> *little value.*

Many other national and local publications were to take up the issues too, both newspapers and periodical magazines, including of course those that were dedicated to, or produced by, women themselves – for example, *The Englishwoman's Journal* (1858–64), *The Women's Suffrage Journal* (1870–90) and later *The Lady's Realm* (1896–1915). This latter magazine played an important part in the debate about the future of marriage in 1898/9. Rather than looking merely at the more traditional views of the benefits a woman gained from marriage – financial security, a home, and children – it set the direct question, '*Does Marriage Hinder a Woman's Development?*' The modern view was emerging that a married woman was to be her own person, not merely taking on the role that someone else wanted her to play, so the magazine editor asked some very famous women of the time to contribute to their series, including the writers Sarah Grand and Mona Caird.

Like many others before her Sarah Grand was to assert that a woman who retained her independence, in every way:

> ...not only makes the best wife for a man, but he finds himself forced to adopt an attitude of respect towards her, he discovers that he has a real and charming companion in the house, he feels a pride in his marriage, and he does his utmost to secure for woman every advantage that shall aid her further development. If a woman be married to a right-minded man, then marriage will not hinder self development.

Mona Caird decided to write her contribution in fictional form, a short story based on role reversal. Her opening gambit was:

> Perhaps it might throw some light on the question whether marriage interferes with a woman's self development and career, if we were to ask ourselves honestly how a man would fare in the position, say, of his wife.

Rather than choosing an extreme, shocking example to use as a comparison, she swapped the roles in very normal circumstances. The quietly suffering house husband, John, watches the over-indulgence of the working wife towards the children when she is able to spend time with them, and blames her husband for any faults in them, while she claims the credit for their good points. He is aware of his self-sacrifice, remembering his interest in chemical experiments before his marriage and how he had to give them up, and wonders if he is a good husband. Then one of his daughters develops a real interest in the subject, eventually becoming a distinguished professor, while his own little ventures are laughed at and he is told 'a man's constitution is not fitted for severe brain work'. It makes him ill. To his chagrin his daughter makes a discovery similar to one he had made previously, yet she gets all the acclaim, and he never got the opportunity to do any more.

Mona Caird ended her story with a question:

> Did his marriage interfere with his self-development and his career, and would many other Johns, in his circumstances, have succeeded much better?

It was a very poignant story, well told.

This was not the first role-reversal story by a woman – I have come across several during my research, including one called bluntly *'Man's Rights or How Would You Like It?'* by Annie Denton Cridge (1871), where, in a series of dreams, a country 'in America' was run by women along exactly the same lines that men had used. Women ran the government, went to work, and had all the fun and opportunities in life; men stayed at home in restrictive clothing and spent much of their time doing little of real worth and staring idly out of windows.

Asking the question 'How would you like it?' had been tried in women's literature from the early eighteenth century, regarding limited opportunities in life, subjection in marriage, lack of personal control of finances, absence of civil rights, and so on. When Georgina Weldon was finally able to sue her husband, regarding the restitution of conjugal rights, in effect she was asking the same question. Not only would her husband *not* have liked it but the judge and those in Parliament who helped rush through the Weldon Relief Act worked very quickly to show that *they* would not like it, or prison, as a possibility either. Increasingly, women from the 1860s onwards were to look towards the gaining of the vote as a means to ensure they could put a stop to laws that worked against women, and the system that allowed them to, and they would work with supportive men to achieve it. When George Jacob Holyoake, a socialist and a secularist, wrote his memoirs, he too considered a role reversal:

> *Were women to legislate for men, and exclude them from their Parliament while doing it, and suffer no information of the rights or claims of men to come before them save through their wives – what an outcry there would be from men against what they would call one-sided, ignorant, blundering, unjust, insolent feminine legislation.* [65]

I am pretty sure he was right. However marriage as an institution was to develop in the future, women would have to work <u>with</u> men, and men would have to adjust, in time, to the new roles that evolved for them. Whether they all liked it or not was another matter. The

---

[65] George Jacob Holyoake, *Sixty Years of an Agitator's Life*, 1893

comment by Edward Blease was delightful: 'I have seen something of the New Woman and I am not afraid'.[66]

While the challenge to the rules and laws concerning marriage had been taking place during the course of the nineteenth century, there had been many other changes for both girls and women regarding education and employment opportunities. I am afraid I have sadly neglected this area in my work, but will redress the fault by devoting my third book, the final part of this trilogy, to it. In the meantime I will give a simple outline of these developments, for these changes too were to have a direct impact on the views and expectations of women in their marriages.

During the Victorian period education had been seen as an increasing priority for girls – but no longer merely the traditional accomplishments, the decorative skills a girl might need to catch a husband (singing, playing an instrument, drawing and so on), but a real education including the academic subjects, the classics, and some physical education. There were many women reformers involved who not only helped provide good secondary schools but who fought to establish further educational rights for girls too, both within newly established girls' colleges or, within those traditional bastions of male territory, the universities. Educational opportunities were vastly expanded and alongside them, thanks to the dedication and hard work of some very determined women, employment opportunities for women expanded too.

Florence Nightingale opened up a whole new career for women with training and qualifications in nursing and the establishment of teacher training courses for women offered a new profession too, particularly as compulsory education, up to the age of ten, had been introduced on a national level in 1880. New inventions like the typewriter and the telephone would have a dramatic impact for women in the world of the office and the bicycle would set a girl free from chaperones. The New Women of the day enjoyed their freedom. Being a single woman offered an opportunity for personal development; it was no longer necessarily a curse. By the end of the century marriage was not considered to be the only option for a girl in the way of a career. Olive Schreiner put it bluntly:

---

[66] *The Emancipation of the English Woman*

I am not in so great a hurry to put my neck under a man's foot and
I do not so greatly admire the cry of babies... There are other women
glad of such work. [67]

Most women would eventually marry, but over time attitudes had had to change about marriage being the be-all and end-all of a woman's life. Way back in 1851 the official census figures had revealed some disturbing facts. Out of a population of a little under twenty million it was shown that there were 500,000 more women in the country than men and there were actually 2,500,000 unmarried women at the time the census was undertaken. For the foreseeable future there would continue to be far more marriageable women than men. The implications of this were to be considered in some of the women's literature of the time:

Is it not an unpleasant reflection that in Great Britain we are
supposed to be three females against every male? No wonder men
think so much of themselves; no wonder it is considered more
honourable in a young woman to possess as betrothed or lord ever
so pock-marked, broken-winded, weak-kneed or soft-brained man
than none at all. [68]

In 1885 the *Girls Own Paper* even warned its readers: 'It is as well to regard marriage as a mere possibility rather than as a certainty'. [69] Huge numbers of women would never get a chance to marry; it was a myth therefore that all women were destined to marry and take care of their husbands. They would not, in fact, be failures if they remained old maids; they had no choice in the matter – it was inevitable that some would have to remain so. This fact gave rise to all sorts of questions – were some women actually superfluous to the needs of men? Were women redundant? What should one do with all the surplus women? There were suggestions they should be sent en masse to the colonies – India had loads of single men out there, soldiers and colonial officers, just waiting for a wife. Many women indeed left England purely to go and 'find a husband' out there. Others tried their luck in Australia.

---

[67]   *The Story of an African Farm*
[68]   Helen Mathers, *Comin' Thro' the Rye*
[69]   *Girls Own Paper*, Vol 6, January 1885

Considering alternatives to a career in marriage became essential for many. Without a husband to support them, it was necessary to earn a living; women's employment agencies had opened up around the country, and newspapers and magazines had pages of advertisements.

It became possible to compare the pros and cons of marriage in a way that had not existed before. *The Daily Telegraph* feature had thousands of letters that did just that. Some women made the decision to remain spinsters – single for their entire lives because they enjoyed the financial independence and personal freedom. They enjoyed the experience of working and the pleasures of living independently – so why indeed *should* they marry? Was it *really* necessary now? What was the personal benefit *to them*? What would they *actually* get out of it? Rather than asking what was the nature of marriage, some women were asking a completely different set of questions and, it is true, there were numbers of men who asked themselves the same things – especially after the legal changes covered in this book.

Other women chose to work *until* their marriage, for having a husband and a home of one's own was still considered a full-time job, but they took their new ideas of independence and freedom with them. Their whole attitude towards marriage could be very different to the traditional conditioned response that was expected of a girl at the onset of Victoria's reign.

The future looked bright; it held lots of promise, particularly to a young girl. No longer would she be the chattel of her chosen husband; she had rights and aspirations of her own, and women had already started down the long path to equality. In 1895 a very modern, well-educated young lady called Edith Lanchester made the decision that she definitely did *not* want to get married; she wanted to make a radical move and live with her working-class lover. Her family was shocked on two fronts and decided that it was absolutely necessary to assess the state of her mental health.

You may remember that in 1890 Lunacy Law reform had instigated a magistrate's involvement in any permanent incarceration – the production of two medical certificates was no longer enough to keep someone in a madhouse or asylum, but it was enough to get Edith through the doors. (Actually, at the time Edith was forcibly committed, the family had obtained only one certificate, and acquired the other a few days later.) Dr Blandford had considered her decision to be 'social suicide', and felt totally justified by his and the family's actions. When the Commissioners for Lunacy heard the details they ordered her release for they considered her totally sane, even though they did not approve of what she was proposing to do. Once again questions were asked about the implications of the case. Was it right to call someone insane if they chose not to marry and did something different instead? Edith was twenty-four. She was legally an adult. Should she not have the right to make her *own* choices in life, as any man would do? Edith went on to live happily with her lover and produced two children in the fullness of time.

It was a very different world to the one Caroline Norton had experienced. If only she, and others like her, had been born into another era. She would easily have won the separation from her husband, with maintenance and child custody, and without all the aggravation. Her contribution to our world, and that of the others like her whom we have met along the way, should not be underestimated. Some time ago I heard a lady state that things did not really change for women until they gained suffrage rights, after their work during the First World War. She had never heard of Caroline Norton, Rosina Bulwer Lytton, Barbara Leigh Smith, Josephine Butler, Elizabeth Wolstenholme Elmy, Georgina Weldon and all the others. She had no idea what contribution these Victorian ladies had made to the lives of married women like herself. I think we commit a grave injustice to these brave and strong-minded nineteenth-century women if we fail to remember them.

At the beginning of this work I took up the idea of marriage as a game. By the time Queen Victoria came to the throne it had already been described as a lottery, a game of chance. Looking back that seems to have been an apt description, but by the end of her reign the weighted dice had been disclosed. One of the players had had all the advantages and knew all the rules; the other player was given no choice but to play. Because of women like Caroline, and men who themselves questioned the fairness of play, those who had made the rules were now under scrutiny, and slowly, very slowly, the rulebook *was* being rewritten. As my work drew to a close, I realised that another game could be used to illustrate a woman's changing position within marriage: the strategic game of chess. A woman could now choose not to play, for there were other opportunities open to her. If she did, though, she may not have had control of the board, but she was no longer a mere pawn in the game.

Appendix One
Key Texts

Unless otherwise stated only the original publication date has been given.

Fiction

Aguilar, Grace. *Home Influence*, 1847
Allen, Grant. *The Woman Who Did*, 1895
Benson, E F. *David Blaize*, 1916
Braddon, Mary Elizabeth. *Lady Audley's Secret*, 1862
Braddon, Mary Elizabeth. *The Lady's Mile*, 1866
Braddon, Mary Elizabeth. *Milly Darrell*, 1873
Braddon, Mary Elizabeth. *Strangers and Pilgrims*, 1873
Braddon, Mary Elizabeth. *Taken at the Flood*, 1874
Braeme, C M. *Dora Thorne*, 1877
Brittain, Vera. *Honourable Estate,* 1936
Brontë, Anne. *Agnes Grey*, 1847
Brontë, Anne. *The Tenant of Wildfell Hall*, 1848
Brontë, Charlotte. *Jane Eyre*, 1847
Brooke, Emma Frances. *A Superfluous Woman*, 1894
Brunton, Mary, *Self Control*, 1810
Caird, Mona. *The Wing of Azrael*, 1889
Caird, Mona. *Daughters of Danaus*, 1894
Carey, Rosa Nouchette. *Only the Governess*, 1840
Carey, Rosa Nouchette. *Queenie's Whim*, 1881
Carey, Rosa Nouchette. *Not Like Other Girls*, 1884
Carey, Rosa Nouchette. *For Lilias,* 1885
Cholmondley, Mary. *Diana Tempest*, 1893
Cleeve, Lucas. *The Woman Who Wouldn't,* 1895
Collins, Wilkie. *The Woman in White*, 1859

Collins, Wilkie. *Man and Wife*, 1870

Corelli, Marie. *The Murder of Delicia*, 1896

Craik, Dinah Mulock. *Agatha's Husband,* 1853

Craik, Dinah Mulock. *A Brave Lady*, 1870

Craik, Dinah Mulock. *Hannah*, 1871

Cridge, Alice Denton. *Man's Rights or How Would You Like It?*, 1871

Cross, Victoria. *The Woman Who Didn't*, 1895

Dickens, Charles. *Dombey and Son*, 1848

Dickens, Charles. *David Copperfield,* 1850

Dickens, Charles. *Bleak House*, 1853

Dowie, Menie Muriel. *Gallia*, 1895

Egerton, George. *Virgin Soil*, 1893

Eliot, George. *Adam Bede*, 1859

Eliot, George. *The Mill on the Floss,* 1860

Ewing, Julia. *Jackanapes*, 1884

Farrar, Frederick W. *Eric, or Little by Little*, 1858

Ferguson, Rachel. *Alas Poor Lady*, 1937 (reprinted Persephone Books, 2006)

Gardener, Helen H. *A Thoughtless Yes*, 1890

Gardener, Helen H. *Is This Your Son, My Lord?*, 1890

Gardener, Helen H. *Pray You, Sir, Whose Daughter?*, 1892

Gaskell, Elizabeth. *Ruth*, 1853

Gaskell, Elizabeth. *Wives and Daughters*, 1864

Gosse, Edmund. *Father and Son*, 1907

Gould, Sabine Baring. *The Red Spider*, 1887

Grand, Sarah. *Ideala*, *A Study from Life,* 1889

Grand, Sarah. *The Heavenly Twins*, 1893

Grand, Sarah. *The Beth Book*, 1897

Griffiths, Elizabeth. *The Delicate Distress*, 1769

Hardy, Thomas. The Mayor of Casterbridge, 1886

Hays, Matilda M. *Adrienne Hope, The Story of a Life*, 1865

Haywood, Eliza. *The History of Betsey Thoughtless*, 1751

Hughes, Thomas. *Tom Brown's Schooldays*, 1857

Hungerford, Margaret. *Lady Verner's Flight*, 1893

Iota. *A Yellow Aster*, 1894

Linton, Eliza Lynn. *Realities*, 1851

Linton, Eliza Lynn. *Sowing the Wind*, 1867

Linton, Eliza Lynn. *Rebel of the Family*, 1880

Linton, Eliza Lynn. *The One Too Many*, 1894

Lytton, Edward Bulwer. *Night and Morning*, 1841
Lytton, Rosina Bulwer. *Cheveley: or The Man of Honour*, 1839
Lytton, Rosina Bulwer. *Miriam Sedley,* 1851
Lytton, Rosina Bulwer. *School for Husbands*, 1852
Lytton, Rosina Bulwer. *Very Successful,* 1856
Lytton, Rosina Bulwer. *The World and His Wife*, 1858
Marryat, Florence. *Love's Conflict*, 1865
Marryat, Florence. *Too Good for Him*, 1865
Marryat, Florence. *Her World Against a Lie*, 1878
Marryat, Florence. *The Root of All Evil,* 1879
Marryat, Florence. *On Circumstantial Evidence*, 1889
Marryat, Florence. *The Nobler Sex*, 1892
Marryat, Florence. *At Heart a Rake*, 1895
Martineau, Harriet. *The Crofton Boys,* 1841
Mathers, Helen. *Comin' Thro' the Rye*, 1875
Maupassant, Guy de. *A Woman's Life*, 1883
Meade, L T. *Bel Marjory*, 1878
Meredith, George. *The Ordeal of Richard Peverel*, 1859
Molesworth, Mrs. *White Turrets,* 1896
Moore, George. A Drama in Muslin, 1886
Moore, George. Esther Waters, 1894
Norton, Caroline. *The Wife and Woman's Reward*, 1835
Norton, Caroline. *Stuart of Dunleath*, 1851
Norton, Caroline. *Lost and Saved*, 1863
Oliphant, Margaret. *The Perpetual Curate*, 1864
Oliphant, Margaret. *Phoebe Junior*, 1876
Oliphant, Margaret. *The Ladies Lindores*, 1883
Oliphant, Margaret. *Kirsteen*, 1890
Oliphant, Margaret. The Marriage of Elinor, 1891
Paston, George. *A Writer of Books*, 1898
Reade, Charles. *Hard Cash*, 1863
Reed, Talbot Baines. *The Fifth Form Boys at St Dominic's*, 1881
Reed, Talbot Baines. *Tom, Dick and Harry*, 1894
Richardson, Samuel. *Clarissa*, 1748
Riddell, Charlotte. *Too Much Alone*, 1860
Robinson, Emma. *Mauleverer's Divorce: A Story of Woman's Wrongs*, 1863
Schreiner, Olive. *The Story of an African Farm*, 1883
Sedgwick, Catherine Maria. *Married or Single*, 1857

Sewell, Elizabeth Missing. *Ursula,* 1858
Sharp, Evelyn. *The Making of a Schoolgirl,* OUP, 1898, (1989 edition)
Stowe, Harriet Beecher. *Uncle Tom's Cabin*, 1852
Taylor, Mary. *Miss Miles*, 1890
Thackeray, William Makepeace. *Pendennis*, 1849
Trollope, Anthony. *The Bertrams*, 1859
Trollope, Frances. *One Fault*, 1840
Trollope, Frances. *Jessie Phillips*, 1843
Trollope, Frances. *Petticoat Government*, 1852
Trollope, Frances. *The Life and Adventures of a Clever Woman*, 1854
Vaizey, Mrs George de Horne. *A Houseful of Girls*, 1902
Ward, Mrs Humphrey. *Marcella*, 1894
Worboise, Emma. *Husbands and Wives*, 1873
Yonge, Charlotte M. *Scenes and Characters*, 1847
Yonge, Charlotte M. *The Daisy Chain*, 1856
Yonge, Charlotte M. *Chantry House*, 1886

Autobiographical Works

Hughes, Molly Vivien. *A London Child of the 1870s*, OUP, 1934
Lewes, Marian. *Brother and Sister Sonnets*, 1869
Lytton, Rosina Bulwer. *A Blighted Life*, 1880
Martineau, Harriet. *Autobiography*, 1877
Sewell, Elizabeth Missing. *The Autobiography of Elizabeth M. Sewell, edited by her niece, Eleanor L. Sewell*, 1907
Thompson, Flora. *Lark Rise to Candleford*, OUP, 1945, (2011 edition)

Non-Fiction – Contemporary Records/Books/Pamphlets

The Book of Common Prayer, 1662

A Brief Exposure of the Most Immoral and Dangerous Tendency of a Bill affecting the Rights of Parents now under Consideration of Parliament, or Summary of Reasons why this Bill, entitled 'Custody of Infants Bill', should not be allowed to become Law of the Land, published by Richard and John E. Taylor, 1838

Acton, Dr William. *Prostitution, Considered in its Moral, Social and Sanitary*

Aspect, in London and other large cities and Garrison Towns, with Proposals for the Control and Prevention of Attendant Evils, originally published 1857, updated 1870

Acton, Dr William. *The Functions and Disorders of the Reproductive Organs*, 1875

Besant, Annie. *The Legislation of Female Slavery in England*, 1876

Blease, Walter Lyon. *The Emancipation of English Women*, 1910

Bluet, Leon Paul. See Max O'Rell

Bodichon, Barbara Leigh Smith. *A Brief Summary, in Plain Language, of the Most Important Laws of England Concerning Women*, 1854

Bodichon, Barbara Leigh Smith. *Women and Work*, 1857

Bray, Mrs Charles. *Elements of Morality in Essay Lessons, for Home and School Teaching*, 1897

Brown, Dr Isaac. *On Some Diseases of Women Admitting Surgical Treatment*, 1866

Butler, Josephine. *An Appeal to the People of England on the Recognition and Superintendence of Prostitutes by Governments*, 1870

Butler, Josephine. *Social Purity*, 1879

Butler, Josephine. *Personal Reminiscences of a Great Crusade*, 1896

Caird, Mona. *The Morality of Marriage*, 1897

Chapman, Elizabeth Rachel. *Marriage Questions in Modern Fiction*, 1897

Cobbett, William. *Advice to Young Men, and Incidentally to Young Women, in the Middle and Higher Ranks of Life*, 1829

Conolly, John. *A Remonstrance with the Lord Chief Baron touching the Case of Nottidge versus Ripley*, 1849.

Cunnington, Dr C. Willett. *Feminine Attitudes in the Nineteenth Century*, 1973

Drysdale, Dr George. *The Elements of Social Science, or Physical, Sexual and Natural Religion*, 1861

Duffey, Eliza B. *No Sex in Education; Or, An Equal Chance for Both Boys and Girls*, 1874

Ellis, Sarah. *The Women of England*, 1839

Ellis, Sarah. *The Daughters of England*, 1842

Ellis, Sarah. *The Wives of England*, 1843

Ellis, Sarah. *The Mothers of England*, 1844

Elmy, Elizabeth Wolstenholme. *Opinions of the Press on the Law Relating to the Custody and Guardianship of Children and on the Infants Bill*, 1884

Elmy, Elizabeth Wolstenholme. *The Infants Act 1886, The Record of Three Years' Effort for Legislative Reform, with its results, Women's Printing Society*, 1888

Elmy, Elizabeth Wolstenholme. *The decision in the Clitheroe case and its consequences, A series of five letters reprinted from the Manchester Guardian*, 1891

Elmy, Elizabeth Wolstenholme. *The Human Flower*, 1892

Fenn, Henry Edwin. *Thirty Five Years in The Divorce Court,* 1910

Gardener, Helen. *Men, Women and Gods*, 1885

Gaskell, Elizabeth. *The Life and Works of Charlotte Brontë and Her Sisters*, ca.1895

Hale, Sir Matthew. *History of the Pleas of the Crown*, 1736

Hewitt, Emma. *Woman's Duty*, 1899

Holyoake, George Jacob. *Sixty Years of an Agitator's Life*, 1893

Kelly, William. *Lectures on the Epistle of Paul the Apostle to the Ephesians*, pre 1906

Landels, William. *How Men Are Made*, 1859

Landels, William. *The True Glory of Woman*, 1871

Landels, William. *The Marriage Ring*, 1883

Lecky, William. *History of European Morals*, 1869

Lewes, George Henry. *A Gentle Hint to Writing Women*, 1850

Linton, Eliza Lynn. *Ourselves, A Series of Essays on Women*, 1870

Lowe, Louisa. *The Bastilles of England, or The Lunacy Laws at Work*, 1883

Martin, Sir Theodore, *Queen Victoria, As I Knew Her*, 1901

Martineau, Harriet. *Household Education,* 1849

Martineau, Harriet. *A History of the Thirty Years' Peace, A.D. 1816-46,* 1878

Matthews, Joseph Bridges. *A Manual of The Law Relating to Married Women, 1892*

Mence Esq, R. *The Mutual Rights of Husband and Wife with the draft of a Bill, to replace that of Serjeant Talfourd, for the Custody of Infants,* 1838

Mill, John Stuart. *On Liberty*, 1859

Mill, John Stuart. *The Subjection of Women*, 1869

Mill, John Stuart, and Taylor, H. *Early Essays on Marriage and Divorce*, 1832

Morgan, Ann J (ed.). *The Mother's Friend*, 1864

Nightingale, Florence. *Cassandra*, 1854

Norton, Caroline. *Observations on the Natural Claim of the Mother to the Custody of her Infant Children, as affected by the Common Law Right of the Father,* 1837

Norton, Caroline. *The Separation of the Mother and the Child by the Law of Custody of Infants, considered*, 1838

Norton, Caroline. *A Plain Letter to the Lord Chancellor on the Infant Custody Bill,* 1839

Norton, Caroline. *English Laws for Women in the Nineteenth Century*, 1854

Norton, Caroline. *A Letter to the Queen on Lord Chancellor Cranworth's Marriage and Divorce Bill*, 1855

O'Rell, Max (Leon Paul Blouet). *Les Filles de John Bull,* 1884

Quilter, Harry. *Is Marriage a Failure? Edited, with a preface by H. Quilter. Containing the most important letters on this subject in the Daily Telegraph (written in consequence of an article 'Is Marriage A Failure?' by Mrs Mona Caird)*, 1888

Randall, Mary Ann. *The Female Advocate,* 1799

Reid, Marion. *A Plea for Woman*, 1843

Ruskin, John. *Of Queen's Gardens*, 1865

Shorter, Clement King. *The Brontes and their Circle*, 1914

Smiles, Samuel. *Self Help*, 1855

Strachey, Ray. *The Cause*, 1928

Stephen, James Fitzjames. *Liberty, Equality, Fraternity*, 1874

Thayer, William M. *Women who Win: Or, Making Things Happen*, 1897

Thompson, William and Wheeler, Anna. *Appeal of One Half of the Human Race, Women, Against the Pretensions of the Other Half, Men, to Retain Them in Political, and Thence in Civil and Domestic Slavery,* 1825

Tweedie, Rev W K. *Daily Duty, A Book for the Nursery, Fireside and School,* 1855

Weldon, Georgina. *How I escaped The Mad Doctors*, 1878

Wilde, Lady. *Social Studies*, 1893

Wollstonecraft, Mary. *A Vindication of the Rights of Woman*, 1792

Contemporary Newspapers/Periodicals

Athenaeum
Blackwood's Edinburgh Magazine
British and Foreign Review
Contemporary Review
Cornhill Magazine
Daily News

Daily Telegraph
Englishman's Review
English Woman's Journal
Englishwoman's Review of Social and Industrial Questions
Fraser's Magazine
Girl's Own Paper
Household Words
Lady's Realm
Law Quarterly Review
Law Review
Law Times
Macmillan's Magazine
Medical Press and Circular
Morning Chronicle
Nineteenth Century
Pall Mall Gazette
Saturday Review
Sentinel
Spectator
The English Republic
The Times
Theological Review
Victoria Magazine
Westminster Review

Contemporary Articles

Boerio, Countess De. 'Some Marriage Thorns and How to Avoid Them', *Girls Own Paper* vol 14, 1893

Browne, Matthew. 'The Subjection of Women', *Contemporary Review*, 1870

Caird, Mona. 'Marriage', *Westminster Review*, August 1888

Cecil, Robert (?), 'Law for Ladies', *Saturday Review*, May, 1856

Chapman, John. 'The Law in Relation to Women', *Westminster Review*, vol 128, 1887

Cobbe, Frances Power. 'Criminals, Idiots, Women and Minors', *Fraser's Magazine*, December, 1868

Cobbe, Frances Power. 'The Subjection of Women', *Theological Review*, 1869

Cobbe, Frances Power. (Letter), *Spectator*, 50, 1877

Cobbe, Frances Power. 'Wife Torture in England', *Contemporary Review*, April, 1878

Dixon, W H. 'The Subjection of Women', *Athenaeum*, June 1869

Elmy, Elizabeth Wolstenholme, 'The Law of Scotland with regard to The Property of Married Women', *The Englishwoman's Review*, Vol 12, September 1881

Elmy, Elizabeth Wolstenholme (Ignota). 'Judicial Sex Bias', *Westminster Review*, March 1898

Faithfull, Emily, 'Admission of Women to the Electoral Franchise', *Victoria Magazine*, 1867, Vol 9, p243

Handley, Edwin Hill. 'Custody of Infants Bill', *British and Foreign Review*, Vol 7, July 1838

Linton, Eliza Lynn. 'Mary Wollstonecraft', *The English Republic*, 1854

Linton, Eliza Lynn. 'One of Our Legal Fictions', *Household Words*, April, 1854

Linton, Eliza Lynn. 'Marriage Gaolers', *Household Words*, July 1856

Linton, Eliza Lynn. 'The Modern Revolt', *Macmillan's Magazine*, 1870

Linton, Eliza Lynn. 'Our Civilisation', *Cornhill Magazine*, 1873

Linton, Eliza Lynn. 'The Philosophy of Marriage', (included in H. Quilter. *Is Marriage a Failure?*, 1888)

Linton, Eliza Lynn. 'The Judicial Shock to Marriage', *Nineteenth Century*, May, 1891

Manson, Edward. 'Marital Authority', *Law Quarterly Review*, 1891

McCarthy, Justin. 'Novels with a Purpose', *Westminster Review*, 1864

Mill, John Stuart Mill and Taylor, Harriet. 'William Burn', *Morning Chronicle*, 1846

Mill, John Stuart Mill and Taylor, Harriet. 'Assault Law', *Morning Chronicle*, 1850

Mill, John Stuart Mill and Taylor, Harriet. 'Wife Murder' *Morning Chronicle*, 1851

Oliphant, Margaret. 'The Laws Concerning Women', *Blackwood's Edinburgh Magazine*, 1856

Oliphant, Margaret. 'The Great Unrepresented', *Blackwood's Edinburgh Magazine*, 1866

Oliphant, Margaret. 'The Grievances of Women', *Fraser's Magazine*, May 1880

Richardson, Samuel. *The Rambler*, No. 97, 1751

Stead, W J. 'The Maiden Tribute of Modern Babylon', *Pall Mall Gazette*, 1885

Taylor, Harriet. 'The Enfranchisement of Women', *Westminster Review*, July 1851

'Womens Law: Mrs Norton's Letter to the Queen', *The Law Review 23*, 1855/6

Secondary Sources –

Public Documents

Great Britain, Hansard, *Parliamentary Debates*

The following books are also highly recommended

Banks, JA and Olive. *Feminism and Family Planning in Victorian England*, Liverpool University Press, 1964

Beetham, Margaret and Kay Boardman (ed.). *Victorian Women's Magazines*, Manchester University Press, 2001

Doggett, Maeve E. *Marriage, Wife Beating and the Law in Victorian England: 'sub virga viri'*, Weidenfeld and Nicolson, London, 1992

Fisher, Trevor. *Prostitution and the Victorians*, Sutton Publishing Limited, Stroud, 1997

Griffin, Ben. *The Politics of Gender in Victorian Britain: Masculinity, Political Culture and the Struggle for Women's Rights,* Cambridge University Press, 2014

Hamilton, Susan (ed.). *Criminals, Idiots, Women and Minors*, Broadview Press, Hadleigh, 1995

Holcombe, Lee. *Wives and Property,* Toronto UP, 1983

Jacobs Jo Ellen (ed.). *The Complete Works of Harriet Taylor*, Indiana University Press, Bloomington, 1998

Jeffreys, Sheila (ed.). *The Sexuality Debates*, Routledge and Kegan Paul, London, 1997

Kent, Susan Kingsley. *Sex and Suffrage 1860–1914*, Routledge, London, 1990

Pinchbeck, Ivy and Margaret Hewitt. *Children in English Society: From the eighteenth century to the Children Act 1948,* Routledge and Kegan Paul, 1973

Pyle, Andrew (ed.). *The Subjection of Women, Contemporary Responses to John Stuart Mill,* Thoemmes Press, Bristol, 1995

Rossi, Alice S (ed.), *John Stuart Mill and Harriet Taylor Mill, Essays on Sex Equality,* University of Chicago Press, 1970

Shanley, Mary Lyndon. *Feminism, Marriage, and the Law in Victorian England,* Tauris, London, 1989

Tosh, John. *A Man's Place: Masculinity and the Middle-Class Home in Victorian England,* Yale University Press, London, 1999

Wroath, John. *Until They Are Seven, the Origins of Women's Legal Rights,* Waterside, Winchester, 1998

Appendix Two
Key Women Players

Josephine Butler (née Grey, 1828–1906)

Happily married in 1852, Josephine became involved in working for destitute women and prostitutes after the tragic death of her young six-year-old daughter, even setting up a House of Rest and an Industrial Home for them. Like many others she saw a strong link between prostitution and poverty, due to the lack of adequate employment opportunities for women. Josephine was a great believer in higher education and was appointed president of the North of England Council for the Higher Education of Women, joining the campaign to persuade Cambridge University to admit females, which eventually led to the establishment of Newnham College. She wrote a pamphlet on *The Education and Employment of Women* (1868) and also edited *Women's Work and Women's Culture* (1869), a series of essays by key women of the time. Josephine's great crusade was the abolition of the Contagious Diseases Acts, believing that it was wrong to legalise prostitution and thereby pander to men's sexual wants at the expense of women's rights. Her husband was the principal of Liverpool College and he received much criticism because of her involvement in such activities. Rather than trying to stop her, he encouraged her to continue. Josephine extended her work throughout Europe and within the empire. She became Secretary of the National Association for Repeal, wrote many books and pamphlets, and gave lectures on the subject. She was also involved in the campaign against child prostitution. Later she set up her own periodicals, *The Dawn* and *The Storm Bell,* and edited them. She also wrote *Personal Reminiscences of a Great Crusade* in 1896.

Barbara Leigh Smith Bodichon (1827–91)

Barbara was the illegitimate daughter of politician Benjamin Leigh Smith. Inspired by the activities of Caroline Norton, she published

A Brief Summary of the Laws of England Concerning Women in 1854, which drew public attention to the legal position of women in this country. She became part of the Langham Place Group – a group of women friends who used to meet regularly to discuss women's rights. Barbara drafted a petition in support of married women's property rights and obtained three thousand women's signatures in support of it. She was a leading member of the Married Women's Property Committee, which fought strenuously to gain financial independence for women in the mid-1850s. After the failure to achieve this she set up the *English Woman's Journal* (1858–64), and was a great supporter of higher education for women, helping with the establishment of what became Girton College, Cambridge. She married in 1857. She was also involved in the moves for women's suffrage and again was responsible for petitioning to that effect. Barbara was a close friend of George Eliot and John Stuart Mill.

Jessie Boucherett (1825–1905)

Inspired by contents of the *English Women's Journal*, Jessie became interested in women's issues; she moved to London and joined forces with the women who worked on it. In 1859 she, Barbara Bodichon and another woman, Adelaide Proctor, started the Society for the Promotion of the Employment of Women. Jessie also funded a small clerical school for women workers. She launched *The Englishwoman's Review* (1866–1910), which joined forces with *The English Woman's Journal* (1858–64), and continued to write articles on women's employment for other publications. She was an active suffragist and campaigner on the women's property issue.

Mary Elizabeth Braddon (1835–1915)

Mary began work as an actress, although she had started writing before that. In 1860 she met the publisher John Maxwell and wrote stories for several periodicals. She wrote many novels, but her greatest success was with *Lady Audley's Secret* (1862) followed by *Aurora Floyd* (1863). Best known as a writer of sensational fiction where such incidences as murder and bigamy were common occurrences; she was also an extremely intelligent woman writer including many subtle criticisms and challenges to the patriarchal society in her work. Her female characters were often strong, independent women. Mary's own personal life was somewhat sensational living with Mr Maxwell openly in Richmond, London, while his wife was still alive – although being cared for by relatives in Ireland, due to her apparent mental ill health. Some reports say she was actually in an asylum, others in private care. There was a major scandal when the death of the real Mrs Maxwell was announced – but Mary became the second Mrs Maxwell in 1874.

Mona Caird (1854–1932)

Mona was a Scottish writer with very strong feminist views. She married in 1877 and her husband was very supportive to her. Her famous article 'Marriage' triggered a huge debate in *The Daily Telegraph* in 1888, which was then published in a collection edited by Harry Quilter. A collection of her essays on marriage was later published in 1897 under the title *The Morality of Marriage and Other Essays on the Status and Destiny of Women*. Her New Woman novels covered controversial subjects including marital rape, *The Wing of Azrael* (1889), and the frustrations of married women being unable to pursue their own interests and ambitions, *The Daughters of Danaus* (1894). She was strongly committed to women's suffrage.

Rosa Nouchette Carey (1840–1909)

Rosa came from a large family and was a prolific writer of stories for women and girls. Her first novel, *Nellie's Memories,* sold 50,000 copies. Unlike most of the other writers in this work she remained a spinster for her entire life, and consequently her novels generally show the strength and capabilities of the single woman, alongside the problems faced by women in their roles as mother, wife and daughter. *Queenies Whim* (1881) included issues of married women's property, and the desire (rather than just the need) to work; *For Lilias* (1885) included the desire for independence and the moral superiority of women. Two of Rosa's closest friends were also novelists, the devout writer Charlotte Yonge – who has been mentioned in the book – and the notorious Mrs Henry Wood – author of *East Lynne*, which was one of the most successful Victorian melodramas of the day.

Frances Power Cobbe (1822–1904)

Apart from a two-year spell at school Frances was educated at home. She became a journalist and her outspoken articles on women's rights led to involvement with Barbara Leigh Smith Bodichon and others. Her articles 'Wife Torture in England', and 'Criminals, Idiots, Women and Minors' had a significant impact at the time. Frances was a member of the Married Women's Property Committee and the London Society for Women's Suffrage, and she founded the Kensington Discussion Society – whose members included Barbara Bodichon, Elizabeth Wolstenholme Elmy, Elizabeth Garrett (the first woman physician in this country) and other key supporters of women's education, like Emily Davies. Later Frances became more concerned with animal rights, founded the animal right's movement and was an active anti vivisectionist. John Stuart Mill was a personal friend of hers. Her partner was Marie Lloyd the sculptor.

Dinah Mulock Craik (1826–87)

At the age of nineteen Dinah became responsible for financially supporting her family as her parents had previously separated and her mother had died. She had started teaching when she was only thirteen and began her writing career by writing for children. Some of her novels were directly concerned with women's issues: for example, *Mistress and Maid* (1862) examined the life of a spinster; *The Woman's Kingdom* (1868) compared the marriages of twin sisters; *A Brave Lady* (1870) was written in direct support of the Married Women's Property Bill and has been much quoted throughout this book; *Hannah* (1871) looked at the controversial issue of being able to marry a deceased partner's spouse.

Elizabeth Wolstenholme Elmy (1833–1918)

Even though she was the daughter of a Methodist minister who did not believe in girls' education, Elizabeth had wanted to go to college, a new idea for women, but was not allowed to go, so she educated herself. Elizabeth is one of the great but generally unknown names of women's history, tirelessly involved in all the major campaigns and renowned for her hard work and enthusiasm. Along with Josephine Butler, she helped establish the North of England Council for the Higher Education of Women, and the Ladies Association for the Repeal of the Contagious Diseases Acts. She developed a thorough knowledge of the judicial and legal system in this country and became a parliamentary watchdog constantly concerned with women's issues. She became the secretary of the Married Women's Property Committee in 1868, and was strongly involved with campaigns for women's suffrage. Elizabeth became pregnant but agreed to marry the father of her child only when other members of the women's groups put pressure on her to do so. Even so she still kept her independence, retaining her surname and refusing to make the vow to obey. Her contribution to the women's campaigns cannot be underestimated – hundreds of thousands of leaflets were sent out, and thousands of signatures were collated, by her hands – and she also gave lectures and wrote many articles and pamphlets on the various issues covered in this work.

Elizabeth Gaskell (née Stevenson, 1810–65)

After the death of her mother, she was adopted by an aunt, who lived in Knutsford, Cheshire. Her novel *Cranford* was based here. Elizabeth was religious, well educated and married Rev William Gaskell in 1832. She began serious writing after the death of her only son from scarlet fever in 1845 and, although she found it hard to find a publisher for *Mary Barton* (1848), the book was very successful. It concerned industrial life in Manchester and included a strike, which was somewhat unusual in a woman's story. Charles Dickens liked this work and invited her to contribute to his own magazine, *Household Words*. Her novels *Mary Barton* and *Ruth* (1853) were both concerned with the need for social reform. *Ruth* is significant for its sympathetic portrayal of an unmarried mother and the belief that fallen women were not social rejects for life. Elizabeth was also known for writing ghost stories. Apart from her fiction she wrote a biography of Charlotte Bronte after her death; Charlotte had been a close friend.

Sarah Grand (real name Frances Elizabeth Mcfall, née Clarke, 1854–1943)

Sarah married when she was only sixteen, and subsequently discovered her husband was one of the Lock Hospital doctors, forcibly examining women under the Contagious Diseases Acts. She left her husband after the success of her first book, *Ideala* (1888), and moved to London. Her novels *The Heavenly Twins* (1893) and *The Beth Book* (1897) were considered very controversial, dealing with such topics as venereal disease and the CDA after she had supported Josephine

Butler in her quest for the repeal of these acts. Sarah also took up work as a lecturer on women's issues, was vice president of the Women's Suffrage Society and became local president of the National Council of Women. In 1920 she became Lady Mayoress of Bath.

Eliza Lynn Linton (1822–98)

Self-taught, Eliza went to London in 1845. She started work as a journalist, but her early novels were unsuccessful. Her novel *Realities* (1851), a very interesting work for a modern reader, was particularly badly received because of its radical ideas criticising both Church and State. In 1858 she married an engraver/artist called William Linton, who already had seven children. The marriage failed. Eliza was a supporter of limited rights for women, believing in the need for married women to hold their own property, and also felt that it should be possible to obtain a divorce for incompatibility. From 1866 onwards she worked on *The Saturday Review,* writing many largely antifeminist articles, including 'The Girl of the Period' (1868). From this point on she also worked as a novelist and her works were very successful, including *Grasp Your Nettle* (1865), *Joshua Davidson* (1872) and *The Autobiography of Christopher Kirkland* (1885). Her later novels were very critical of college-educated girls, *The One Too Many* (1894), and women's suffrage and women's clubs, *In Haste and At Leisure* (1895). She was the first woman journalist in this country to receive a salary.

Rosina Bulwer Lytton (1802–88)

Rosina was the daughter of Anna Wheeler (who co-wrote *The Appeal of One Half of the Human Race, Women, Against the Pretensions of the Other Half, Men* with William Thompson in 1825), but she and her mother were not that close. Rosina married Edward Bulwer in 1827. He took a mistress and after a public scandal they separated. She was forced to write for a living, and used the opportunity to make direct and satirical comments about him, and very critical comments about male-dominated society. She wrote many novels; the key ones were *Cheveley: or the Man of Honour* (1839), *Miriam Sedley* (1851), and *Very Successful* (1856). Her *Appeal to the Public* was included in the second edition of the latter, and reprinted twice. Her husband made life very difficult for her at times by persuading publishers to refuse to publish her work. The combination of this with, but largely due to, her public deformation of his character at the Hertford election hustings led Edward to have Rosina committed to a lunatic asylum in Brentford, Middlesex. She was released due to the public outcry it provoked. Her history of these events was later published, without her direct permission, as *A Blighted Life*, in 1880. Her granddaughter was Lady Constance Lytton, a famous suffragette, imprisoned and force-fed during the struggle for emancipation.

Florence Marryat (1833–99)

Florence married twice, the first time when she was only sixteen to T. Ross Church, who was serving in the army, and she travelled widely in India with him. She was a prolific writer completing around seventy works, as well as being a successful actress, editor and businesswoman. Some of her novels were concerned with women's issues, where she included such topics as adultery and abuse, which she said were based on her own experience. Her works have been referred to many times in this book: *Her World a Lie* (1878); *The Nobler Sex* (1892); *At Heart a Rake* (1895) to name but a few. She and her husband divorced in 1879. She later married an army colonel. In addition to her writing she was interested in spiritualism and some of her works were concerned with that. For anyone particularly interested in Florence, Dr Catherine Pope runs an excellent website on her: http://www.florencemarryat.org

Harriet Taylor Mill (née Hardy, 1807–58)

Harriet was twice married; it was during her first marriage that she became close friends with John Stuart Mill. She was a keen advocate of women's rights and J.S. Mill agreed with her ideas. Although Harriet wrote articles herself, including 'The Enfranchisement of Women' in 1851, they collaborated on various works that were published under his name, with her agreement, including the famous *The Subjection of Women* (1869). She completely decried the principle of separate spheres believing that women should be able to enter every career and should receive a suitable education, rather than merely being educated to be submissive wives. Two years after her first husband died, she married J.S. Mill, who publically revoked any claim he legally held over her at the time (property rights, etc.). After her death, her daughter Helen helped J.S. Mill with the production of his works including *The Subjection of Women*.

Caroline Norton (née Sheridan, 1808–77)

In 1827 Caroline married George, but the marriage was a disaster. He accused her of infidelity with Lord Melbourne and took her to court, although it was not proven. She fought for child custody and her actions led to the passing of the Infant Custody Act of 1839, including the publication of *A Plain Letter*. Caroline later also fought for better financial treatment for those women like herself who had separated from their husbands, and her pamphlet *A Letter to the Queen* was influential in changing the laws regarding that, some of the main points being included virtually word for word in the Matrimonial Causes Act of 1857. Some of her own experiences were included in her novels, e.g. *The Wife, and Woman's Reward* (1835) and the more successful *Stuart of Dunleath* (1851) and *Lost and Saved* (1863). She also wrote poetry. Caroline remarried when her first husband died in 1875.

Margaret Oliphant (née Wilson, 1828–97)

Born in Edinburgh, she later moved to London. Her brother tried to take credit for her first novel, *Margaret Maitland*, which was published in 1849. She was a prolific writer of novels, and was taken on by *Blackwood's Edinburgh Magazine*. Margaret was well known in London literary circles, and was best known by her contemporaries as the author of the *Carlingford* series. Many of her novels are subtly concerned with women's issues, but later in life she became more openly critical in both her novels (e.g. *Kirsteen* 1890) and her journalism. Margaret married her cousin Francis in 1852. Her earnings had to help support the family as well as her own brother who was an alcoholic. Some years later her husband became ill suddenly and died of consumption, and her earnings became even more important, especially when she also took on the care of her brother's children. Tragically, she outlived all her own children. Apart from the success of her novels she wrote in a variety of genres, including travel stories and ones concerning the supernatural.

Frances Trollope (née Milton, 1780–1863)

In 1809 she married Thomas Trollope, and had five children – Anthony being the most famous as a successful Victorian novelist, who is still widely read. Her husband was not good with money, so Frances had to support the family with her writing. One of her friends had set up a commune in America and Frances went to join her there. It was not a successful venture, but her book that resulted from her experiences there was – *The Domestic Manners of the Americans* (1832). It is said that Charles Dickens was so taken by it that he wrote a similar travel book, *American Notes*, based on his own experiences there in 1840–2. Frances wrote other travel books, and a wide variety of novels – some of which called for changes in society, including the laws that affected women and working children. The key ones here were *Life and Adventures of Michael Armstrong, Factory Boy* (1840) and *Jessie Phillips* (1840), both of which may have helped to influence the legal changes of the time.

Georgina Weldon (née Thomas, 1837–1914)

Before she married Georgina was a soprano and hoped to continue her career afterwards, however her husband, William, did not approve and so Georgina was then only able to take part in amateur events. They had no children and she became interested in teaching music and setting up an orphanage. The French composer Charles Gounod moved in with the Weldon household and there were whispers of scandal, but he eventually returned to his wife in Paris. Georgina also developed a keen interest in spiritualism and her husband moved out. Later William tried to have her locked up in a lunatic asylum, but the attempt failed and Georgina used the experience to help fight for changes in Lunacy Laws. In 1882 she wrote *The History of my Orphanage, or the Outpourings of an Alleged Lunatic and How I Escaped from Mad Doctors*. After the passing of the 1882 Married Women's Property Act, Georgina developed a keen interest in law and later successfully sued those involved in the attempted abduction. She also sued her husband for the restitution of her conjugal rights, and won that case, although he did not end up going to prison as a new law, nicknamed the Weldon Relief Act, was swiftly brought in to prevent that happening. Her notoriety in the law courts led her to become known as 'Portia of the Law Courts'. On several occasions she ended up in court for libel and had to serve a couple of short-term prison sentences. Her actions played a significant part in both legal and institutional reform.